Gun Control
and Gun Rights

Gun Control and Gun Rights

Constance Emerson Crooker

Historical Guides to Controversial Issues in America
Ron Chepesiuk, Series Editor

GREENWOOD PRESS
Westport, Connecticut · London

Library of Congress Cataloging-in-Publication Data

Crooker, Constance Emerson.
 Gun control and gun rights / Constance Emerson Crooker.
  p. cm.—(Historical guides to controversial issues in America)
 Includes bibliographical references and index.
 ISBN 0–313–32174–4 (alk. paper)
 1. Gun conrol—United States—History. 2. Firearms—Law and legislation—United
States—History. 3. Firearms—Social aspects—United States. 4. Social movements—United
States. I. Title. II. Series.
HV7436 .C76 2003
363.3′3′0973—dc21   2002035213

British Library Cataloguing in Publication Data is available.

Library of Congress Catalog Card Number: 2002035213

ISBN: 0-313-32174-4
ISSN: 1541–0021

First published in 2003

Greenwood Press, 88 Post Road West, Westport, CT 06881
An imprint of Greenwood Publishing Group, Inc.
www.greenwood.com

Printed in the United States of America

The paper used in this book complies with the
Permanent Paper Standard issued by the National
Information Standards Organization (Z39.48-1984).

10 9 8 7 6 5 4 3 2 1

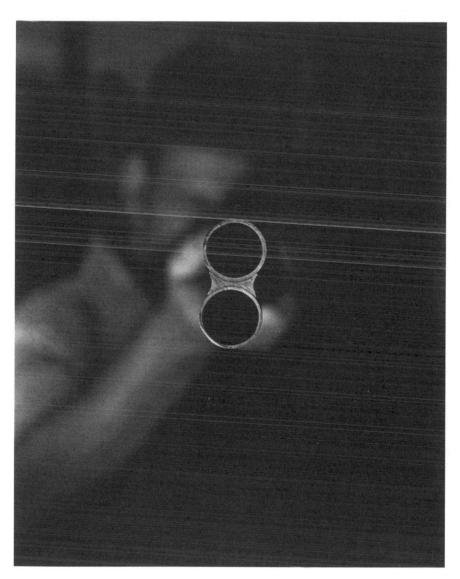

Down the Barrel (A Master Image, Inc.)

Contents

Introduction

In America, there is a great divide between gun control and gun rights advocates. Animosity runs deep. The two groups are less likely to compromise and more likely to vilify each other than those who oppose each other on most other civic issues. The gap is more than intellectual or philosophical. It is cultural. Although not everyone fits these generalizations, it is often true that gun control and gun rights advocates dress differently, talk differently, think differently, and even live in different parts of the country.

Gun control advocates tend, on the whole, to be urban, often eastern, or from an eastern background, and educated in the liberal arts.[1] In their culture, few hunt or target shoot, and only criminals have guns. They do not generally keep guns for self-protection. They believe that in this technological age, we don't survive by brute, physical force, but by our access to information within cooperative communities, and that, as members of such systems, be they government, businesses, or neighborhoods, we enjoy sufficient security. Because we need no longer rely on the personal power of the brave frontiersman to defend the cabin and bring game to the table, gun control advocates distrust those who tout individualism, and who fear a tyrannical central government.

Specifically, when gun control advocates hear gun rights proponents talk of the right to self-defense, they suspect that this is pretense. They distrust those who appear obsessed with killing tools. They suspect that gun rights advocates secretly lust to go on the offensive, like Clint Eastwood when he said, "Go ahead, make my day." Gun rights advocates call their political foes "gun nuts" and suspect they are only one fantasy away from mass murder. In the words of a Senator's aide who had answered many violent calls laden with death threats, "The one thing you learn about this issue is that the most active people for gun rights are also the most violent people, the people you don't want to have guns."[2]

On the other hand, gun rights advocates, on the whole, tend to be from southern and western states.[3] They are more likely to come from a rural, hunting tradition, or a military or law-enforcement background, and they are predominantly male.[4] As Idaho Senator Larry Craig has said, "In Idaho, the second thing you put in your pickup is a gun rack. I do believe there is a different understanding of the use of firearms with folks who come from the West, or from a background where their families have been active in hunting."[5]

Gun ownership in that culture is common, and skill at shooting is a source of pride. And, although most of their neighbors own guns, they, for the most part, live peaceably with each other. Because they view guns as common objects that are seldom misused, they wonder, "Why all the firearms fuss?" Guns do not cause violence. Criminality, in their view, causes violence.

In their culture, guns are multipurpose tools for hunting, putting down livestock, defending against attack, and for recreational target practice. Guns also have value as collectors' items, especially those of historical interest. Besides their practical value, guns are, to them, great icons that symbolize frontier freedom and rugged individualism.

They believe that gun control proponents, who they sometimes call "gun grabbers," are naive about the rules of physical force. Gun rights proponents see all systems as based on force. Even a judge's most solemn decree could go unheeded if it were not backed by the armed might of the state. And if a powerful state disarms its people, the people cannot stand against its inevitable drift toward tyranny over them. Personal power is seen as a crucial safeguard of liberty.

Gun rights proponents tend to enshrine these selected words of the Second Amendment to the U.S. Constitution: "the right of the people to keep and bear Arms, shall not be infringed." But the full wording is, "A well regulated militia, being necessary to the security of a free state, the right of the people to keep and bear Arms, shall not be infringed." And, although gun rights proponents argue that our founding fathers intended to guarantee their gun rights, and although that argument has been accepted by one federal circuit court, the U.S. Supreme Court has not yet interpreted the Second Amendment as a guarantee of personal rights to possess arms. The vast majority of courts limit the Second Amendment right. The courts require some relationship to membership in a government-sanctioned militia (now the National

Guard) before the right attaches. In spite of this, the mantra of gun rights proponents, as emblazoned on the front of the National Rifle Association's Washington, D.C., headquarters, is that the right of the people to keep and bear arms shall not be infringed.

Gun rights advocates also believe in the natural right of any living thing to self-defense. This means that, before there was a constitutionally guaranteed right to bear arms, there was a natural right to self-defense. This can take on religious overtones when they refer to this as a God-given right. For example, Timothy McVeigh, the convicted Oklahoma City bomber, once wrote a letter to his congressman complaining that a certain gun control law violated his "God given right to self-defense."[6] Because a firearm is a primary tool of self-defense, gun rights proponents claim *any* government encroachment on the right to gun ownership is intolerable. It is, in their view, the "first step down a slippery slope that ends in virtual slavery at the hands of a totalitarian regime."[7]

This has been referred to as the "potato chip" theory of gun control, because of the prediction made by Harlon Carter, former head of the National Rifle Association, who warned Congress that a fourteen-day waiting period, when it didn't work, would stretch to ninety, and so on, until all guns were outlawed. He said bureaucracies work like the old potato chip commercial: "It is a little nibble first, and I'll bet you can't eat just one."[8]

This is why gun rights advocates allow no room for compromise. This is also why their struggle takes on the fervor and single-mindedness of a holy war. Their strongly held views are bolstered by the economic interests of gun manufacturers and by the strident language of urgent fundraising letters designed to feed the bureaucracy of the nation's largest (approximately 3 million members) gun lobby, the National Rifle Association.

During the 1970s and the early 1980s, gun rights advocates were politically almost invincible. They successfully halted most legislative efforts to control guns, and they succeeded in crafting laws favorable to their views.

But the tide turned in the late 1980s and in the 1990s. Their "take no prisoners" stance on gun control began to marginalize them while a blood-spattered nation cried out for a stop to gun-related violence.

Now we have federal laws that mandate instant criminal background checks of gun purchasers, and which ban certain semiautomatic weapons, "plastic" guns (said to be undetectable by metal detectors), and armor-piercing bullets. Laws that already criminalized a convicted felon's gun possession were extended to include those people subject to domestic-violence-restraining orders and those convicted of misdemeanors of domestic violence. Possession of firearms within a certain distance of public schools was federally criminalized, then overturned by the Supreme Court, then criminalized again in another federal law. All this in spite of strong opposition from the previously invincible gun lobby.

There are moderates who try to bridge the gap between the two groups. They agree that gun rights exist, but that, as with most other rights, we can tolerate reasonable restrictions on those rights in the interests of public safety, especially in view of the technological advances that have made guns more effective killing machines. Still, the rhetoric that divides the camps prevails. The two groups, being culturally distinct, distrust one another, and resort to name-calling and stereotyping, thus muddying the debate. An example of the perceived cultural conflict is seen in the comments of gun rights proponent Charley Reese, who asserted that gun control proposals stem from mistrust of ordinary gun owners. He wrote, "Gun control is not about guns or crime. It is about an elite that fears and despises the common people...."[9]

The head of a Washington think tank on criminal justice, Eric Sterling, has said:

It's a cultural, urban versus rural thing. We make fun of [people who own guns]. "It's a penis substitute. It's a fetish. They're sickos."

The flip side—from the NRA point of view—is of these urban socialist reformers who are...willing to sacrifice the Constitution for their one-world, UN, commie-pinko stuff.

But can we look at guns in a nonjudgmental way?...How do we minimize harm without blaming people—without saying you're evil, you're perverted, you're a gun nut?[10]

The intent of this book is to explore the issues of gun violence, gun control, and gun rights in a reasoned way, without the name-calling. As in most human endeavors, we solve problems better when we walk in the other guy's shoes than when we dig in our heels. This book is an honest attempt to shine light on all sides of these difficult issues.

1
Gun Violence in America

GUN-RELATED DEATHS AND INJURIES

The controversy between gun control and gun rights advocates starts with gun casualty statistics in America. Gun control proponents cite spiraling casualties as the reason for government intervention, while gun rights proponents downplay the carnage.

Statistics compiled in the 1990s show that each day in the United States, a person dies by gunshot every eighteen minutes, totaling nearly 30,000 deaths per year. About half of those are suicides, another 11,000 are murders, and about 1,500 are gunshot accidents. It only takes two years for such deaths to top the number of Americans killed in the Vietnam War.[1]

Not everybody dies, but rates of injury and the threat of injury are high. During the 1990s criminals used guns during aggravated assaults more than 164,000 times per year, and during assaults on police officers more than 2,700 times per year, and during robberies more than 181,000 times per year.[2]

Things were also bad during the 1980s when, in America, a total of 330,000 people were killed by guns. That tops the number who died from AIDS during the same period.[3]

The Violence Policy Center has reported the following figures on firearms deaths and injuries:

Firearms are the second leading cause of traumatic death related to a consumer product in the United States and are the second most frequent cause of death *overall* for

Americans ages 15 to 24. Since 1960, more than a million Americans have died in firearm suicides, homicides, and unintentional injuries. In 1998 alone, 30,708 Americans died by gunfire: 17,424 in firearm suicides, 12,102 in firearm homicides, 866 in unintentional shootings, and 316 in firearm deaths of unknown intent, according to the National Center for Health Statistics. More than twice that number are treated in emergency rooms each year for nonfatal firearm injuries.[4]

The cost from gunshot deaths and injuries is not only emotional, but is also economic. Treating gunshot wounds is expensive. It has been noted that to save the life of a single victim of a serious gunshot wound can cost $150,000 to $200,000, and it is often the taxpayer or the hospital that foots the emergency-room bill. MedSTAR nurse Barbara Ozmar has said that gunshot wounds are "draining this country's healthcare system."[5]

GUNS AND DOMESTIC VIOLENCE

Gun control proponents argue that a gun in the home increases the likelihood that a family member will be seriously injured or killed by another family member. The figures seem to support that conclusion.

The U.S. Congress made this finding regarding domestic violence when it passed a law prohibiting those subject to domestic restraining orders from possessing firearms:[6]

Congress finds with respect to this provision that domestic violence is the leading cause of injury to women in the United States between the ages of 15 and 44; firearms are used by the abuser in 7 percent of domestic violence incidents....[7]

A woman is at a five times greater risk of being murdered if there is a history of battering and a gun in the house according to a report in the *New England Journal of Medicine*.[8] Data from 1996 reveals that more women are killed with handguns than with all other weapons combined.[9]

A 1994 study showed that 68 percent of domestic violence homicides are from firearms.[10] One study (1993)[11] showed that domestic violence homicides are 7.8 times more likely to occur in homes with guns than homes without, and a later study (1997)[12] found that when there were one or more guns in the house, the risk of domestic homicide increased more than three times. One study found that when a gun is present in a home, there is a five times greater likelihood that one of the residents will commit suicide than in a gun-free home.[13] Similarly, a gun kept in the home is forty-three times more likely to kill a member of the household or a friend than an intruder.[14]

DEATH RATE HIGHER WITH GUNS

The death rate when a firearm is used is much higher than when knives or other weapons are used in an assault. Domestic violence assaults involving guns are twelve times more likely to result in death than are those without guns, according to an article in the *Journal of the American Medical Association*.[15] The same report concluded that when firearms were used, death was three times more likely than when knives were used, and 23.4 times more likely than in family assaults involving other weapons or bodily force.

These statistics should not be surprising. Shooters generally shoot to kill, and, even if they shoot to maim or warn, the unpredictable trajectory of bullets can still kill.

Gun rights advocates point out that these statistics fail to answer an important question: Are guns more lethal in murders because of their design or because a person shooting a gun has the determination to kill? In other words, would every firearm murder happen anyway by other means if the killer had no access to a gun?

Researcher Jeffrey A. Roth noted that gun murders often occur during a temporary rage and when the murderer is under the influence of alcohol.[16] The mixture of alcohol and temporary rage presumably would make the murderer less effective if he resorted to a knife or his hands alone. This researcher also noted that 80 percent of gun victims in a given sample were wounded only once, which would suggest that the killer did not forge ahead using the full capacity of the gun.[17] The researcher concludes cautiously that "properties of weapons, rather than intentions of attackers, account for at least some of the difference in lethality between guns and other weapons."[18]

GUN RIGHTS PROPONENTS RESPOND TO THE STATISTICS

Gun rights proponents respond differently to these numbers depending on the argument they are making at the moment. They often claim that the numbers are inflated or that the conclusions gun control advocates draw from them are misleading. But sometimes they agree there is a high level of gun violence in America which proves the need for keeping firearms for self-defense. Even when they admit the problem is severe, they dispute the solution, always turning the focus back to individual responsibility and off the hardware.

For example, Wayne LaPierre, executive director of the National Rifle Association, has written:

Daily, the cry, "Stop the violence!" grows louder and more strident. Although the problem is plain, it is also complex. A pervasive sense of lawlessness has settled on our society, especially among young people. The real problem is more a matter of heart than of hardware.[19]

The CATO Institute claims that the annual death rate of children from gun accidents is not in the thousands but in the hundreds. The CATO Institute picks fifteen as the upper age and says that only 142 children under fifteen died from gun *accidents* in 1997. Then it admits that, in 1997, 642 children under fifteen died from accidental and intentional shootings combined. Then, it agrees that twelve American children per day die from gun violence, but implies that some of them can be discounted because this figure includes "children" up to twenty years of age, "the great majority of whom are young adult males who die in gang-related violence."[20] The CATO Institute, in its cynical underassessment of gun violence, apparently believes that some of our children deserve to live more than do others.

Similarly, John R. Lott, author of *More Guns, Less Crime,* agrees that only 13 percent of all murders are committed by complete strangers, but disputes the impression left that the others were all committed by close acquaintances. He implies that these figures should be discounted because they include killings by gang members and drug dealers who know each other. In the same context he says that "we cannot ignore the fact that... violent crime, and especially murder... is disproportionately committed by blacks against blacks."[21] The implications of Lott's view should be troubling. He seems to suggest that when blacks or gang members are killed by somebody they know, it is of such little concern that they should be excluded from the body count.

COMPARE OTHER NATIONS

In 1997, the Centers for Disease Control reported that the firearm death rate of children in the United States is twelve times higher than the firearms death rate of children in twenty-five other industrialized countries combined.[22]

In 1990 there were 10,567 handgun murders in the United States. That number has been compared to the total of all handgun murders in the same year in Japan, Great Britain, Switzerland, Canada, Sweden, and Australia, which, combined, contain close to the same population as that of the United States. The total of handgun murders in all of those nations in 1990 was 291.[23] So, if these figures are accurate, the United States suffered 10,276 more handgun murders in 1990 than all those nations put together.

In Switzerland, nearly all males possess guns because of Switzerland's militia requirements. Yet Switzerland has a low murder rate. The conservative CATO Institute points out that Switzerland's homicide rate is low despite a rate of home firearm ownership which is "at least as high as in the United States."[24] Does this suggest that nearly universal availability of guns deters crime, as suggested by some?[25] This explanation would not account for the sharp difference in murder rates between two countries where guns are equally available. Perhaps, instead, the difference in crime rates is due to the fact that Swiss militia members are required to keep their guns locked up and to account for all ammunition, so they are less likely to use their guns in the heat of passion.[26] In Switzerland, the ammunition must be sealed and it is a punishable offense to unseal it.[27] This is a far cry from America where promoters of armed self-defense tout the need to keep your weapon armed and at hand.

Similarly, a study about the effect of gun laws on crime rates in an American city, Seattle, and a Canadian city, Vancouver, could lead to conflicting conclusions. Seattle and Vancouver have similar economic profiles. Seattle has far less restrictive gun possession laws than Vancouver, so more guns are presumably available. Yet the rates of burglary and assault were similar in each city. Does that mean gun possession has little effect on crime rates? Maybe not. Seattle also had a 400 percent higher rate of homicide by firearm than Vancouver.[28] But that still does not settle the question of cause and effect. Where many factors simultaneously contribute to the cause of the murder rate, any study, to be valid, must take into account these factors before concluding the extent to which one or another is a contributing cause. But surely, the number of available guns is one important factor. For example, if there were none available, there could be no murders by firearm, so any that get added into the available pool will make it possible for the murder by firearm rate to increase.

Gun control proponents often point out that countries such as Great Britain and Canada, which have strong gun control laws also have lower rates of violent crime. Their critics accuse them of juggling numbers and misconstruing causes. Nobody, however, can claim that our gun casualties are not shockingly high, and everyone agrees that we must act. The question is, how? The gun control camp would remove the guns from society, while the gun rights camp would remove the criminals.

2

Why Guns Should Not Be Controlled

NOBLE USES OF GUNS

Gun rights proponents fear that the din of the debate over gun control will drown out the reasons people choose to own guns. They refer to the "noble and respectable place firearms hold and have always held in American life."[1] First on the list is always the defense of self and family. Keeping a firearm in the home to protect against an unlawful intruder is so common that it is estimated that at least half the U.S. households keep guns for personal protection.

Closely related is the desire to prevent and deter crime. For example, in states where concealed weapons permits are issued to qualified individuals, many private citizens, while out in public, carry guns in purses or in concealed holsters to protect against assaults and robberies. Gun rights proponents argue that would-be criminals in such jurisdictions are deterred from crime because they know that any potential victim might be packing a gun.[2]

Next on most lists comes hunting, for its value as outdoor recreation and for its comradery, as well as for sustenance in some rural areas. Guns are also useful for putting down sick livestock and for varmint control on farms and ranches.

Target shooting builds skills and provides recreation. Many people enjoy competitions that range from the local level to shooting events in the Olympics.

Other benign uses of firearms are mentioned by pro-gun activists. Because guns may be valuable, unusual, or historically worth preserving, enthusiasts like to keep them as collectors' items.

Next on the list, and possibly fueling much of the debate, is the economic value of the gun industry itself. The manufacture and sale of guns creates jobs and contributes to commerce, and the taxable proceeds go toward the common good. Of course, gun control advocates have questioned whether these benefits outweigh the costs to society from gun-caused deaths and injuries, and, much like tobacco companies today, the fate of an entire industry may hang on society's answer to this cost/benefit question, which gives the gun industry reason to rear up and fight back.

The last of the gun's "noble" uses is the most controversial, and does not make every gun rights list. Guns are sometimes said to be useful for their value in "overcoming tyranny."[3] This stems from the view that guns in early America were the bastion of individual liberty. The theory goes that, without guns in the hands of the early patriots, the fledgling republic might quickly have turned tyrannical, and might have disarmed the people at will. According to this view, the almost universal possession of arms in early America[4] was seen as a necessary deterrent to those who would centralize all power in the federal government, disarm the people, and snatch away the liberty so recently won.

The extent to which this view is historically accurate is hotly debated. Also, the extent to which its rationale still applies is open to question in an age when the United States has amassed the most powerful military arsenal in human history, including nuclear weapons and satellite-based targeting systems. How can a modern patriot with a rifle be effective against all that? Of course, the enormity of modern military power can lead to opposite conclusions about how to counter a government's tendency toward tyranny. One view is that, the more mighty an unchecked military becomes, the greater becomes its potential for abuse, and thus citizens should at least be sufficiently armed to defend themselves in the event unlawful storm troopers come beating down their doors. The other view is that the people, even banded together, are no conceivable match for the modern military, and it is time to forget firearms and resort to our long-established political checks and balances to curb any governmental tendency toward tyranny.

MOST FIREARMS OWNERS ARE RESPONSIBLE

The gun rights proponents say that the majority of gun owners are responsible, and that you cannot blame crime on the tool, but on the criminal using the tool.

An author who studied the history of the National Rifle Association from an unbiased perspective concluded:

Certainly, the facts are on the NRA's side when it argues that the overwhelming majority of gun owners are responsible individuals who commit no crimes with their

Johanathan Thornton, three-time New Mexican champion of the high-power rifle competition. (Photo by Constance Crooker)

firearms. Despite the opposition's many attempts to blame gun owners in general for crime, that is not the case.[5]

WE HAVE ENOUGH LAWS TO PROTECT US

A repeated theme of gun rights groups is that we have enough laws on the books already, and that we should focus on enforcing the ones we have. There is much truth to this assertion. Gun laws are such a tangle of state, federal, and local regulations that it is a wonder anybody chooses to own a gun at all. After two decades of brisk activity in gun legislation, there are no major new federal gun-law proposals on the horizon. And the federal government is taking the lead in enforcing the ones we have. The U.S. Justice Department spearheads a program called Project Safe Neighborhoods (described in the Conclusion) designed to educate police and local prosecutors in gun laws so that the laws can be enforced uniformly. Perhaps this will be the next stage in our nation's attempt to reduce gun violence—enforcing the laws we already have.

Another theme of gun rights proponents is that it is people who commit crimes, so we should focus on punishing the criminal. Gun rights groups have long supported mandatory minimum and enhanced sentencing laws to keep violent, armed criminals out of circulation. A mandatory minimum law is one that a judge must impose on the convicted person. The judge has no discretion to impose less than the term the law mandates. An enhanced sentence is one in which a person receives additional time on top of the normal sentence if the person, for example, used a firearm in the commission of the crime. During the same two decades in which gun legislation has been at its most active, mandatory minimum sentencing and enhanced sentencing laws have also grown by leaps and bounds.

Clearly gun rights proponents have the edge in this argument. We do have an abundance of gun laws on the books, and we have tough sentencing laws to go after the criminals. These can be effective tools for reducing gun violence in our society.

SELF-DEFENSE

Gun rights advocates are fierce defenders of the right to self-defense. They claim that it is a natural, God-given right, inherent in the species. They claim it is one of the rights reserved to the people in the Tenth Amendment to the U.S. Constitution. Therefore, according to this view, *any* government infringement of that right is unconstitutional.

One gun rights author, Alan Korwin, has expressed the right to self-defense this way:

Self-defense against criminal assault is guaranteed in all 50 states and federally,[6] as it should be, and is as old as the first written laws of civilization. Denying the fundamental right to self preservation is unjust, immoral, dangerous and should not be tolerated.[7]

Whether or not the Constitution guarantees a natural right to self-defense, guns can be highly effective tools for this purpose. A person skilled in the use of guns, although possibly too weak to prevail in hand-to-hand combat, can maintain a safe distance while overcoming an attacker. And if the person gains the element of surprise by suddenly producing a gun at a crucial moment, that person may fend off an attack without having to fire. This is why some people call a gun "the great equalizer."

Gun rights advocates speak often of the need to be self-sufficient in defending oneself in light of the fact that the police cannot be everywhere. Paxton Quigley, author of the book *Armed and Female*,[8] wrote, "If crime happens,...know beforehand that in almost every instance no one will be there to protect you but yourself. Police will not be there unless officers are accidentally nearby, and witnesses can be counted on not to interfere."[9]

Gun rights advocates also tout the deterrence aspect of displaying a gun when necessary. Although nobody should pull a gun unless circumstances warrant firing it, it may be that the sight of a firearm in the hands of a potential victim will scare off an attacker. Paxton Quigley reports on a study in which, of 150 cases of armed resistance by citizens against criminal attackers, 50 percent were captured or driven off with no shots fired.[10]

As a matter of public policy it would be helpful to know how useful guns have been in self-defense scenarios. This is a hard matter to quantify. Attacks that go unreported go uncounted. And claims of self-defense can be a matter of opinion. For example, a survey of prisoners who fired guns during the commission of their crimes shows that 48 percent claim they fired in self-defense, but their location in a penitentiary suggests that jurors begged to differ.[11] The CATO Institute has claimed that "guns are used for self-defense more than 2 million times a year, three to five times the estimated number of violent crimes committed with guns."[12]

Depending on who is doing the counting, the estimated annual defensive gun use in the United States ranges from the U.S. Department of Justice figure of only 110,000, to national polls that range from 760,000 to 3.6 million defensive uses of guns per year.[13] This is such a huge discrepancy that the only reasonable conclusion is that the actual number is not known.

Much of the information presented by gun rights advocates regarding self-defense is anecdotal rather than numerical. This does not lessen the fact that such stories, if true, indicate that people can and do successfully and lawfully defend themselves with guns.

In the book, *Armed and Female*, author Quigley reports on cases where women successfully defended themselves with firearms. In one story, a woman who had been ordered by a knife-wielding home intruder to don lingerie instead reached in the bureau drawer and pulled out a loaded gun. She forced the would-be rapist to call 911 while she kept him in her sight until police came to the rescue.[14]

In another case, an elderly woman lawfully killed her assailant. Two burglars, one of them armed with a gun, had entered her home and had broken her husband's nose when she and her husband couldn't produce enough cash. The woman said she would get more cash, and instead, got a loaded gun, which she pointed at one of the burglars. He lunged for the gun that he had placed on a counter and she shot him in the chest, killing him. The accomplice fled but was soon captured.[15] The killing was deemed legally justified.

Similarly, Wayne LaPierre, in his book *Guns, Crime, and Freedom,* cites cases of successful self-defense. For example, he describes an incident where an attacker pointed a gun at a woman seated in her car and said, "I'm going to kill you, bitch." As the attacker got in her car, she pulled her own gun and said, "No, I'm going to kill you." He dropped his gun, ran, and was later captured by police.[16] In the book *Guns for Women,*[17] authors George Flynn and Alan Gottlieb have compiled more than one hundred scenarios in which people have successfully and presumably lawfully defended themselves or their loved ones with firearms.

Whatever the defects in counting cases of self-defense by firearms, such numbers that exist suggest that self-defense with a gun can be effective. One study concluded that one third of all surviving robbery victims included in the study were injured. Of the robbery victims who offered no resistance, one quarter were injured. Of the robbery victims who defended themselves with guns, only 17 percent were injured. Similarly, 30 percent of assault victims were injured. Twenty-seven percent of assault victims who offered no resistance were injured, and only 12 percent of assault victims who defended themselves with guns were injured.[18]

On the other hand, gun control advocates point out the many deficiencies of relying on a gun for self-defense. To use a gun in an emergency situation, it must be near at hand and loaded. A gun might prove ineffective for home protection, if it is stored unloaded and under lock and key. In that case it would not be readily available, for example, to protect against a nighttime intruder. If, on the other hand, the gun is kept loaded and near at hand, there is always the danger that children can get at it or that a burglar could steal it.

Quigley has summed up the problem this way:

Having a gun for security and keeping it safe from others are mutually antagonistic. The safer the gun is, the less ready it is for emergency use; conversely, the more ready a gun is to be fired, the more opportunity there is for mishaps. In other words, an unloaded gun that is perfectly safe is perfectly useless. If you plan to have a loaded gun available, then availability in itself is going to dictate that you will have to assume some risk and make changes in your home and in your life style.[19]

This same author laments, "I wish there were a number of methods to store a gun in a ready condition and at the same time have it absolutely child-proof, but there isn't even one."[20]

There are further complications with relying on a gun for self-defense when traveling outside of the home. A gun may be no protection against a surprise ambush, and even less against a random public shooting that erupts without warning, say, during a bank robbery, a school shooting, or an office-place massacre. A gun helps only if the victim is able to draw and shoot first.

Mike Miller was an FBI agent who, along with other officers, was gunned down inside Washington, D.C.'s police headquarters by a TEC-9-wielding assailant who stormed the office. A TEC-9 is considered an assault weapon because of its capacity to fire multiple rounds in rapid sequence. Mike's brother, Bryan Miller, now executive director of the gun control group, Cease Fire New Jersey, has said:

What happened to Mike and his colleagues is completely full of irony in the sense that this man was able to walk into the least likely place in the world, a police head-quarters full of trained and armed public servants, and exact that kind of damage. The NRA and its apologists ignore that. This case flies in the face of the argument that people can protect themselves if they're armed. Mike and his colleagues were not only armed, but trained to handle these situations. But in the face of the incredible firepower of a TEC-9, they were helpless.[21]

Self-defense instructor Martha J. Langelan teaches women to rely on their wits and whatever objects might come to hand during an attack, and, in her experience with thousands of women, has concluded that "we are safer with-out a gun."[22] She explains that guns do not work in real life situations. Attacks happen too fast, and even if a woman grabs her gun, it's hard to hold onto if the attacker tries to take it. In addition, since more than 70 percent of sexual assaults are committed by an acquaintance, and since women are psychologi-cally reluctant to shoot someone they know, "guns don't help, they hurt."[23] Langelan says, "The pro-gun advocates are living in some kind of Wild West fantasy. . . . [I]t is unrealistic and completely irresponsible to tell women that a gun will be any use at all."[24]

Also, there are risks inherent in shooting in any public place. Bullets are notorious for ricocheting unpredictably, and the same shot that saves the shooter's life could kill an innocent bystander.

Then there are the legal problems involved in transporting a gun. Most places bar carrying a concealed weapon without a permit, and more and more are barring the open carrying of guns. And to transport a gun in a vehicle, a person must usually carry it unloaded and in the trunk or in a locked compartment where it is not available in case of a carjacking or of violent road rage. Even if a person obtains a permit to carry a concealed weapon, there are many places the permit does not apply, such as government buildings and airports.

In addition, there is the risk that the shooter will overstep the legal bounds of self-defense and find himself subject to criminal prosecution. The laws on the amount of force permitted to defend oneself or one's property may not be uniform from state to state, and, although a person may feel fearful when faced with a criminal, the legal right to respond with deadly force may be insufficient in a given case. For example, in Oregon, the right to use deadly force in self-defense is reserved to situations in which an attacker is about to use deadly force or is burglarizing an occupied home or is committing a felony involving threatened physical force against the person, such as rape.[25] The use of deadly force to defend only property or to defend against intrusion into a non-dwelling is not permitted, unless the intruder is threatening arson or a crime of violence.[26]

One study reported that only 2 of 743 gunshot deaths occurring in the home were inflicted on an unknown intruder. And only nine of those deaths were legally justified.[27] In other words, murder and manslaughter of family and friends happen so much more frequently in the home than cases of true self-defense that the risks from gun ownership at home outweigh the risks from intruders.

In spite of limitations on the right to use deadly force in defense of property, the chief executive officer of the National Rifle Association (NRA), Wayne LaPierre, has written approvingly of Florida residents who, after suffering the property destruction wrought by Hurricane Andrew, protected their property at gunpoint and posted signs saying, "You loot, we shoot." While LaPierre may admire their spirit, he should acknowledge that he might be approving the same criminal conduct he so often rebukes when he cries out for tougher sentencing laws, because the use of deadly force to protect mere property is usually a criminal offense. If the head of the NRA is confused about when a person may legally shoot a criminal, the average person shoots at his or her own risk.

Then there is the risk that the assailant will grab the weapon and use it against the victim, or that the victim will accidentally shoot himself for any of a number of reasons. All in all, say the gun control proponents, it is a risky matter to rely on guns for self-defense.

When it comes to self-defense then, a gun is a two-edged sword. You could never convince those who have successfully defended themselves with a firearm that disarming themselves might be to their benefit. Why would a person willingly give up the tool that gives him the edge in a life and death struggle? On the other hand, the vast number of guns in our society, coupled with their risks, and factoring in the volatility of human nature, means our acceptance of their risks comes with a high price tag.

DETERRENCE TO CRIME

One controversial author, John R. Lott, Jr., claims that the more guns that exist in the hands of law-abiding citizens, the more criminals are deterred from committing crimes of violence. In *More Guns, Less Crime*,[28] he claims that the numbers show that, in the jurisdictions where law-abiding citizens may obtain permits to carry concealed weapons in public places, the rate of certain violent crimes plummets. This is especially true for rape and aggravated assaults. Murder appears to be discouraged, but the rate is not always statistically significant. Robbery rates are inconsistent and may go up,[29] while property crime rates increase by about 5 percent.[30]

Lott claims that in his analysis, he factored in other reasons why the rates of violent crime might have dropped, such as increased sentencing penalties and waiting periods,[31] and that he found a statistically significant correlation between the passage of concealed-carry laws and the resulting drop in violent crimes. His overall conclusion is that criminals are deterred from violent crime by the passage of concealed-carry laws, because they fear that a potential victim might be armed. He also concludes that the more that people take advantage of the concealed-carry laws, the more the violent crime rate drops.

Lott also examines what happens in adjacent states when one state's concealed-carry law causes violent crime rates to drop. He claims the rates go up in adjacent states which have no concealed-carry laws. His explanation is that the laws displace criminals, who move from one state to another to take advantage of the more gun-free environment. He postulates (without supporting evidence) that "criminals who commit murder, rape, and robbery apparently move to adjacent states without the laws."[32] Note that he does not consider whether the crime rates in adjacent states might have gone up for different reasons, nor that the perpetrators there might be an entirely different set of criminals. He seems to view criminals as a calculating set of professionals who, if thwarted in one place, will transfer their skills elsewhere, rather than viewing them as the opportunistic, impulsive, antisocial characters that fill our penitentiaries.

In the introduction to *More Guns, Less Crime*,[33] Lott compares the rates of "hot burglaries" in Britain and Canada, which have tough gun control laws, and in the United States, which has fewer gun restrictions. A hot burglary is one in which the resident is home when the burglar enters. Lott claims that almost half the burglaries in Britain and Canada are hot, compared to only 13 percent in the United States. This, he says, points to gun ownership as a deterrent. Lott says that American burglars spend more time casing a house to ensure that nobody is home because they fear their victims might be armed.

Academicians have disputed Lott's conclusions. For example, Professor Stephen Teret has claimed that the original Lott and Mustard studies, which formed the basis for Lott's book, used "incorrect and discredited methodology."[34] The Lott study claimed that laws authorizing qualified applicants to carry concealed weapons ("shall issue" laws) have a deterrent effect on criminals and thus reduce crimes of violence. Yet the study showed no deterrent effect on robbery rates; only a supposed deterrent effect on rape, aggravated assault, and murder. This suggests that the conclusions Lott draws from the numbers may be flawed for the following reasons.

"Shall issue" laws are designed to permit self-defense against predatory street crimes by a stranger, such as a robber. Most rapes and aggravated assaults are committed by someone known to the victim, so the perpetrator would be likely to know whether or not the victim is armed. Similarly, only a small percentage of murders are stranger-to-stranger crimes. The lack of a deterrent effect on the one crime that predominantly involves strangers weakens Lott's theory. Isn't it the robber who, knowing his victim might be armed, would be expected to be deterred by laws that permit people to carry concealed firearms?

Lott attempts to answer this criticism by, first, backing off from his original conclusions that "shall issue" laws have little or no effect on robbery rates, but he does not clarify what, if any, their effect might be.[35] Then he makes the surprising assertion that "it is not clear that robbery should exhibit the largest impacts, primarily because the term *robbery* encompasses many crimes that are not street robberies. For instance, we do not expect bank or residential robberies to decrease; in fact, they could even rise."[36]

This assertion points out a problem when an economist, such as Lott, strays into the arena of criminal law. The law does not recognize any such thing as a "residential robbery." Any robbery in a residence would be a burglary, and Lott has already accounted for burglaries in his statistics. And, if "shall issue" laws deter, why wouldn't a bank robber fear being shot in the back by an armed customer while demanding money at the teller's window? Robberies are, in fact, crimes that should be particularly sensitive to his deterrence theory. Robberies tend to occur in public places and tend to be perpetrated against strangers. Yet the numbers show no correlation. Therefore, Lott's deterrence conclusions may be incorrect.

Similarly, other crimes of violence which are supposedly reduced by "shall issue" laws include home and business burglaries. But there is little reason such crime rates should have been impacted. One Lott critic has pointed out:

Handguns were freely available for home and business use in all the shall-issue juris-dictions prior to the new laws. The new carrying privilege would thus not affect home or business self-defense but should have most of its preventive impact on street crime and offenses occurring in other public places. But the [Lott] study contains no qualitative analysis of different patterns within crime categories to corroborate the right-to-carry prevention hypothesis.[37]

In other words, if Lott had not analyzed a broad class of violent crime, and had instead focused on stranger-to-stranger street crime, he would have been better able to prove or disprove the relationship between "shall issue" laws and deterrence.

Another problem noted by critic Harold W. Anderson is that the Lott study leaps to the conclusion that, because A happened (passage of the con-cealed weapons law), and then B happened (reduction in violent crime), that A must have caused B. But many factors could cause B, and A might have nothing to do with B.

For example, in Portland, Oregon, which has a concealed-weapons-permit law, arrests for assaults with a firearm dropped from 663 in 1997 to 271 in 2000, but experts attribute the drop to "harsher sentences, the aging of baby boomers, a decline in the crack cocaine market, low unemployment and in-creased community involvement."[38] They do not cite deterrence by armed citizens as a cause.

Lott has responded to this criticism by saying he has tried to account for a number of the variables that could cause drops in crime rates. He also says that by measuring statistical significance he is gauging the likelihood that two events may have occurred randomly.[39] But this was a nationwide study, so it did not include local variables such as local unemployment rates or local ille-gal drug markets. The ambitious scope of the project may mean that Lott bit off more than he could chew, in terms of identifying and accounting for all relevant variables which might contribute to changes in the crime rate.

Teret points out that there is also no logical reason why a criminal, know-ing people carry concealed weapons, would substitute a property crime for a crime of violence as claimed by Lott.[40] What is the supposed criminal think-ing? "I'm afraid to assault and rape you, so I guess I'll go rob a 7–11 instead?" Teret points out that "there is no credible criminologic theory"[41] that could account for this type of behavioral displacement.

Teret also criticizes the study for ignoring other gun laws that were passed at the same time as the "shall issue" laws. For example, Florida, Oregon, and Virginia all adopted strict background checks to screen handgun purchasers for criminal convictions during the same periods that those states adopted "shall issue" laws. Perhaps it is the background checks that are responsible for any reduction in violent crime rates, but the Lott-Mustard study fails to consider their effects.[42]

Another puzzling aspect of Lott's conclusions stems from the fact that his study focused on one of two types of concealed-carry law. He distinguishes between so-called "discretionary" and "non-discretionary" or "shall issue" laws. In a "discretionary" jurisdiction, a citizen who meets all the statutory criteria that justify issuance of a concealed-weapons permit might still be denied the permit because the law allows the administrator to exercise discretion whether to issue it. In a nondiscretionary jurisdiction, if the citizen meets all listed criteria, the administrator must issue the permit.

Lott made much of the fact that he was focusing on "shall issue" or nondiscretionary jurisdictions (the system generally favored by the more ardent gun rights proponents). He repeatedly refers to the actual numbers of permits being issued as having relevance to his results. He also claims that the timing of when the permits are issued has relevance.

This is all puzzling, because his basic thesis is that criminals are deterred by the knowledge that any potential victim might be carrying a hidden gun. So as long as some permits are issued to some citizens, it shouldn't matter to the criminal whether he is in a discretionary or nondiscretionary jurisdiction. The chance of striking at an armed victim would exist in either case. It is as if Lott presumes the criminal in a discretionary jurisdiction sizes up a potential victim by thinking, "If I were a cop, I'd deny that person a concealed-weapons permit, therefore it's safe to attack."

Similarly, Lott's emphasis on the actual number of permits issued is confusing. Does he assume a criminal will first check police department records to determine how many permits were issued and then calculate the odds of getting shot before committing a crime? The fact that some permits are issued to some people should be the only reason why concealed-carry laws would exert an alleged deterrent effect. Yet Lott makes much of the supposed "spillover" benefit conferred by each additional person who carries a concealed weapon.[43] He claims that each concealed-weapons' carrier spreads a halo of protection over those who go unarmed, since the criminal does not know which is which. But why would a greater number of armed people affect the criminal's behavior, since the criminal would presumably not know who or how many are actually armed? It is the chance that *some* might be armed which would deter.

It would be interesting to recalculate Lott's numbers to see, in both discretionary and nondiscretionary jurisdictions, and controlling for a broad range of factors that are known to affect crime rates, whether there might be a statistically significant correlation between all concealed-carry jurisdictions and the reduction specifically in stranger-to-stranger crimes of violence. Such a

Dylan Kliebold (R) and Eric Harris are shown in the Columbine High School cafeteria on the day they killed 12 students and one teacher before killing themselves, in a still image from a security camera, May 17, 2002. (Photo by Littleton HS/ZUMA Press. © Copyright 1999 by Littleton HS.)

study might more accurately reveal whether the passage of right to carry laws deters criminals. There might well prove to be such a relationship, but Lott did not do this study, and criticism of his methods is warranted.

Finally, gun control proponents point out that when we have more guns in our society, legitimately or not, the pool of weapons available to criminals is larger. To put it concisely, more guns means more guns.

In 1994, the FBI's National Crime Information Center added 306,000 entries to its list of stolen firearms.[44] Though the majority were purchased legally, they ended up in the hands of criminals. If 306,000 legally owned guns weren't available in the first place, it would mean that many fewer guns in the hands of criminals every year. And, if it is difficult to get a gun legally, the cost of illegal guns goes up and the availability goes down. In other words, a society awash with a glut of guns will certainly experience more guns in the hands of criminals than a society where guns are scarce.

Gun control proponents also point out that family squabbles that escalate into shootings might have ended nonviolently if guns were not present in the home. They argue that the school shootings in which young people use guns taken from their parents' homes might not have ended in tragedy if guns were less available to kids.

The CATO Institute has argued that school shootings do not illustrate a need for tougher gun control laws. At Columbine High School, where Eric Harris and Dylan Kliebold sprayed their fellow students with gunfire, they violated close to twenty firearms laws just in amassing their arsenal, "so it seems rather dubious to argue that additional laws might have prevented this tragedy."[45]

Gun control proponents would reply that this begs the question as to whether gun laws, which help reduce the overall pool of weapons, might have helped prevent this tragedy. Could mere high school kids violate twenty firearms laws in amassing such an arsenal if the guns weren't so readily available?

Since the United States does not register guns, nobody knows how many guns there are or who owns them.[46] Rough guesses have been made based on polls, gun sales, and other indicators. More than a decade ago in 1989, a study by the Bureau of Alcohol, Tobacco, and Firearms concluded that there were then 66.7 million handguns and 200 million firearms of all kinds in circulation in the United States.[47] Common wisdom holds that roughly half of U.S. homes contain at least one gun.[48]

Some studies point to the opposite conclusion from Lott's. Namely, more guns mean more crime. In *Lethal Passage,* author Erik Larson says, "[T]here is an abundance of credible evidence that where there are more guns, there are more deaths from guns."[49] Larson points to a study conducted by Dr. Arthur Kellerman in which Kellerman compared rates of homicide and assault in Vancouver, British Columbia, and in Seattle, Washington, from 1980 to 1986. Vancouver restricted gun sales to those who can show a legitimate need, while Seattle had few regulations. Although their assault rates proved similar, Seattle attackers were eight times more likely to use a handgun. Furthermore, Seattle's homicide rate was five times higher than that of Vancouver.[50]

Similarly, criminologist Philip J. Cook studied whether gun availability influenced crime in fifty of the largest U.S. cities. He compared the percentage of homicides and suicides with the prevalence of gun ownership and found that the cities with low gun ownership rates had lower percentages of homicides and suicides. And, although gun availability did not impact robbery rates, in areas where guns were more available, the robber was more likely to use a gun to commit the robbery.[51]

So, does widespread gun ownership deter criminals? Perhaps. Is the benefit to society offset by the harm caused when some of the many millions of guns in America get into the hands of the unstable, the unskilled, and the predatory? That is up to us as a people to decide.

3

Political and Public Voices on Gun Control

GEORGE W. BUSH

Then presidential candidate George W. Bush said this about gun control:

It starts with enforcing the law. We need to say loud and clear to somebody, if you're going to carry a gun illegally, we're going to arrest you. If you're going to sell a gun illegally you need to be arrested. If you commit a crime with a gun there needs to be absolute certainty in the law. And that means that the local law enforcement officials need help at the federal level. Programs like Project Exile, where the federal government intensifies arresting people who illegally use guns. And we haven't done a very good job of that at the federal level recently. And I'm going to make it a priority.

Secondly, I don't think we ought to be selling guns to people who shouldn't have them. That's why I support instant background checks at gun shows....There's a lot of talk about trigger locks being on guns sold in the future. I support that....So we're distributing them in our state of Texas for free. I think we ought to raise the age at which a juvenile can carry a handgun from 18 to 21. I disagree with [Gore] on [registration of guns]...the criminal is not going to show up and say hey, give me my I.D. card. It's the law-abiding citizens who will do that. And I don't think that is going to be an effective tool to make the—keep our society safe.[1]

HILLARY RODHAM CLINTON

Senator Hillary Rodham Clinton spoke in support of Senator Charles Schumer's proposal that states should issue photo licenses to purchasers of handguns:

One of many full-size billboards in the Metro Denver area for the NRA Annual Convention, 1999. (Photo by Mike Osborn/Zuma Press.)

I stand in support of this common sense legislation to license everyone who wishes to purchase a gun. I also believe that every new handgun sale or transfer should be registered in a national registry, such as Chuck is proposing.[2]

RUDOLPH GIULIANI

Former New York Mayor Rudolph Giuliani has supported a written test plus licensing for gun owners:

I do not think the government should cut off the right to bear arms. My position for many years has been that, just as a motorist must have a license, a gun owner should be required to pass a written exam that shows that they know how to use a gun, that they're intelligent enough and responsible enough to handle a gun.[3]

JESSE VENTURA

The former wrestler, Minnesota Governor Jesse Ventura, has said:

I'm all for gun control, I just define it a little differently. If you can put 2 rounds into the same hole from 25 meters, that's gun control![4]

Shooting range at the NRA's Whittington Center. (Photo by Constance Crooker.)

PAT BUCHANAN

Former presidential candidate Pat Buchanan disapproves of gun control laws:

The urban barbarism that has turned our streets into battlegrounds and our classrooms into killing fields will not be stopped by an assault on the Second Amendment right of American gunowners to keep and bear arms.[5]

CHARLTON HESTON

Charlton Heston, movie actor and president of the National Rifle Association was asked whether gun purchases should be limited to one per month. He replied,

It's the camel's nose in the tent. Look at Stalin, Mussolini, Hitler, Mao Zedong, Pol Pot, Idi Amin—every one of these monsters, on seizing power, their first act was to confiscate all firearms in private hands....[6]

WARREN CASSIDY

NRA writer Warren Cassidy has said of the NRA:

You would get a far better understanding if you approached us as if you were approaching one of the great religions of the world.[7]

MINNESOTA SENATOR PAUL WELLSTONE

In 1994, U.S. Senator Paul Wellstone of Minnesota introduced to the Senate an amendment to the Violence Against Women Act,[8] barring persons subject to domestic violence restraining orders from possessing certain firearms. In speaking of the importance of the amendment, Senator Wellstone said:

I think the best way I can summarize the importance of this amendment...is to make it crystal clear that in all too many cases, the only difference between a battered woman and a dead woman is a gun....Over 4,000 women are killed each year at the hands of their spouse or a relative or a friend, and each year an estimated 150,000 incidents of domestic violence involve use of a weapon.[9]

ALABAMA'S ASSISTANT ATTORNEY GENERAL CHARLES J. COOPER

The government of Alabama, speaking about the Second Amendment through its Assistant Attorney General Charles J. Cooper in a court case,[10] sided with gun rights advocates and blasted gun control proponents, saying:

[The opposing party] urges the radical proposition that the Second Amendment creates no individual right, or that if it does create such a right, it may be infringed wherever a "rational basis" exists for the restriction....[The opposing party] would have this Court literally denude one provision of the Bill of Rights of all legal significance.[11]

HUBERT H. HUMPHREY

Former Senator Hubert H. Humphrey appeared to agree with the antityranny rationale for the Second Amendment when he said, "[T]he right of citizens to bear arms is just one more guarantee against arbitrary government, and one more safeguard against a tyranny which now appears remote in America, but which historically has proved to be always possible."[12]

OREGON REPRESENTATIVE WAYNE KRIEGER

Oregon legislator, Representative Wayne Krieger, caused a scandal by stuffing legislators' mailboxes with an anonymous letter, dated April 1, 2001, describing a fictitious female lawmaker who was bound and gagged, stripped to her underwear, and tarred and feathered for her crimes against the Constitution; namely, proposing gun control legislation.[13]

SWITTERS

A fictional character, a renegade undercover agent named Switters, created by novelist Tom Robbins, had this to say about firearms:

Firearms are to Americans what fine food and drink are to the French: can't hold a proper celebration without them.[14]

JANET RENO

The former Attorney General of the United States, Janet Reno, has said, "Gun registration is not enough. I've always proposed state licensing… with some federal standards."[15]

PAXTON QUIGLEY

Paxton Quigley, author of *Armed and Female*[16] and a noted firearms training instructor, has taken a middle ground. She supports gun ownership, but does not object to proposed requirements that a person's firearms skills be first proven:

You might say that all laws in some ways restrict someone's freedom. Yet we recognize the need for demonstrating the skills necessary to drive a car or fly a plane or perform open-heart surgery. So why is it so unacceptable to have enforceable laws that require gun owners to demonstrate their abilities—both emotional and physical—to operate such deadly weapons? And why do some people so ardently want to prohibit gun ownership, even in light of convincing evidence that handguns deter and terminate so much violent crime?[17]

WAYNE LaPIERRE

Wayne LaPierre, chief executive officer of the National Rifle Association and author of *Guns, Crime and Freedom* has written:

[G]un ownership doesn't cause crime. Criminals do. Whether a firearm has a long or short barrel, fires single or multiple rounds, its capacity for "good" or "evil" rests solely with the user. No gun ban has ever kept guns out of the hands of criminals—only prisons do.[18]

Wayne LaPierre has also said, "A ban on any firearm is a vehicle for banning all firearms."[19]

ERIK LARSON

Erik Larson, author of *Lethal Passage*[20] and a proponent of gun control, believes gun owners should be licensed:

Where I run afoul of the tenets of the National Rifle Association is in my belief that people should be allowed to acquire guns only after going through a licensing process *at least* as rigorous as a driver's license.[21]

Erik Larson has also written:

When will we as a culture stop seeing gun ownership as a God-granted right, so precious as to be nurtured and preserved at the cost of thirty thousand corpses a year; when will we at last demand that all those armed patriots out there first demonstrate a little responsibility and recognize that while they are in the woods waiting for that eight-point buck to wander within range, a newly released felon in Nebraska is buying a gun to blow his ex-girlfriend away, a kid in East Baltimore is tucking a .45 into his belt to defend his lunch money, a toddler in Chicago is aiming the family gun at his baby brother, and a drunken husband in Beverly Hills is climbing the stairs to teach his wife a lesson she will not soon forget?...The place to start is with guns themselves, and the time is now.[22]

KATHERINE KAUFFER CHRISTOFFEL

Katherine Kauffer Christoffel is a pediatrician concerned with children's gunshot injuries. She is the medical director for HELP, or Handgun Epidemic Lowering Plan, and she is ardently pro-regulation:

My emphasis is that handguns are just too dangerous for civilian use. Stranger danger does not show up very often, but the family is at home every day. A handgun in the home turns so many ordinary situations lethal.[23]

SCOTT HARSHBARGER

Scott Harshbarger, Attorney General for Massachusetts, is tough on crime, but has supported an assault-weapons ban and product safety rules for handguns. He notes irony in the fact that the gun lobby usually says firearms policies should be dealt with at the state, not federal level, until Harshbarger acts. Then they switch gears and say the state is overreaching. He says, "They have tremendous lobbying power and influence, but one thing they lack is common sense."[24]

RICHARD AND HOLLEY GALLAND HAYMAKER

Richard and Holley Galland Haymaker had hosted a Japanese exchange student, Yoshihiro Hattori. While trick or treating on Halloween, Hattori was shot and killed when the owner of the home he was approaching mistook him for a burglar. This spurred the Haymakers to become active gun control advocates. At Hattori's funeral they said, "The thing we really must despise, more than the criminal, is the American law that permits people to own guns."[25]

(It should be noted that a jury found the homeowner not guilty of manslaughter. The homeowner testified he saw Hattori approaching in the carport and ordered him to stop, but Hattori kept advancing.)

SUZANNA GRATIA HUPP

Texas State Representative Suzanna Gratia Hupp lost both her parents to a mass murderer as she and her parents were dining in a Killeen, Texas, restaurant in 1991. Hupp, in obedience to the prohibition on carrying concealed weapons, had left her handgun in the car rather than carry it in her purse. She regrets not having it with her so she could have at least changed the odds. She said, "I had made an incredibly stupid decision. I'd rather be sitting in jail with a felony offense on my head and have my parents alive to see their grandchildren."[26]

PHILLIP B. JOURNEY

Phillip B. Journey, an attorney and former board member of the National Rifle Association criticizes those on his own side of the gun debate who go to extremes:

There are people involved in this issue who don't seem to get along with people on the other side. These are our opponents, not our enemies, and there's a great distinction. The absolutist philosophy taken by some gun rights activists is a detriment. We build a public perception that we're intolerant. It allows our opponents to label us as extremists and that hurts us....[27]

NEAL KNOX

Although he denies planning it, Neal Knox, along with Harlon Carter, helped engineer the now-famous 1977 "Cincinnati Revolt" within the National Rifle Association, and together they turned the NRA from a target-shooting and sportsman's club into a powerful national gun lobby.[28] Knox speaks in military terms about the perceived enemy. He brags that "[W]e bumped several foes out of Congress, and scared many more."[29] But he has proved a bit much, even for his own beloved organization. Because of his uncompromising stances, he's been fired from his NRA job, booted off the board of directors and defeated by Charlton Heston for an NRA office. Still, he comes up swinging. One of his recent salvos is, "Registration of guns or their owners is an assault on the Second Amendment and an insult to freedom-loving Americans."[30]

JOHN ASHCROFT

The Attorney General of the United States, John Ashcroft, who is also a member of the NRA,[31] wrote a controversial letter to the executive director of the National Rifle Association. On May 17, 2001, Ashcroft wrote to James Baker on government stationery expressing his opinion that, while some have argued that the Second Amendment guarantees only a "collective right" of the states to maintain militias, the historical evidence and the "preponderance of legal scholarship on the subject" make clear that the Constitution was intended to protect "the private ownership of firearms for lawful purposes."[32] In the letter, Ashcroft did not mention the fact that most federal circuit courts that have examined the issue have ruled to the contrary, and have conditioned Second Amendment firearms rights on a reasonable relationship to membership in a state-sanctioned militia. See the Second Amendment discussion in Chapter 4.

Ashcroft subsequently made public that the official position of the U.S. Justice Department was that the Second Amendment guarantees individual gun rights.

This announcement is controversial, because it comes from the head of the office of federal prosecutors. These are the lawyers who prosecute people accused of violating federal firearms laws. Those who are accused frequently argue that the Second Amendment protects the individual's right to bear arms. The government attorneys generally counter by citing the federal courts that restrict such rights to militia related activities. The government normally urges the court to rule that individuals enjoy no Second Amendment protection unless engaged in militia activity. So Ashcroft's letter has turned federal prosecutorial policy on its head.[33] One can only conclude that Ashcroft is soft on crime, or he is pandering to a political constituency for reasons not related to his role as the country's top prosecutor, or that he sincerely believes that this is the correct legal position, in spite of the harm it might do to ongoing federal gun prosecutions.

Even if Ashcroft is sincere that this is the correct legal position, attorneys may not speak for themselves if their views contradict the interests of their

U.S. Attorney General John Ashcroft testifies on Capitol Hill before the House Select Homeland Security Committee's hearing on "Transforming the Federal Government to Protect America from Terrorism," July 11, 2002. (Photo by Isaac Menashe/Zuma Press.)

clients. Ashcroft represents the people of the United States, not the individuals accused of gun crimes. The implications of his views became apparent when the so-called American Taliban, John Walker Lindh, raised his Second Amendment individual right to arms as a defense to his federal prosecution. It remains to be seen what the effect will be on federal firearms prosecutions when the nation's chief prosecutor takes the side of the criminal defendant on the question of the individual's right to arms.

JUDGE WILL GARWOOD

On October 16, 2001, Judge Will Garwood, a Reagan appointee to the U.S. Court of Appeals for the Fifth Circuit, wrote in support of the individual rights view of the Second Amendment. Judge Garwood ruled that:

... [T]he Second Amendment protects the rights of individuals to privately keep and bear their own firearms that are suitable as individual, personal weapons ... regardless of whether the person is then actually a member of the militia.[34]

The Fifth Circuit stands alone among the federal courts in this regard.

JUDGE STEPHEN REINHARDT

On December 5, 2002, Judge Stephen Reinhardt, who sits on the U.S. Court of Appeals for the Ninth Circuit, ruled that the Second Amendment "protects the people's right to maintain an effective state militia, and does not establish an individual right to own or possess firearms for personal or other use."[35] This is the prevailing view of judges who have ruled on this issue.

ALAN GOTTLIEB

Alan Gottlieb, author, frequent talk-show guest, chairman of the Citizens Committee for the Right to Keep and Bear Arms, and harsh critic of those he collectively refers to as the "gun grabbers," responded to Judge Reinhart's ruling in a fundraising letter for the Second Amendment Foundation in which Gottlieb said,

The ultra-liberal federal 9th Circuit Court of Appeals just ruled that *the Second Amendment doesn't protect an individual right to bear arms.*
This is an outrageous lie. It is very urgent that we overturn this *radical anti-gun ruling.*
[We must petition] the *U.S. Supreme Court* and tell them to protect our Constitutional rights against the ultra-liberal anti-gun rights federal court in California.[36]

Gottlieb also has this to say about gun control laws:

There's nothing sillier than disarming our society with anti-gun laws which crooks never obey. Waiting periods give criminals a grace period for murder, gun turn-ins merely help gun manufacturers sell new guns, gun bans prompt gun-buying rushes— stupid, stupid, stupid.
Gun control instead of criminal control has to be the Mother of All Stupidity.[37]

Gottlieb asserts that the Second Amendment guarantees a right to self-defense:

"The right to defend your life and property is pretty basic. The right to keep and bear arms is about as rock-bottom as you can get for self-protection."[38]

GANG VOICES FROM LOS ANGELES

Youthful members of gangs often make headlines for being involved in gang-related shootings. It is useful to see what they, themselves, have to say about guns. Here are some of their own voices. The first is the voice of Javier Vidal, nicknamed Cisco, a member of the TMC gang in Los Angeles.

I'll tell you a story. About two weeks ago we were all at a group meeting for TMC, kicking back. And some of the homies said, "Okay. Who's going to pitch in to buy guns?" And I said, "I ain't gang banging no more so I can't do it."...They got $900 from everybody else who was there. And they bought three Uzis together with clips that hold about 250 bullets. When they got them we were all at a party. I got to say, they looked nice, Uzis brand new in the box.[39]

After two of his friends were shot and killed, the same gang member said, "It ain't the same without them. They used to make me laugh. I go every weekend to the cemetery and talk to them. I ask them how they're feeling. What's happening up there. I tell them what's going on in the projects. And I tell them that we love them."[40]

A young man named Dreamer, a gang member from the Clarence neighborhood, has this to say about guns:

I thought that probably the only way they could stop the shooting is if they didn't have gun stores. See 'cause people rob the gun stores. Then they take the guns and they go sell them. And then also, they smuggle them in from another country, and they get on the street. But the only way to stop the shooting is if we couldn't get the guns....

But see, it's like a game. That's the way the game is played. And you have to play the way your enemies play or you ain't gonna survive. If you don't play it the way they play it, you're going to die and they're going to laugh.[41]

While walking home from a Christmas celebration, a priest and several youngsters were caught in the middle of a gunfight between rival gangs. One of the youngsters later said, "Sometimes I wish that everybody that had a gun would come outside and hold the gun up to the air. And then the guns would float up to the sky and we'd never see them again."[42]

COMPARE AFGHANISTAN

Present-day Afghanistan is instructive because it reflects a distorted image of what can happen when a gun culture becomes so pervasive that social stability is threatened by the multiplicity of competing, armed groups.

Prior to September 11, Afghanistan was wracked by nearly thirty years of armed civil strife among rival ethnic groups who were themselves supported (and armed) by competing outside powers such as the former Soviet Union, the United States, Saudi Arabia, China, and Pakistan. The internal arms race among rivals resulted in what has been termed the "Kalashnikovization" of Afghanistan. A Kalashnikov is a Russian AK-47, deadly for its capacity to fire multiple rounds with one pull of the trigger. During that long war, many military weapons that flowed into the country leaked from their intended destinations into the hands of anybody who had the power or money to grab

them, resulting in the widespread arming of the previously civilian population.[43] As one Afghan scholar, Larry P. Goodson, noted:

The long Afghan war profoundly altered...important components of Afghanistan's...framework.... [T]he war transformed the role of violence in society, even in
non-combat situations. Not only did Afghan citizens become more inured to everyday
violence, but also the collapse of functioning government and social institutions made
violence a more common means of settling disputes. The near anarchy that resulted was
made possible by the proliferation of high-technology weapons in the country; accord-
ingly, it was dubbed "Kalashnikovization."[44]

    Prior to the Afghan war, most rural Afghan men possessed weapons, but generally
the most advanced were Lee Enfield .303 rifles. Those days are gone forever.[45]

    Kalashnikovization contributed to the splintering of power from a central
military to local militia groups. After the rise of the Pushtun Taliban militia
(augmented by Pakistani "volunteers"), the power struggle at the time the
United States entered the war in the fall of 2001, consisted of the prevailing
southern Taliban forces who were trying to annihilate multiple ethnic groups
in the north.[46] "...Kalashnikovization has contributed to ethnic cleansing
and even genocide there."[47]

    Some Afghans are proud of their guns. The Pushtun people have a saying,
"A gun is the jewelry of a man."[48] But there are sentiments to the contrary.
After the Taliban ouster, one shopkeeper said, "They should send peacekeep-
ers to take the weapons, because Afghanistan is full of weapons."[49] There are
also mixed feelings. A young Afghani whose brother was murdered said, "We
don't like to carry weapons. We hate weapons. Of course [a gun] would be
good for the security of my family."[50]

    There are proposals to disarm the Afghan population. Starting January 14,
2002, the interim government required that government identification cards
be issued to people whose jobs required them to carry guns. The authorities
plan to require civilians to register their weapons with police, but are up in
the air over who will be allowed to keep guns at home. In a country full of
armed banditry, the people do not feel secure without guns, but lawlessness is
so extreme that armed attacks on convoys are hampering UN relief efforts to
feed the people. The military is beginning to confiscate weapons from soldiers
before sending them home, and the interim government is considering a gun
buy-back program, but estimates it would cost $200 million, which the new
government cannot afford.[51]

    The extent of any disarmament of the Afghan population remains to be
seen, but the issue raises, in microcosm, many of the questions with which
our own system has struggled. Is it the prevalence of the deadly AK-47s that
has caused the problem, or is it all guns? Is the anarchy that has resulted from

the weapons glut peculiar to Afghan society, or could it happen here? Is it a good idea to seize guns from citizens when armed bandits far outnumber the police? When, if ever, is police protection a sufficient substitute for personal protection? Is there good reason to track all guns by having them registered? Must soldiers disarm themselves when the conflict has ended? Do buy-back programs work well enough to justify the expense?

LAW ENFORCEMENT VEERS TOWARD GUN CONTROL

Until the 1980s, members of law enforcement had a long-standing affinity with the National Rifle Association. The NRA had long provided firearms instruction to the police. Furthermore, the NRA pleased the police by supporting tough-on-crime measures; it did this to advance its position that society should punish criminals, not law-abiding gun owners. Additionally, police and NRA members made natural allies due to their mutual interest in weapons.[52]

Sometimes, however, their interests have split. Members of law enforcement are constantly in harm's way, and have a strong interest in any laws that might make them safer while on the job. Law enforcement and the NRA engaged in their first face-off in the early 1980s when the groups took opposite stances over one such proposed law.

Certain bullets, nicknamed "apple greens" for the pleasing color of their Teflon tips, soon came to be called by the more sinister name of "cop-killers." These bullets were designed to pierce metal, the idea being that police could use them to get at suspects who would be shooting at them from within the relative safety of a car's interior. Unfortunately, they were so effective that they could pass into a car and out again, ricocheting wildly while retaining their deadly force, thus endangering bystanders. The law enforcement agencies that tried out the apple greens soon abandoned their use at about the same time that the crime world learned that the apple greens could pass through the supposedly bulletproof Kevlar vests worn by the cops.[53]

Alarmed by this new danger, a New York police union promoted a federal bill to ban these "cop-killers." The NRA, knowing it would stir police animosity, still took its predictable make-no-inroads position, explaining, "There is no such thing as a good or bad bullet."[54] The lines were drawn. When the dust settled, a restriction on manufacturers and importers of armor-piercing bullets had passed.[55] The police won, while the NRA suffered a bloody nose at the hands of its former ally.

Similarly, in the mid-1980s, law-enforcement groups opposed NRA-backed legislation designed to roll back the clock by repealing key provisions of the 1968 Gun Control Act. On the day the Senate voted on this bill, called the McClure-Volkmer bill, the senators had to file by uniformed police who stood at attention outside the chamber to remind senators to support the interests of law enforcement. But this time the NRA prevailed. As one Senator said, "You guys will forgive and forget. They [the NRA] never do."[56]

Another battle line was drawn over proposed restrictions on the Glock 17, referred to as a "plastic" gun because it contains a minimal amount of metal compared to its plastic parts. When it was learned that the Glock 17 might pass undetected through airport security devices, law enforcement became interested in the antiterrorism aspect of the problem, and supported the proposed ban. The NRA, on the other hand, claimed the gun still had enough metal to make it detectable, and that any form of gun ban would set a dangerous precedent.

After compromises in which the detectability standard was lowered from 8.5 ounces of steel to only 3.7 ounces of steel, President Ronald Reagan signed the undetectable-weapon bill into law in 1988. Both sides claimed victory, although the NRA lost more than it gained, especially in the area of public relations, because, during the heat of the legislative battle, it had vilified many upstanding law-enforcement officials.[57]

Eleven national law-enforcement organizations joined with the Center to Prevent Handgun Violence in the case of *United States v. Emerson* (discussed in Chapter 4 in relation to the Second Amendment). In *Emerson,* the Center argued that the Second Amendment is restricted to protecting only those arms related to service in a government-authorized militia. Their legal brief stated that these law-enforcement organizations "represent hundreds of thousands of law enforcement officers who face the daily threat of handgun violence and who rely upon gun control laws in the ongoing war against violent crime. [They are] committed to preventing handgun violence and to keeping prohibited persons from possessing handguns and other weapons. The gun control laws of the United States provide law enforcement with a valuable tool in this effort."[58]

Sometimes, when individual law-enforcement officers have taken positions that they regard as moderate and that gun rights groups regard as traitorous, the officers have had their lives threatened. One such officer is Baltimore's Colonel Leonard Supenski. Although Supenski is himself a gun aficionado, he angered gun rights groups by supporting the 1993 Brady law's mandatory waiting period and background checks. A pro-gun group twice threatened to kill him.[59] Supenski takes a practical view. He feels that, unless some such "moderate" laws go through, a momentum for truly restrictive laws will lead to the bans so feared by the hard-liners.[60]

Supenski decries the fact that the gun industry is unregulated by consumer safety rules that regulate everything else in America from mattresses to aspirin. He sees a difference between well-designed guns such as a Smith &

Wesson nine-millimeter and "garbage" like the Cobray M-11/9 semi-automatic. "If you had industry regulations, or if you had safety regulations or product-liability regulations, you better believe they'd see the light [and stop producing the Cobray].... [Y]ou wouldn't need the California assault-weapon ban, you wouldn't need a New Jersey ban, a Maryland Saturday-night-special law. You wouldn't need them because that kind of garbage would never be released into the mainstream."[61]

The hard-line position of some gun rights advocates is that the police want everybody disarmed, not for their personal safety, but so the state can exercise its power to tyrannize the unarmed populace. The voices of the officers themselves sound more moderate. On the whole, they are generally sympathetic to America's gun culture, since they are closely allied with it, but many see no reason not to impose reasonable restrictions for the safety of themselves and of society.

THE IMPACT OF MEDIA VIOLENCE

When people search for the cause of gun-related violence, they point to many sources. Guns themselves, moral decay, criminal subcultures, poor parenting, alcohol and drug addiction, carelessness, and greedy gun manufacturers have all been blamed. Also making everybody's list, no matter which side of the debate one comes from, is media violence. Everyone seems to ask the same questions. How influential is it and what can be done about it? To what extent does violent content in music lyrics, films, and video games affect violent behavior? If there is a proven link, should the government limit such violent expression in the interests of public health, or does the First Amendment to the U.S. Constitution protect its free expression? Are there effective methods of limiting such expressions of violence without government-mandated censorship?

Regarding video games, Grossman and DeGaetano, the authors of *Stop Teaching Our Kids to Kill*, claim that modern video games have become so realistic, and their interactive aspect so "educational" that they teach kids to kill as effectively as astronauts learned to fly to the moon before leaving earth. In some of the games, the player pulls a trigger and is rewarded for killing life-like figures, who are seen to fall and die. The player is also rewarded for quickly switching from one target to another to kill multiple victims.[62] Games like "Time Crisis" and "Doom" are so effective that the military and law enforcement use modified versions for actual combat training.[63]

Is the training effective? In Paducah, Kentucky, a fourteen-year-old named Michael Carneal stole a gun, brought it to school and fired eight shots. He had never fired a real weapon before, yet of eight shots fired, he hit eight dif-

ferent children. Five were head shots and three were upper torso shots. Three
children died and one was paralyzed for life. The FBI says that in a real setting, an average experienced officer, at seven yards, will only make one out of
five shots, so Carneal's skill was exceptional.[64]

Furthermore, Carneal did not follow instinct, which would dictate that he
fire continuously at one "threat" until eliminated. Instead, he moved quickly
from target to target, shooting only once at each, as if firing at whatever
popped up on his "screen."[65] It was later learned that Carneal had spent hundreds of hours playing point-and-shoot video games.[66]

Similarly, prior to the Columbine High School massacre, Dylan Kliebold
and Eric Harris had spent hundreds of hours playing "Doom," and Eric had
even reprogrammed his game so that it looked like his own neighborhood,
complete with the houses of people he hated.[67]

The difference between military training and the training children receive
on video games, according to the authors of *Stop Teaching Our Kids to Kill,* is
that there are no safeguards with video games. Military and law-enforcement
agencies use "shoot, don't shoot" scenarios to train personnel when to hold
their fire, whereas video games reward players for shooting everything in
sight. For example, the "Duke Nukem" series awards bonus points for killing
naked prostitutes tied to columns, and games like "Postal" and "Redneck
Rampage" give points for killing innocent victims while they beg for mercy.[68]

Video game producers claim that games with violence carry warnings that
they are for "mature" audiences only. But children usually do not need to provide proof of age to buy these products, and many are readily available online.[69]

As far as violent films and song lyrics are concerned, the interactive aspect
is missing, so it would seem such forms of entertainment would be less likely
to promote violent behavior in the audience. Common experience tells us
that many people exposed to such violent imagery are not incited to violence.
But can such entertainment lead to violence in some? And if it can, should society be complacent about the risk of setting off powder kegs in those who are
susceptible?

Grossman and DeGaetano list multiple medical and governmental studies conducted from 1952 to the present that reach the conclusion that
media violence is in fact one of the risk factors that contributes to real violence. The studies include a 1969 report by The National Commission on
the Causes and Prevention of Violence, a 1972 report by the Surgeon General, a 1976 resolution by the House of Delegates of the American Medical
Association, a 1982 report by the National Institute of Mental Health, the
conclusions of a 1984 attorney general's Task Force on Family Violence, the
conclusions of The American Academy of Pediatrics' Task Force on Chil-

dren and Television, research in 1985 by The American Psychological Association's Commission on Youth and Violence, and an American Psychological Association report, all of which link TV violence to real-life violence.[70]

One of the astounding conclusions appeared in the *Journal of the American Medical Association* in 1992, and involved a study of the change in the violence rate in previously television-free communities after television was introduced. Dr. Brandon Centerwall's study concluded that, "the introduction of television in the 1950s caused a subsequent doubling of the homicide rate.... [I]f, hypothetically, television technology had never been developed, there would today be 10,000 fewer murders each year in the United States, 70,000 fewer rapes, and 700,000 fewer injurious assaults."[71]

Similarly, in a study reported in the January 2001 *Archives of Pediatrics and Adolescent Medicine*,[72] one group of third- and fourth-grade students participated in a "TV turnoff" program that included limiting video games and videotapes as well. A control group of schoolchildren did not. The children's behavior was assessed before and after the TV turnoff. The children in the turnoff group showed a statistically significant decrease in peer ratings of aggression and in observed playground verbal aggression, while the control group did not. The reduction in aggression was greatest for the children who had displayed the most aggression before the TV turnoff. The authors of the study claim that, since they targeted media use without focusing on violent media, the causal effects of media on children's aggressive behavior is even more clear.

On March 28, 2002, the CBS news program *Eye on America* reported that a recent study has found a direct link between watching more than one hour of television a day and reported incidents of violence. Seven hundred people were followed from age fourteen through age thirty, and, taking into account differences in their economic conditions and their neighborhoods, there was still a direct link between violence and watching television.

Some media figures agree. CBS President Leslie Moonves, when asked if he thought the media had anything to do with the Columbine High School shooting, said, "Anyone who thinks the media has nothing to do with it is an idiot."[73] Even the chief executive officer of the NRA has acknowledged a link between media violence and real-life violence. Wayne LaPierre has written, "It's the 'TV-educated' juveniles who emulate the gratuitous violence in the media that are causing the problem."[74]

Predictably, the counterarguments, though few and far between, seem to come from those with financial interests to protect. One Web site that hosts computer games has commented on a Clinton-era surgeon general's report on the relationship between media and violence. It notes that the report cites media as only one of the causes of youth violence, and that "in respect to video games and other interactive media, the [surgeon general's] report stated that the number and type of studies that have investigated the effect of violent games are insufficient to determine the impact of such games on violent behavior."[75]

Similarly, the chairman of the film division in Columbia's School of the Arts has said, "attempts to prove that the media cause—rather than simply influence—behavior are hopelessly inconclusive. First, the question of what constitutes violence is arguable. Studies quantifying the extent of violence on television notoriously group together shows as different as 'Cops' and 'Bugs Bunny.' "[76]

In spite of these protests, the overwhelming weight of the scientific studies show a correlation between media violence and aggressive behavior. If we assume the scientific data is correct, and that violence in the media is a risk factor that increases the likelihood of real violence, what role should society take to protect itself?

In the United States, we abhor censorship. The First Amendment guarantees the constitutional right to express unpopular and even dangerous ideas.[77] The dividing line is not one of content, but of intent. If a person incites another to unlawful conduct, he may cross the First Amendment's line of protection, but if he sets out merely to "entertain," shouldn't the First Amendment protect even the most gory expressions of violence?

Military-trainer and author, Lieutenant Colonel Dave Grossman, advocates that we censure, but not censor, those who exploit violence for profit. He advocates community education including mass refusal to purchase products that glamorize violence. He says we must "turn entirely away from these ugly people, defeating them by refusing them tolerance or respectability."[78] He says that, as we learn the harmful effects of media violence that its deglamorization and condemnation will be done "in simple self-defense as our society rises up against the enabling of the violent crimes that are destroying our lives, our cities, and our civilization."[79] But, in his caution not to recommend treading on First Amendment rights, he suggests that there might come a point where the safety of society should take precedence over freedom of expression. The dividing line for him lies in the degree to which advances in technology make fantasy so real that they desensitize the viewer's moral restraint while stimulating the desire for violence. He acknowledges that not even "the most rabid defender of the Second Amendment" would claim a private right to own nuclear, biological, and highly explosive weapons, so, similarly, regarding media violence:

There is no more need to constrain the print media than there is to control bowie knives, tomahawks or flintlock rifles, but there might just be a justification for controlling,...in the realm of media technology...,TV, movies and video games.[80]

Grossman and DeGaetano, in *Stop Teaching Our Kids to Kill*, conclude that, "[T]he selling of violence to children for profit needs to become a true national issue."[81]

GUN PLAY: SHOULD CHILDREN BE EXPOSED TO FIREARMS?

Federal law does not permit the sale of firearms to those under eighteen years of age nor of handguns to those under twenty-one.[82] Federal law also makes it a crime for those under eighteen to possess a handgun or handgun ammunition, although there are so many exceptions that they almost swallow the rule.[83] For example, minors may temporarily possess handguns for work, in farming, target practice, hunting or firearms training, with parental written consent, as long as state and local laws do not impose additional restrictions.[84] Gun rights proponents often tout firearms training for children as the panacea for preventing firearms accidents among the young and for teaching proper respect for and use of guns. Some also advocate make-believe gunplay as a character-building activity.

Chairman of the Committee for the Right to Keep and Bear Arms, Alan Gottlieb, says, "Playing with guns as a kid helps to develop a strong sense of self—and parents who instill respect for guns and provide firearms training are creating competent and responsible future adults."[85] On the other hand, former surgeon general, Jocelyn Elders, referring to the epidemic level of death by gunfire in America, said, "Please think twice before buying that toy gun for a child. These toy guns are not child's play."[86]

One conservative journalist has suggested that children's gun play is a natural expression of the rough and tumble aggressive play observed in the young of many mammals. He posits the concept that if aggressive play is suppressed, we are fooling with Mother Nature. He predicts that suppressing childhood aggression might have disastrous consequences since "Mother Nature has a way of fighting back when she is thwarted."[87]

On the other hand, the Oxnard, California, police department warns that disastrous consequences follow when toy guns are mistaken for real guns. The Oxnard PD Web site reports that an airport was shut down due to security concerns over a six-year-old's toy gun, a sixteen year old was shot by police when his water pistol was mistaken for a real gun, and an eleven year old was expelled under "zero tolerance" rules for bringing a realistic-looking toy gun to school.[88] Some jurisdictions have proposed bans on toy guns that are designed to look real,[89] and others have proposed gun buy-back programs for toy guns.[90]

Some parents make the decision that their children will not be permitted to own toy guns, nor will they knowingly expose them to real ones. Others suggest that, when children begin to show an interest in guns, they should be taken to a firing range and taught to handle guns safely. According to the Americans for Gun Safety Foundation, "this removes the 'forbidden fruit' attraction from firearms. It replaces it with knowledge and discipline."[91]

The National Rifle Association advocates teaching gun safety to children through its Eddie Eagle Gun Safety Program (if you see a gun, stop, don't touch, leave the area, and tell an adult). The NRA claims the Eddie Eagle program does not teach young children to shoot.[92] At the same time, the NRA is proud that "more than one million youth participate in NRA shooting sports events and affiliated programs."[93]

Paxton Quigley, author of *Armed and Female,* says that telling a child never to touch a gun is not enough to insure safety. She recommends firearms training for the young:

Although it may sound radical at first, the ideal strategy is first to show your children how your gun works while you're cleaning it, and then, later, to go to a range and show them how to shoot a gun.... From the outset make it clear that they are never to handle a real gun when you are not with them, and, of course never to point even a toy gun at anyone. At the same time, tell them that if they want to handle—not play with—a gun in your presence, they will be allowed to do so.[94]

Gun control proponents would respond that because we do not train children early in dangerous activities such as driving, why make an exception for firearms?

Emory University researcher Dr. Arthur Kellerman pointed out the innate emotional volatility of the young when he said, "Teaching a child respect for a gun doesn't change the child's willingness to use it if he's depressed, if he just failed a test that he felt the rest of his life depended on, or just broke up with his girlfriend or he's mad at his best friend."[95]

A parent's decision regarding a child's exposure to guns must be made carefully and within the bounds of local and federal law.

4

Does the Second Amendment Guarantee an Individual Right?

INTRODUCTION

Do we have a Second Amendment constitutional right to keep and carry firearms? This question has plagued legal scholars, gun rights advocates, and gun control proponents for several decades.

Gun control proponents assert that the legal precedents clearly say no. Courts have repeatedly ruled that the Second Amendment to the U.S. Constitution speaks of the militia, and unless a firearm reasonably relates to a person's membership in a government-sponsored militia, individuals have no such guaranteed rights.

But legal precedent has not ended the debate. Gun rights advocates argue that history reveals the clear intent of those who drafted the Second Amendment. Individuals, regardless of their involvement with a militia, were meant to have the right to keep and bear arms. Those advocates urge courts to change course and adopt an individual rights view of the Second Amendment.

Gun control proponents and gun rights advocates engage in heated disagreements over the meaning of the Second Amendment's wording. They argue about how common gun ownership was in early America. One side sees the early government heavily regulating guns, while the other extols the historical protection accorded our "natural right" to self-defense. One side says the fledgling Union would not have tolerated insurrection, while the other says the Second Amendment was meant to insure that an armed populace could overthrow a tyrannous regime. Historians on both sides cite facts and quote sources that best support their views, and little history is universally agreed upon.

Because the U.S. Supreme Court has announced no individual right, courts have not had reason to explore the extent of, nor the limitations on, any such right. So, even assuming that the Supreme Court is persuaded to someday acknowledge such an individual right, the extent to which the right may be curtailed would still be an open question. This is true because our constitutional rights may be curtailed if competing societal interests are strong enough.

For example, our First Amendment right to free speech must be exercised responsibly. If we harm others with our words, we can be sued for slander or defamation, in spite of the First Amendment. If the Supreme Court decides someday that an individual has a Second Amendment right to keep and bear arms, courts will still need to decide the extent to which gun control regulations may limit that constitutional right.

LEGAL CONTEXT OF THE SECOND AMENDMENT

In analyzing the Second Amendment, it is most helpful to begin with a simple legal truth. The meaning of the Second Amendment is whatever the courts say it is. Therefore, the Second Amendment may not mean what its words seem to express if the courts say otherwise. Neither does it mean what private individuals wish it means, no matter how well-reasoned their arguments. The legal "meaning" of the Constitution is the exclusive province of federal court judges, for the simple reason that our system grants them the power to determine constitutional meaning.

America's political system is famous for its checks and balances. We have three branches of government: the executive, the legislative, and the judicial. Each has its own role, but each can look over the shoulder of the other and keep it in check. For example, the president is chief of the executive branch, which exists to enforce laws, but the president may veto laws passed by the legislative branch. The federal courts may declare that a law passed by the legislative branch is unconstitutional. In return, the legislative branch may remove the unconstitutional provision and pass the law again. At its best, our system is a finely crafted dance of power.

In this system, the top two tiers of the federal court system, consisting of the circuit courts of appeals and, above them, the Supreme Court of the United States, have the power to interpret and declare the meaning of laws and of the Constitution of the United States. This has been clear since 1803 when Chief Justice Marshall of the U.S. Supreme Court, in the famous case of *Marbury v. Madison,* declared that it was the judiciary's duty "to say what the law is."[1]

When appellate-level judges declare the meaning of the Constitution, judges in the same jurisdiction must follow that rule in later cases. This system of following legal precedent bears the Latin name *stare decisis.* Exceptions to *stare decisis*—following precedent—may occur if a court in a later case modifies or overturns one of its own prior decisions.

In the hierarchy of the judicial system, the Supreme Court of the United States has the last word on the meaning of the U.S. Constitution. The Supreme Court's ruling is nationally binding and is final, unless the Supreme Court itself later changes its own prior ruling. Therefore, the dispute over the meaning of the Second Amendment focuses on cases decided by the U.S. Supreme Court, and the heart of the debate lies in that court's few pronouncements.

What are those pronouncements? First, let us look at the language of the Second Amendment itself. The Second Amendment says:

A well regulated Militia, being necessary to the security of a free State, the right of the people to keep and bear Arms, shall not be infringed.[2]

It was not until 1875 that the U.S. Supreme Court first spoke on the meaning of the Second Amendment. The Court reversed the convictions of southern whites charged with conspiring to deprive blacks of a constitutional right to keep and bear arms. It held that the Second Amendment could not be violated by individuals. It was meant only to limit the power of the federal government with respect to state militias.[3] Then, in 1886, the Court upheld a man's conviction for violating a state law prohibiting military assemblies without a permit, noting that the Second Amendment established no individual right to bear arms.[4]

In 1939, in the now-famous case of *United States v. Miller,*[5] the U.S. Supreme Court was asked to decide on the constitutionality of a federal law called the National Firearms Act.[6] Section 11 of that law made it a crime to transport in interstate commerce certain types of unregistered weapons, in this case a "sawed-off shotgun." The Court ruled that, unless possession or use of a firearm "has some reasonable relationship to the preservation or efficiency of a well regulated militia, we cannot say that the Second Amendment guarantees the right to keep and bear such an instrument."[7] The Court said there had been no proof that this shotgun was "any part of the ordinary military equipment or that its use could contribute to the common defense."[8] Therefore, when the Act criminalized interstate transportation of the unregistered, short-barreled shotgun, the Act did not violate the Second Amendment.

In reaching its conclusion, the Supreme Court noted that the U.S. Constitution had given Congress the power to call forth the state militia for federal purposes, leaving the states with authority to appoint the officers and to train and discipline the militia.[9] Next, the Court declared that the Second Amendment had the "obvious purpose to assure the continuation and render possible the effectiveness of such forces."[10] It was against this backdrop that the Court upheld the constitutionality of the National Firearms Act.

Since the *Miller* case was decided, the Supreme Court has only twice addressed the Second Amendment. In a 1961 case,[11] the Supreme Court approved of the way that, in *Miller,* it had looked to historical sources to decide that the Second Amendment guaranteed rights, not to the people, but to the militia. In 1980, in *Lewis v. United States,*[12] the Supreme Court cited *Miller* in a footnote, when it noted, in passing, that a challenged law[13] passed Second Amendment constitutional muster.[14] The only other times the Supreme Court has mentioned *Miller* are in concurring or dissenting opinions,[15] which are not binding law under the principle of *stare decisis.*

Although Supreme Court decisions regarding the Second Amendment have been sparse, there have been many cases[16] decided by the federal circuit courts of appeals affirming the proposition that the Second Amendment does not expressly guarantee a personal right to possess a firearm. The Amendment encompasses only possession of weapons reasonably related to the activity of the militia. Only recently has one federal circuit, the Fifth Circuit Court of Appeals, ruled to the contrary. Its lone decision and the effect of its decision is discussed later in this chapter.

To give an example of the presently prevailing view, note this language from a 2002 federal appellate court ruling from the Ninth Circuit:

The [Second] Amendment protects the people's right to maintain an effective state militia, and does not establish an individual right to own or possess firearms for personal or other use.[17]

In spite of, or perhaps because of, the relative silence of the Supreme Court, a large body of legal and lay Second Amendment analysis has sprung up in the form of law review articles, books, legal briefs, online discussion groups, radio talk shows, and letters to the editor. In fact, the media has been saturated with the subject in recent years, spurred by high profile shootings and by the resulting proliferation of gun control proposals. Even the Supreme Court has noticed its own silence in relation to the public din. Justice Clarence Thomas said, in 1997, "Although somewhat overlooked in our jurisprudence, the [Second] Amendment has certainly engendered considerable academic, as well as public debate."[18] It is against this legal backdrop that the debate over the Second Amendment roars on.

EARLY GUN CONTROL IN ENGLAND AND AMERICA

Gun control proponents have amassed much information about the history of gun control laws in England and in the early American colonies. They use the information to bolster their argument that gun control was an expected and even an intended aspect of the Second Amendment. Gun rights advocates, on the other hand, argue that much gun control legislation has been passed in violation of the Second Amendment's guarantees, which hold gun owners' rights sacrosanct.

In order to understand the intent behind the Second Amendment, we will first examine historical attitudes toward gun control. While some argue that the English enjoyed a broad right to possess firearms, others point to early English restrictions intended to keep firearms out of the hands of the masses of poor people, and to restrict their possession to the social elite and the government-controlled military.

For example, during the reigns of Henry VII and Henry VIII, the wheel lock was outlawed, for fear it would give too much power to the poor. Under Henry VIII, royal permission was needed to shoot firearms. In 1541, parliament limited possession of firearms to the nobility and certain wealthy freeholders. Not only was the possession of firearms limited, but the crown sought to monitor the distribution of firearms. In 1660, Charles II tracked the sale of firearms by requiring gun makers to report all gun sales including the person to whom guns were sold, and to list all guns held in stock.[19]

On the other side of the argument, when referring to historical England, one author has said that "many, if not most common people had arms."[20] This does not explain why, in early modern England, a thorough review of popular rebellions reveals no instances of people firing at government authorities. It appears they went up against armed troops with only farm implements. And when they did turn out for militia duty, as they were sometimes required to do, they brought only pikes and clubs, but not firearms. The English government had to provide any firearms. Therefore, the argument goes, it is unlikely that the majority of English commoners owned firearms.[21] In fact, the English Declaration of Rights limited the possession of firearms to high-ranking Protestants "as allowed" by parliament.[22]

Gun control proponents argue that gun control was the norm in the colonial era. The American colonies legislated who could and could not own firearms. For example, in 1637, Massachusetts disarmed all but certain Protestants. Maryland disarmed its Catholics in 1670. The colonies restricted slaves and indentured servants from bearing arms.[23] Colonial governments severely penalized the sale of firearms to Indians.[24]

Other early government controls on firearms included prohibitions against using firearms in connection with alcohol, and against frivolous shooting of a musket.[25] Colonial Virginia allowed expropriation of firearms during times of crisis, and allowed its governor to conduct gun censuses.[26]

Although free white males were encouraged to own firearms in support of militias, the government reserved to itself the right to impress those arms on any occasion.[27] And the militias were under exclusive control of the government. It was illegal in the British empire for groups to form their own private military bodies. Such groups would have been prosecuted as rioters or insurrectionists.[28]

After the Revolution, Congress passed the Uniform Militia Act of 1792, which limited who could bear arms in state militias to free, able-bodied, white male citizens between the ages of eighteen and forty-five.[29] Gun control proponents argue that this means no Second Amendment guarantee was intended to apply outside of that group.

BACKGROUND OF THE SECOND AMENDMENT

After the American Revolution, the Constitutional Convention met in Philadelphia in 1787 to draw up the U.S. Constitution. The proposed Constitution was sent to the states for ratification. Its provisions were hotly debated between the Federalists, who generally supported a strong national government, and the Anti-Federalists, who feared their newfound liberty would be lost to a centralized power. The Anti-Federalists objected that the Constitution did not enumerate and protect individual rights. A sufficient number of states ratified the Constitution, and it went into effect on September 17, 1787.

In 1789, Congress responded to the Anti-Federalists' concerns by proposing the first ten amendments to the Constitution. These amendments are called the Bill of Rights. While the body of the Constitution delineates the powers accorded the three branches of government, the Bill of Rights describes the relationship of the newly formed government to its people. These ten amendments were ratified by the states in 1791.

The right to bear arms is described in the Second Amendment, which says:

A well regulated Militia, being necessary to the security of a free State, the right of the people to keep and bear Arms, shall not be infringed.[30]

At the time of the American Revolution, the colonies had their own militias. In fact, the famous Revolutionary battles at Lexington and Concord, Massachusetts, were fought by militiamen. For the period in question, the

Oxford English Dictionary defines "militia" as "a citizen army as distinguished from a body of mercenaries or professional soldiers."[31]

In 1776, Adam Smith described a militia this way:

[The state] may...oblige either all the citizens of the military age, or a certain number of them to join in some measure the trade of a soldier to whatever other trade or profession they happen to carry on. Its military force is then said to consist in a militia.[32]

Similarly, in 1787, Attorney General Luther Martin wrote a letter to the Maryland legislature in which he said that, if the states were to cede all control of their militias to Congress, the citizens might actually be grateful, "as thereby they would be freed from the burdens of militia duties, and left to their own private occupations and pleasures."[33] So it is clear that membership in a militia was a part-time duty owed to the state by citizens who had other occupations.

The state militias had their roots in the colonies. A law enacted in 1649 in the colony of Massachusetts declared that the infantry would be made up of musketeers and pikemen. The musketeers were required to carry a "good fixed musket" of a certain length, a priming wire, a scourer and mould, a sword, rest, bandoleers, one pound of powder, twenty bullets, and two fathoms of match. The pikemen were required to carry a pike, corselet, headpiece, sword, and knapsack.[34]

In 1784, Massachusetts law provided for a militia. Its militia included a "Train Band," made up of all able-bodied men, from sixteen to forty years old, and an "Alarm list" made up of all other men under sixty. Each officer and soldier in the militia who had "sufficient ability in the judgment of the Selectmen of the town" where he lived was required to "equip himself, and be constantly provided with a good fire arm, &c."[35]

In 1785, Virginia required all free males between eighteen and fifty years of age (with exceptions) to enroll in a company of the state's militia. The companies would meet once every two months.[36] The militiamen were to report for duty with a musket of a certain length, a "good bayonet" with iron ramrod, a cartridge box, and twenty cartridges, a "good knapsack and canteen," one pound of "good powder," and four pounds of lead, including twenty blind cartridges. In the counties west of the Blue Ridge, a rifle could substitute for a musket. If any private could not afford the required arms, he could apply to the court, which would allow the purchase with money collected from fining those who failed to comply with this law.[37]

In 1786, New York required all able-bodied male citizens who were between sixteen and forty-five years of age to enroll in a local "Beat" of the state militia and to provide themselves, at their own expense, "a Musket or Fire-

lock, a sufficient Bayonet and Belt, a Pouch with a Box therein to contain not
less than Twenty-four Cartridges suited to the Bore of his Musket or Firelock,
each Cartridge containing a proper Quantity of Powder and Ball, two spare
Flints, a Blanket and Knapsack...."[38]

These laws did not ensure, however, that all men were armed as required.
Patrick Henry, who said that "the great object is, that every man be armed,"[39]
went on to say:

But we have learned, by experience, that necessary as it is to have arms, and though
our assembly has, by a succession of laws for many years, endeavored to have the militia completely armed, it is still far from being the case.[40]

Controversy has arisen over the number of guns actually in the possession
of private citizens in our early history. Were we primarily a nation of self-
reliant, armed citizens who hunted, defended the homestead, and banded together with neighbors in the militia? Or were firearms an expensive and rare
feature of early American life?

Michael Bellesiles, the author of *Arming America: The Origins of a National Gun Culture*,[41] studied old records of wills from the era and found that
only a small percentage of deceased males listed firearms in their inventories.
He also studied "militia records, legislative materials—colonial, imperial,
local, state, and federal—police and court files, travel accounts, diaries, newspapers and journals, personal letters and official correspondence, account
books and production records, novels and short stories, and woodcuts and
paintings"[42] to piece together a cultural picture of how the early Americans as
a whole viewed firearms and their relationship to firearms.

Bellesiles concluded that firearms, which, for most of early American history were manufactured exclusively in Europe, primarily for the wealthy or
the military, were expensive and rare objects. Early firearms were also techno-
logically troublesome, cumbersome and difficult to aim. As for hunting, the
author asserts that early Americans were famously well-fed, not from the in-
efficient art of hunting with unreliable firearms (he says they tended more toward trapping game), but from farming and raising domestic livestock.[43] He
asserts that by the 1740s there were probably more guns per capita among the
Indians than among the whites.[44]

Bellesiles does not claim that there were no guns or even few guns in early
America, but that there were fewer than we have been led to believe, and that
Americans on the whole displayed little interest in guns. For example, he cites
Massachusetts records regarding privately owned muskets, and compares it
with population estimates of the era, and concludes that only 23 percent of
white Massachusetts males over sixteen owned guns in 1789.[45] Of the people

who did own firearms, they often let them fall into disrepair due to the lack of gunsmiths in early America.

According to Bellesiles, the militia system became so notoriously ineffective, due to lack of sufficient serviceable firearms and due to civilian avoidance of military service, that the colonies began to arm and to pay professional soldiers instead.[46] And at the famous battle of Lexington, which began America's Revolutionary War, out of 130 militiamen gathered, only 7 Americans fired their weapons at the advancing British forces.[47] As for the American militia's supposed superior skill at marksmanship, these farmer/militiamen had little practice at shooting. As the Lexington battle spread to surrounding towns, 3,763 Americans in all participated, but only 273 British were hit.[48]

Bellesiles concludes that a distinctive American gun culture did not arise until the Civil War era.[49] It was not until then that technological advances, including mass production techniques, created a fervor for guns. Until that time, American gun makers could not produce large numbers of firearms. Most guns available to colonists and to early Americans came from Europe. The few early gun makers on this continent each produced only a handful of handmade weapons per year. Most supplemented their income by engaging in other trades. Therefore, in America's early days, there was no economic push to create a major market for firearms.[50]

Then, in 1848, Samuel Colt opened a new gun factory in Hartford, Connecticut, and began to manufacture his newly invented, rapid-shooting revolver, which he cleverly decorated with Wild West images and which he marketed as the tool that opened the West, although most of his sales were in the East and in Europe. The guns were designed for personal self-defense, not for hunting. He combined machine production with traditional handcraft techniques to produce them by the thousands.[51]

In 1857, Congress refused to renew Colt's patent, and companies such as Remington, Starr, Whitney, and Smith & Wesson rushed into the revolver-making business. According to Bellesiles, these gun companies promoted the mystique of the hardy, self-reliant, armed American male to boost sales. Gun makers "convinced an ever-wider audience that they needed guns in order to be real Americans."[52] This, according to Bellesiles, was the real beginning of the American gun culture, not America's reliance on the militia. It was not until mass production entered the equation that guns began to be made plentifully and locally. Bellesiles asserts that these new American gun manufacturers spurred our distinctive American gun culture, by promoting "Wild West" shows of shooting skill, and by popularizing the newly invented six-shooter for self-defense.[53]

The implications of this thesis on the intent behind the Second Amendment are strong, although Bellesiles says he takes no position on this issue.

But, if he is correct that no predominant gun culture existed in the late 1700s, and if the government heavily controlled the firearms that did exist, a concern for individual rights to keep firearms could not have been what spurred the Second Amendment.

Bellesiles received accolades from the academic community for this new view of America's gun culture, and he was awarded the prestigious Bancroft Prize in 2001.[54] Then the National Rifle Association and other gun rights groups chimed in, and the debate over gun ownership in early America spilled over into the political arena. Once controversy erupted, academics began to take a second look to see whether or not they had been duped by Bellesiles and his research.

First, gun rights groups took a stand. They countered that firearms possession was nearly universal. Focusing on Bellesiles' count of guns in probate records (which takes up five paragraphs of his lengthy book), they attacked his conclusions. They argue that, just because a firearm is not mentioned in a will, it does not mean the person did not own one. None of the inventories of Thomas Jefferson's three estates lists any firearms, yet Jefferson owned dozens of guns during his life.[55]

After the gun rights groups jumped into the fray, the academics followed. The historical journal *The William and Mary Quarterly*[56] published a forum in which historians explored the controversy.

One historian, Gloria L. Main, claims that Bellesiles did not do his homework when it came to probate records of gun ownership.[57] She cites her own studies of probate records in which she claims that, between 1650 to 1720, 76 percent of young Maryland fathers owned "arms of some sort," as compared to Bellesiles' claim that only 7 percent of Maryland wills mentioned guns.[58] She admits she was counting all arms, including swords and pikes, which she did not count separately, claiming only that swords and pikes were "rare." She also does not explain why she looked at the probate records of "young" males as opposed to all records, but because the young might be of a more fit age to go hunting, this might skew the overall percentages upward, whereas Bellesiles included records of the old and of women, and he counted only guns. In other words, she seems to be comparing apples and oranges.

Interestingly, this same historian agrees with Bellesiles that most guns were imported by way of the long sea voyage from Europe because there were few American gun makers, and that the wealthy few were almost twice as likely as the more numerous poor to own guns.[59] Yet she concludes that American consumers "clearly wanted their guns" and that they "did not have to wait for domestic mass production to supply their demand,"[60] without explaining where the supply came from nor how people could afford guns.

Another historian, Ira D. Gruber, criticizes Bellesiles' research as "biased" and "careless" and says that Bellesiles minimizes the importance of some of his facts while exaggerating others.[61] Yet Gruber seems to agree with Bellesiles' key points. For example, he does not contend that the musket was a finely crafted, accurate weapon, but rather that Bellesiles "exaggerated" its weaknesses.[62] Similarly, he does not dispute Bellesiles' claim that there were battles in which the use of the bayonet was more important to the outcome than firepower, but asserts only that, in some battles, firepower was more important.[63] Gruber agrees that history proves that "the militia was not well trained" and that "the militia was not an effective military force" and that "the militia was never completely armed," but concludes that Bellesiles "overemphasized the weaknesses of the militia."[64] This historian's criticisms fall in the area of context and nuance, not in the area of substance.

A more detailed and substantive critique by another historian, Randolph Roth, claims that Bellesiles' research methods were flawed, but, again, Roth focuses on the issue of counting guns listed in probate inventories, a small fraction of Bellesiles' argument.[65] Bellesiles admits that he would use different sampling set methods today,[66] and points to significant flaws in his critic's own counting methods. Bellesiles reviewed the probate records again and remained firm in his overall conclusions. The most true thing any of them say on this subject is Bellesiles' own comment: "Historians may examine the same records and yet literally be on different pages."[67]

Randolph Roth presents some intriguing evidence in two early-nineteenth-century newspaper clippings about the "dreadful slaughter" of many thousands of squirrels by "enterprising sharpshooters" out for the bounty on those crop-stealing vermin.[68] Those clippings, however, do not provide much counterweight to *Arming America*'s meaty thesis that Americans, in general, showed little interest in firearms until the middle of the nineteenth century.

Finally, a fourth historian, Jack N. Rakove, does not challenge Bellesiles' research, but instead asks the important question, What difference does it make to our understanding of the Second Amendment, if we discover that gun ownership was less widespread than previously assumed, that guns of that era were not well suited for self-protection or hunting, and that "the militia was typically a moribund joke in time of peace and of little military value in time of war?"[69] Rakove concludes that, even if the Second Amendment was designed to express the "aspiration to preserve a citizen militia" in an era when that ideal "had already slipped," that perhaps it is inappropriate to rely on the "original intent" of the writers of the Second Amendment, because "firearms are now more devastating than anyone in the eighteenth century could have plausibly imagined."[70] He asks, What obligation do we now have to defer to the presumed aspirations of that generation?[71]

Although this question reflects a naive view of the seriousness with which courts take their obligation to explore questions of "original intent," courts do sometimes bend with the times, albeit cautiously and slowly, so the eventual outcome of the ongoing courtroom battle over the Second Amendment cannot be predicted.

Bellesiles defends his theories against these critics.[72] He says that he is not primarily concerned with the number of guns in early America, and that his book is not about probate records, because that subject only takes up five paragraphs in his lengthy work.[73] His goal was to research many sources in order to paint a composite picture of the cultural attitude toward firearms, which, he concludes, appears to have been indifference: "Most Americans in the colonial period did not care that much about firearms."[74] The wealthy may have had them, but some groups, such as African Americans, indentured servants, and in some areas Catholics, were prohibited from owning guns, and there is "no evidence that gun ownership was common among the poor."[75]

Bellesiles expresses frustration that, in the face of "all this scholarship . . . gun advocacy groups persist in an unquestioning faith in the militia myth, maintaining that the American Revolution was won by common farmers grabbing their trusty rifles from above the mantle and rushing forth to do battle with King George's redcoats for the next eight years."[76] After all, it is "well documented that the performance of the militia in the American Revolution was generally abysmal after the first few months of the war."[77] Even George Washington's opinion of the militia "started out low and shrank with time."[78]

Bellesiles professes not to promote any single ideology on the subject of the intent of the framers of the Second Amendment for the simple reason that they had no single intent. "[W]e cannot speak of the framers of the Constitution as a single unit, so diverse were their understandings and so wide their disagreements."[79] The Second Amendment, like many of our laws, resulted from compromise in the midst of controversy. As far as he is concerned, if the courts do lean heavily on original intent in interpreting the Second Amendment (which he does not argue for; he believes the Constitution should remain flexible over time), history shows that, at the close of the American Revolution, the militia was placed under the control of the federal government "in an effort to see to its proper organization, training, and arming,"[80] and that "guns remained in the service of the state, subject to many forms of regulation, and limited by racial, ethnic, class, and even religious classifications."[81]

One problem not noted by Bellesiles' critics, but which should not be glossed over, is that he displays some inconsistency in how he describes the early American cultural view of guns. On the one hand, he says that because firearms were scarce, expensive, and clumsy instruments, people had little interest in owning them, and when they did, they let them fall into disrepair for lack of gunsmiths to fix them. But when early Americans do express interest in guns, he sees them as caught up in a gun "mythology" that didn't really exist. So, is he talking about the reality of gun ownership, as in the number and distribution of guns, or is he talking about the cultural attitude toward guns, which does not necessarily depend on the number of available guns?

Guns might have been scarce and unreliable, but couldn't people of that era still have perceived, rightly or wrongly, that guns played an important role in the lives of the colonists? If so, their gun "culture" might differ from their reality. In other words, the "myth" (if it was one) of the armed and self-reliant backwoodsman might have been the cultural perception of those times, and not merely a nostalgic revision of history.

For example, Benjamin Franklin boasted about Pennsylvania's armed citizens in a newspaper article in 1747. Franklin may have believed what he wrote, or may have been motivated to exaggerate the skills of the colonists, or he may have been writing satirically, but in any case, he appears to buy into the "myth." Thus, he wrote:

If this now flourishing City, and greatly improving Colony, is destroy'd and ruin'd it will not be for want of Numbers of Inhabitants able to bear Arms in its defence. 'Tis computed that we have at least (exclusive of Quakers) 60,000 Fighting Men, acquainted with FireArms, many of them Hunters and Marksmen, hardy and bold.[82]

Bellesiles refers to this type of contemporary braggadocio as the "mythology of shooting skill" with which even "sensible people" were swept up.[83] But if "sensible people" such as the founding fathers believed in the hardy and bold, well-armed American, even if it was not an accurate reflection of reality, perhaps the mythology itself prompted the creation of the Second Amendment. In other words, does the historical reality matter if those who drafted the Constitution were, themselves, seduced by the myth? If the intent of the framers was to protect a way of life that never really existed, does that alter the framers' purpose or their ideology? And so, the controversy begins.

TODAY'S ARGUMENTS PRO AND CON

It may appear simplistic to say that there are only two sides to the Second Amendment argument, but, with some exceptions, this debate has become so polarized that an almost religious fervor prevails. Gun control advocates tend to support the argument that the Second Amendment only applies when it relates to a person's participation in a militia (now the National Guard), while

Stephanie Atchison demonstrates a long rifle of the type used on the Lewis and Clark expedition at Fort Clatsop National Memorial, Warrenton, Oregon. (Courtesy National Park Service, Fort Clatsop National Memorial.)

most gun rights advocates believe the Second Amendment guarantees broad protection of an individual's rights to keep and carry guns of all types.

There are people who take a middle ground, and who say that the Second Amendment would support a mix of rights and responsibilities. These people advocate controlling the sale of some types of extra-lethal guns, such as certain assault weapons, and they do not oppose some restrictions on where and how guns may be carried. It should be noted, however, that many gun rights advocates are suspicious of the centrists, viewing them as wolves in sheep's clothing, ready to rob them of their rights.[84] Therefore, it is useful to present the Second Amendment controversy as a two-sided argument between politicized factions, while keeping in mind that there are many nuances.

The gun control proponents have not agreed entirely whether the Second Amendment guarantees rights of individuals in their collective role as militia members (sometimes called the "collective rights theory"), or whether the Second Amendment guarantees the rights of the states to keep their militia members armed (sometimes called the "states rights theory"). In either case, they are talking about rights that only arise to protect the strength of the militia. Therefore, this book will refer to them as the "militia rights" proponents in order to distinguish them from the second group, the "individual rights" proponents.

THE LANGUAGE OF THE SECOND AMENDMENT
Militia Rights or Individual Rights?

Looking solely at the language of the Second Amendment, the militia rights proponents argue that the first clause of the Second Amendment qualifies everything that follows, and cannot be separated from it. One commentator has suggested that the Second Amendment could be paraphrased in modern language this way: "An armed and militarily trained citizenry being conducive to freedom, the right of the electorate to organize itself militarily shall not be infringed."[85] In other words, the federal government cannot restrict militia members from keeping firearms and using (bearing) them while acting as militia members. Because the states, as government bodies, cannot "bear arms," the right is given to individuals in their representative capacity, but the individual has the right to bear arms only to the extent it advances a state's interest in its well-regulated militia.

On the other hand, individual rights advocates would say that the drafters meant something different. They would paraphrase the Second Amendment this way: The right of the people to keep and bear arms shall not be infringed (meaning, shall not be taken from the *individual*), because a well-regulated militia is necessary to the security of a free state. They argue that the Second Amendment's phrase, "A well regulated Militia, being necessary to the security of a free State...," serves only an explanatory purpose. The right of the people to keep and bear arms may be worthy of protection because such a militia is needed. But the right exists regardless of the individual's relationship to a well-regulated militia. If that were not true, the Founders would have written "the right of the militia to keep and bear arms..." instead of "the right of the people to keep and bear arms...."[86] So, the guarantee does not belong, collectively, to militias. It belongs to individuals. In one court case, the National Rifle Association put it this way:

The Second Amendment simply forbids the federal government from infringing the right of individual American citizens to keep and bear arms, and this prohibition contributes to fostering "a well regulated militia" by preserving the armed citizenry from which the framers believed that such a militia should be drawn.[87]

A supporting argument goes this way. The structure of the Second Amendment is equivalent to the following: "A well educated citizenry, being necessary to the culture of a free state, the right of the people to keep and read books, shall not be infringed." That sentence structure means all the people have the right to keep and read books, not a government-selected intelligentsia.[88]

Individual rights proponents also point to evidence from the era. In 1789, a newspaper reporter understood the Second Amendment to mean "that the said constitution be never construed to authorize congress... to prevent the people of the United States, who are peaceable citizens, from keeping their own arms...."[89]

What Does "Bear Arms" Mean?

There is a dispute over the meaning of the phrase "bear arms." It has been argued that "bear arms" is a peculiarly military phrase.[90] In modern times we might say that we "bear arms" against enemy troops, but we do not speak of bearing arms against deer or rabbits, nor do we normally speak of bearing arms in defense of our homes. The question is, how would the drafters of the Second Amendment have used the phrase?

Looking to the *Oxford English Dictionary*'s definition of "bear," we find that the phrase "bear arms" dates back to at least 1568, and has been long used in a military context.[91] James Madison had drafted a proposed version of the Second Amendment in which he used the phrase in its military context. His proposed draft read, "The right of the people to keep and bear arms shall not be infringed; a well armed, and well regulated militia being the best security of a free country: but no person religiously scrupulous of bearing arms, shall be compelled to render military service in person."[92] Militia rights proponents point out that the conscientious objector clause of the proposal shows that James Madison understood the phrase "bear arms" in its military sense.

Standing alone, the word "arms" also has a primarily military meaning, according to this line of argument. The *Oxford English Dictionary* defines "arms" as, "Instruments of offense used in war; weapons,"[93] and that dictionary traces the military usage of the term back to the year 1300 in the quotation (modernized here): "arms he has and shield to fight with upon the field." For more than 150 years, judges, when ruling in legal cases, have also held that the word "arms" is used in its military context in the phrase "bear arms."[94]

The presence of the word "keep," as in "keep and bear arms," does not change the military character of the phrase, according to an argument raised in *United States v. Emerson*.[95] The reasoning goes that, by protecting the right to "keep" as well as "bear" arms, the amendment assures that militiamen are able to store their weapons at home.

Individual rights advocates argue that the phrase "bear arms" did not have an exclusively military meaning. They point out that Pennsylvania and Vermont guaranteed their people the right to "bear arms for the defense of themselves and the state."[96] Thus, the idea of bearing arms for personal defense was not unheard of. These advocates also find mention at state constitutional ratification conventions of the right "to bear arms for defense, or for killing game,"[97] another indication that the phrase "bear arms" had both a military and personal meaning.

One definition of "bear" means to carry or wear. Thomas Jefferson drafted a game bill restricting those convicted of hunting out of season from "bearing" a gun off the person's property.[98] This shows that Jefferson understood "bear" to mean "carry." (It also shows that Thomas Jefferson, idol of the gun rights camp, helped draft a gun control law.)

What Does "Infringed" Mean?

There is debate over the meaning of the word "infringed." The Second Amendment says that the right of the people to keep and bear arms "shall not be infringed."

Militia rights proponents argue that, both before and after the American Revolution, there were many legal restrictions on firearms possession, and the Second Amendment was not intended to alter those restrictions, merely to prevent the federal government from taking away existing rights.[99]

Individual rights advocates agree that the intent was to leave existing rights intact, but they view those existing rights as "natural rights," including the universal, natural right to self-defense. They point out that the word "infringe" is only used in the Constitution in relation to individual rights, not to government bodies. The Constitution "delegates" or "reserves" governmental powers.[100]

So, if the Second Amendment was meant to protect a state's right, or the rights of citizens collectively, the drafters would have written that the state reserves its right to arm its citizens. They wouldn't have tried to prevent the federal government from "infringing" some perceived state's right, because, in our system, governmental bodies do not have "rights" but only powers that the people delegate to those bodies.

What Does "Militia" Mean?

Militia rights proponents say that, in that era, "militia" was not synonymous with "all men." John Adams distinguished between individuals and a legally sanctioned militia this way:

To suppose arms in the hands of citizens, to be used at individual discretion, except in private self-defense, or by partial orders of towns, counties or districts of a state, is to demolish every constitution, and lay the laws prostrate, so that liberty can be enjoyed by no man; it is a dissolution of the government. The fundamental law of the militia is, that it be created, directed and commanded by the laws, and ever for the support of the laws.[101]

Individual rights advocates respond that militia duty was so nearly universal, that the term "militia" encompasses "the people." Furthermore, the phrase "the right of the people" is unambiguous. They say it would be strange to grant a state's right to maintain a militia in the Bill of Rights, which guarantees the rights of individuals.[102] Particularly, the First and Fourth Amendments use the same language as the Second Amendment when they guarantee rights to "the people," and those two Amendments insure individual rights, not collective rights or rights of the states.[103]

What Does "Right" Mean?

Individual rights proponents point out that the Constitution uses the term "right" only in regard to individual rights. The federal and state governments are given "powers," not "rights." Nor does the Constitution use the term "people" to mean a state government.[104]

All this debate over words leaves only one thing clear. The twenty-seven words in the Second Amendment have been dissected and analyzed by excellent minds on both sides of this cultural rift. When the debate rises above mudslinging and name-calling, each side's analysis deserves respect.

GUN CONTROL PROPONENTS AND THE SECOND AMENDMENT

Gun control proponents view gun control as a consistent and expected part of the national fabric. They profess that, even in colonial times, gun ownership was regulated, and that possession of firearms was viewed as a collective duty necessary to the defense of society, not as an individual right.[105] Here is the argument from their point of view.

Historic Precedents for Gun Control

Gun control proponents point out that American firearms laws derived from English law where the right to keep and bear arms was not seen as a fundamental right of the people.[106] The 1689 English Bill of Rights, which was written in response to the king's keeping a standing army without the consent of parliament, and in response to his "endeavor to subvert and extirpate the Protestant religion," guaranteed that "Protestants may have arms for their defense suitable to their conditions and as allowed by law...."[107] This right was intended to guarantee that England's noblemen could form feudal militias, in order to prevent the central government from monopolizing military force.[108] It left intact numerous legal restrictions on gun possession, and did not universally guarantee an individual's rights to possession of arms.[109]

By the time of the American Revolution, colonies such as Virginia and Connecticut reserved the right to impress arms whenever they needed them. To impress arms means to take them by force for public use. No gun belonged unqualifiedly to individuals; the people held their guns in trust for the colony.[110] This historical backdrop, say militia rights proponents, shows that gun control was a natural and expected part of public life.

Founding father James Madison said:

Americans have the right and advantage of being armed, unlike the citizens of other countries, whose governments are afraid to trust the people with arms. . . . A well regulated militia, composed of the people, trained to arms, is the best and most natural defense of a free country.[111]

According to militia rights theorists, in the context in which Madison spoke, he was talking about the balance created when "subordinate governments"[112] (the states) formed militias that could hold in check the potential tyranny of a national standing army, a thing much feared by early American Anti-Federalists.[113] Thus, Madison, in calming Anti-Federalist fears, was referring to collective rights stemming from Americans' participation in state militias, not to individual rights.

History Decries Anti-Tyranny Function of Second Amendment

The preceding does not mean that James Madison was against forming a strong national military presence. To the contrary. He had witnessed agrarian uprisings, such as Shay's Rebellion in Massachusetts, where farmers tried to overthrow the state government by force. Madison was concerned about holding such rebellions in check. He noted that, because "the states neglect their militia now, the discipline of the militia is evidently a *National* concern, and ought to be provided for in the National constitution."[114] He said that "without such a power to suppress insurrections, our liberties might be destroyed by domestic faction."[115]

The framers, having moved on from revolution to the business of building a country, feared insurrection. They expressed shock at Shay's Rebellion.[116] The rebellion was not waged against a government imposed from afar. It began when private individuals demanded debt relief, and it was directed against a government chosen by the people. It was thus an unthinkable outrage to the fledgling Union. In fact, in 1787, two years before Congress proposed the Second Amendment, four states sent their militia to help in quelling Shay's Rebellion.[117]

After the adoption of the Second Amendment, Washington sent militia to put down the Whiskey Rebellion in Pennsylvania. Those rebels did not invoke the protection of the Second Amendment, and they were denounced by both the Federalists and the former Anti-Federalists.[118] Thus, the founders did not intend the Second Amendment to guarantee rights to private persons or groups, and especially not to disaffected citizens who would take up arms against their chosen government.

The Second Amendment Extends Guarantees to the States, Not to Individuals

Along with providing for a national army and navy, the framers of the Constitution provided for a type of national militia. It was to be a hybrid between state militias and the federal government, with the federal government responsible for "organizing, arming and disciplining" the militia, and "governing such part of them as may be employed in the service of the United States," while reserving to the states the appointment of officers and the authority of training the militia according to congressional standards.[119]

This quasi-federal militia was provided for in Article I, Section 8 of the Constitution, before the Second Amendment was written. State militias were later transformed into the National Guard,[120] although some states retain a backup pool of reserves not subject to federal call-up.[121] "Private" militias, those with no government sanction, have been specifically banned in some places.[122] And Oregon has made unlawful "paramilitary activity" a criminal offense.[123]

This background should help in our understanding of how the framers viewed the militia. During ratification debates, Patrick Henry expressed concern that the federal government might disarm the state militias. Madison responded to that concern by assuring Henry that the states would have concurrent constitutional power to arm their militias.[124] Therefore, the Second Amendment was designed to assure the states that the federal government was not taking over the militias; the states would still have concurrent power with the federal government to arm their militias.[125] So the Second Amendment was a guarantee extended to the states, not to individuals.

This argument is bolstered by one of the changes made from the draft version to the final version of the Second Amendment. In a draft phrase, Madison had written, "a well armed, and well regulated militia being the best security of a free country...."[126] In the phrase that made it into the Second Amendment, the word "country" was changed to the word "State." The phrase as it now reads is, "A well regulated militia, being necessary to the security of a free State...."[127] This was changed because the federal government wanted to assure power-jealous states of their right to maintain their state militias.

There was never an intent by the framers to protect an individual's right to firearms, apart from the individual's membership in a militia. Historical support is found in the proposals for constitutional amendments put forth by the states. New York, North Carolina, Rhode Island, and Virginia all put forth proposals that included the phrase "well regulated militia" in contexts similar to the resulting Second Amendment.[128]

New Hampshire alone proposed an amendment that would give broader protection to individuals. New Hampshire's proposed amendment reads, in part, "Congress shall never disarm any citizen, unless such as are or have been in actual rebellion."[129] But Congress chose the proposals that linked the right to bear arms with state militias.

The Anti-Federalists were concerned about the potential for tyranny if a federal standing army were created. They wanted a counterbalance in the form of guaranteed state militias. In the record of the debates of the ratifying conventions there are many pages of discussion concerning standing armies and the militia, and no references to the need to bear arms for purposes other than militia service.[130] The index to Herbert Storing's *The Complete Anti-Federalist,* a collection of Anti-Federalist writings, lists seventy-six references to "standing armies" and only two references to the "right to bear arms."[131] Both those references were to proposals for a right to bear arms for, among other purposes, killing game. Those proposals were rejected and did not become part of the Second Amendment.

The Constitution itself, in Article I, Section 8, reflects the Anti-Federalists' fears of a federal standing army, in that it limits the appropriations for a federal army to two years.[132] Membership in a militia was not something a man could confer upon himself. Legitimate militias were organized by the state to serve the common defense.[133] The Constitution granted the states the authority to appoint the officers of their militia,[134] and the phrase chosen for the Second Amendment was not simply "militia," but "well-regulated Militia." Therefore, even though the militia is drawn from the citizenry, it is as much a mistake to say that the Second Amendment guarantees individuals the right to arm themselves in private militias as it would be to say that, because jurors are drawn from the citizenry, the Seventh Amendment's right to trial by jury grants citizens the right to form private juries to judge their fellows. The Second Amendment guarantees a state's right or a collective right only.

How Gun Control Proponents View *Miller*

Gun control proponents rely on the leading U.S. Supreme Court case of *United States v. Miller*[135] for the following propositions. The right that the

Second Amendment protects is not an individual right. It is the collective right belonging to members of a state-sponsored militia. Private militias are not included within the Second Amendment's zone of protection.

They also point out that *Miller* requires that, in order to achieve Second Amendment protection, the *possession or use* of the weapon must have some reasonable relationship to the preservation or efficiency of a well-regulated militia. The question is not whether the weapon has a military use. The question is whether the person accused of violating a specific gun regulation did in fact possess or use that weapon in connection with a state's militia. Only if he did so, does the Second Amendment protect that gun possession.

Although gun rights advocates argue that the rule in *Miller* should apply only to non-military–type weapons, such as the sawed-off shotgun at issue in that case,[136] gun control proponents reply that, if that is what *Miller* means, then the Second Amendment would expand to protect a private person's right to ordinary military equipment, such as rocket launchers, assault weapons, and other dangerous weapons unsuited for civilian use, and that clearly is not the intent of the Amendment.[137]

Gun control proponents conclude that, for all practical purposes, the Second Amendment is merely a piece of "historical residue."[138] As a parting blow, they blast gun rights advocates for producing a "great volume of pseudoscholarship" regarding the meaning of the Second Amendment.[139]

GUN RIGHTS ADVOCATES AND THE SECOND AMENDMENT

Gun rights advocates and gun control proponents divide most sharply in their view of who or what receives Second Amendment protection. Gun rights advocates assert that the Second Amendment was designed to protect individuals in their private capacities. Their best arguments follow.

The Second Amendment Guarantees Individual Rights

The Second Amendment extends a right to individuals to possess and use firearms in the defense of themselves and their homes.[140] "Believing that the amendment does not authorize an individual's right to keep and bear arms is wrong. The right to bear arms is an individual right."[141] Nineteenth-century constitutional commentators "took it for granted that the Second Amendment protects the right of individuals to keep and bear arms."[142]

The intent of the framers of the Constitution was that every man retain the right to be armed. James Madison spoke of European governments that were "afraid to trust the people with arms," and he spoke of "the advantage of being armed, which the Americans possess over the people of almost every

Jim Messer, owner of J&D Guns, Avon, Montana. (Photo by Constance Crooker.)

other nation."[143] Patrick Henry, who opposed ratification of the Constitution partly out of fear the federal government would seize control over weapons and their use, said, "The great object is that every man be armed.... Everyone who is able may have a gun."[144]

If the Second Amendment means that the states are assured of the right to maintain their own militias, why would the Founders have rejected a Virginia/North Carolina proposal that each state shall have the power to organize, arm, and discipline its own militia when Congress fails to do so? That rejected provision cannot embody the true meaning of the Second Amendment.[145]

The Nature of a Militia and the Prohibition against Civilian Disarmament

Looking to history, each side agrees that, at the time of the American Revolution, there existed a widespread fear of the capacity for abuse by standing armies. They also agree that the militia was composed of citizenry subject to occasional military duty, and that the men called up were to appear with their own firearms and other equipment.[146] But gun rights advocates point out that the militia was viewed as the opposite of a formal military organization. It was a stand-by force made up of armed citizens, who constituted a broad segment of the population.[147] Because standing armies were feared as a dangerous tool of would-be tyrants, an essentially civilian militia was seen as a safer alternative.[148] It remained inactive until its services were needed, and it remained armed while inactive.[149]

This history still echoes in present law. Gun control proponents are quick to point out how the militia described in Article I, Section 8 of the Constitution evolved into the present-day National Guard. Today's "organized militia" consists of the National Guard and the dwindling Naval Militia.[150] Perhaps, they suggest, the guarantees of the Second Amendment extend only to members of those organizations.

But, say gun rights advocates, they miss the fact that we still have an "unorganized militia" in the United States. Starting with the Militia Act of May 8, 1792,[151] and continuing into the present, as embodied in the U.S. Code, the unorganized militia consists of all able-bodied males between ages seventeen and forty-five, who "are not members of the National Guard or the Naval Militia."[152] In other words, the bulk of our male population is still, under federal law, part of our standby militia.

Interestingly, the gun rights advocates do not lean heavily on the existence of this "unorganized militia" as a rationale for the Second Amendment's guarantee. These advocates assert that the Second Amendment's term, "the people" means all the people, and is not limited to a subgroup comprising the organized or unorganized militia. As one pro-rights attorney has said, "The 'people' means the people. What else could it mean?"[153] Even extending the Second Amendment's guarantees to all able-bodied seventeen- to forty-five-year-old males would constitute a restriction on what they view as a universal right.

Gun rights advocates disagree with gun control proponents over the meaning of the phrase "well regulated militia." Control proponents say "well regulated" refers only to an organized militia, such as our present-day National Guard. Rights advocates say that "well regulated" means "not inappropriately regulated" or "not heavily regulated."[154] Because Article I authorizes Congress to standardize the training for the militias, the Second Amendment would not have been created to duplicate such training and regulation. They conclude that the Amendment must be a prohibition against civilian disarmament.[155]

For historical support, they point out that the "shot heard 'round the world" at the start of the Revolutionary War was fired when the British governor sent troops to collect and destroy colonists' firearms in Lexington and Concord, Massachusetts. The governor believed the colonists were too heavily armed. In Lexington, the British force was confronted by "people drawn up in military order." Then, after the British seized firearms in Concord, Concord residents ambushed, shot, and killed the British on their return march to Boston. So the American Revolution began with citizens' resistance when the government attempted to disarm them.[156] A gun rights advocate has asserted, "The historical evidence is unquestionable that the Second Amendment was prompted in part by the British policy of confiscating the firearms of individuals."[157]

But this argument brings us full circle. If the armed colonists of Lexington and Concord were acting as members of their militia, it is just as reasonable to argue that the Founders were concerned about the government seizing weapons from individuals acting in the capacity of militiamen.

No States' Rights Purpose to Second Amendment

According to gun rights advocates, the Second Amendment was not about granting the states power over their militias. When the Constitution granted almost complete federal authority over state militias,[158] the Anti-Federalists were quick to denounce the power shift from the states to the federal government. In 1787, Attorney General Luther Martin commented on Article I, Section 8 of the Constitution, which gave the federal government broad powers to supervise and call up the state militias. Martin referred to the section as "this extraordinary provision, by which the militia, the only defense and protection which the State can have for the security of their rights against arbitrary encroachments of the general government, is taken entirely out of the power of the respective states, and placed under the power of Congress."[159]

So, when Madison made his famous statement about the advantage of Americans being armed,[160] he was trying to placate the Anti-Federalists with the assurance that, although the federal government had already taken considerable constitutional control over the states' militias, the federal government would, under the Second Amendment, still lack the power to disarm citizens. The "Federalists and the Anti-Federalists *shared* the assumption that the new federal government should lack the power to disarm the citizenry."[161]

In other words, the Second Amendment was not designed to guarantee the states that they could maintain power over their militia. The states had already lost much of that power, and both Federalists and Anti-Federalists were well aware of that. Therefore, the purpose of the Second Amendment was to assure Anti-Federalists that, at least, the people could remain armed.[162]

If it were as the gun control proponents argue, it would be a case of the right hand giving while the left hand takes away. Article I, Section 8, Clause 16 of the Constitution grants Congress the power to take substantial control over state militias. Then, in Article I, Section 10, Clause 3, the states are forbidden to keep troops without the consent of Congress. Then, according to gun control proponents, the Second Amendment, without changing those constitutional provisions, somehow shifts control over militias back to the states. Gun rights advocates assert that, logically, that could not have been the purpose of the Second Amendment. "In fact," says one such advocate, "if one took the purpose attributed to the Second Amendment by the states' rights theorists seriously, it would seem to follow that *all* federal gun control regulations are invalid because control over the private possession of arms lies exclusively in the state governments."[163]

Anti-Tyranny Function of Second Amendment

While gun control proponents argue that the Founders feared insurrection, and would not condone any right of individuals to forcefully oppose an elected government, gun rights advocates claim that a primary purpose of the Second Amendment was to allow individuals enough power to overthrow a tyrannical regime.[164] They find support in the language of English legal theorist Sir William Blackstone (later quoted with approval by Samuel Adams), who, a decade before the American Revolution, said that the right to arms serves "the natural right of resistance and self-preservation, when the sanctions of society and laws are found insufficient to restrain the violence of oppression."[165]

A noted Federalist was quoted in a 1789 newspaper with this comment on the recently proposed Second Amendment: "As civil rulers, not having their duty to the people duly before them, may attempt to tyrannize, and as the military forces which must be occasionally raised to defend our country, might pervert their power to the injury of their fellow-citizens, the people are confirmed by [the Second Amendment] in their right to keep and bear their private arms."[166]

This anti-tyranny rationale for the Amendment was stated by Justice Joseph Story who declared, "The right of the citizens to keep and bear arms has justly been considered, as the palladium of the liberties of the republic; since it offers a strong moral check against usurpation and arbitrary power of the rulers; and will generally, even if these are successful in the first instance, enable the people to resist and triumph over them."[167] Story also wrote, "One of the ordinary modes by which tyrants accomplish their purpose without resistance is, by disarming the people, and making it an offense to keep arms...."[168]

Gun control proponents counter this argument by saying that, even if there were an anti-tyranny function of the Second Amendment, it is now outmoded. Today, few worry that the U.S. Army will impose a military dictatorship over Americans. Nor would bands of armed citizens have much chance of defeating such well-armed forces.

Gun rights advocates respond that an armed populace still creates a deterrent to government oppression by raising the potential costs of military force, even where a military dictatorship would prevail with a sufficient investment of resources.[169]

Furthermore, according to Wayne LaPierre, chief executive officer of the National Rifle Association, the argument that the Second Amendment's anti-tyranny function is obsolete is wrong. "The claim that an armed populace cannot successfully resist assault stems from an unproved theory."[170] He cites examples where guerrilla warfare has triumphed over modern armies, and says, "a determined people who have the means to maintain prolonged war against a modern army can battle it to a standstill, subverting major portions of the army or defeating it themselves or with major arms supplied by outside forces."[171] This leaves one wondering which "outside forces" LaPierre imagines might supply major arms to disgruntled Americans who would band together to throw off the perceived "tyranny" of our federal government.

It should be pointed out that, although the gun rights proponents have amassed strong enough historical arguments to sway one federal circuit court to adopt the personal rights interpretation of the Second Amendment, they may have shot themselves in the foot, so to speak. Their legal briefs on the subject of the Second Amendment reflect a sophisticated view of the historical underpinnings of the Second Amendment, but when gun rights proponents make public declarations regarding Second Amendment rights, they have all the depth of advertising slogans. They tend to portray the founding fathers as unanimously and vigorously defending the right to bear arms, when the reality is that the Second Amendment was forged in order to compromise a hotly debated matter.

For example, Wayne LaPierre presents an oversimplified, sound-bite history of the Second Amendment in his book, *Guns, Crime and Freedom.*[172] He compiles only the favorable quotes, ignores their context, and fails to present the contemporaneous countervailing view. For example, La Pierre paints George Washington as a lover of the militia and quotes Washington as saying, "A free people ought not only be armed, but disciplined."[173] But George Washington had come to dislike the undisciplined, untrained militiamen who, in his view, hindered the war effort.[174]

Unfortunately for gun rights advocates, LaPierre's kind of junk history has likely been one reason many historians have not taken the NRA's views seriously. The organization would serve its members better if it acknowledged there was no historical unanimity, but that when the dust of constitutional debate settled, the individual rights proponents had won. Instead, LaPierre writes as if the founding fathers all spoke with one voice: LaPierre's.

The Natural Right to Self-Defense

Gun rights advocates also argue that the personal right to resist violent crime with arms was an important part of the right guaranteed by the Second Amendment. Early Americans lived in a world without organized police forces, and needed to be self-reliant when defending against criminal attacks. And even now, with our large police forces, the police generally arrive after the crime has been reported, too late to prevent violence. Although it appears nowhere in the Constitution, gun rights advocates suggest there is a preexisting natural right, which they call the "well-established and ancient right of self-defense."[175] They speak of a citizen's "fundamental, natural right to self-defense when they are threatened with criminal attack."[176]

How Gun Rights Advocates See *Miller*

Gun rights advocates view the Supreme Court case of *United States v. Miller*[177] quite differently than do gun control proponents. The crucial language in *Miller* is this:

[Without evidence that] possession or use of a [sawed-off shotgun] at this time has some reasonable relationship to the preservation or efficiency of a well regulated militia, we cannot say that the Second Amendment guarantees the right to keep and bear such an instrument. Certainly it is not within judicial notice that this weapon is any part of the ordinary military equipment or that its use could contribute to the common defense.[178]

Gun rights advocates argue that their opponents focus wrongly on the *possession or use* of the weapon being reasonably related to the militia. They say the Supreme Court was more concerned with the type of weapon than with how it could be used. Gun rights advocates focus on the phrases "such an instrument" and "this weapon," to argue that a weapon is outside the scope of Second Amendment protection only if it is not suitable for military use. The *Miller* case was examining the National Firearms Act, which regulated short-barreled shotguns, machine guns, and silencers. Because these devices are particularly suited to criminal use, gun advocates argue that the rule in *Miller* should be applied narrowly.[179] Because many other weapons are suitable for military use, the Second Amendment should broadly protect an individual's right to their possession and use.

A more sweeping understanding of *Miller* would render the Second Amendment a nullity, and lead to absurd results. Does *Miller* imply that, if a criminal in possession of a sawed-off shotgun is preparing for a military career, or is thinking of himself as a militiaman, the Second Amendment protects his possession of the weapon? Surely not. The *Miller* case must be about the non-military nature of the sawed-off shotgun.[180]

Gun rights advocates also argue that, because the *Miller* case defines "militia" as including "all males physically capable of acting in concert for the common defense,"[181] the *Miller* court understood "militia" to be synonymous with "the people" who have the right to bear arms. In other words, they claim that *Miller* supports their argument that the Second Amendment was intended to protect the rights of individuals and not just members of a militia.

The other side would respond that *Miller* does not so define "militia." *Miller* mentions the historical requirement of "enrollment" for a group to constitute a militia. *Miller* says, "the Militia comprised all males physically capable of acting in concert for the common defense. 'A body of citizens enrolled for military discipline.'"[182]

Gun rights advocates also claim that, implicit in the *Miller* holding, is recognition of an individual right to keep and bear arms. If the defendant in *Miller* had shown that his possession or use of the shotgun did have some reasonable relationship to the preservation or efficiency of a well-regulated militia, he presumably could have prevailed.[183]

THE FEDERAL CIRCUITS SPEAK

The Fifth Circuit Court of Appeals is the only federal circuit court to endorse the individual rights view of the Second Amendment. It did so in a case called *United States v. Emerson*.[184] Before exploring that case, we will summarize the language of some of the contrary holdings of other circuit courts to highlight the contrast between the Fifth Circuit and the others.

Turning to the circuit court decisions, the Sixth Circuit Court of Appeals has stated, "Since the Second Amendment right 'to keep and bear Arms' applies only to the right of the State to maintain a militia and not to the individual's right to bear arms, there can be no serious claim to any express constitutional right of an individual to possess a firearm."[185]

The Seventh Circuit found that a law prohibiting those convicted of domestic violence from possessing firearms did not violate the Second Amendment because, under no "plausible set of facts" would "the viability and efficacy of state militias...be undermined" by that law.[186]

The Ninth Circuit has said that the "Second Amendment is a right held by the states, and does not protect the possession of a weapon by a private citizen."[187] More recently it has ruled that the Second Amendment "protects the people's right to maintain an effective state militia, and does not establish an individual right to own or possess firearms for personal or other use."[188]

The First Circuit has held that the Second Amendment was not infringed because there was no evidence that an accused person "was or ever had been a member of any military organization or that his use of the weapon...was in preparation for a military career, [and where the evidence showed that he was] on a frolic of his own and without any thought or intention of contributing to the efficiency of the well regulated militia."[189]

The Third Circuit found that a defendant's possession of a machine gun was not protected by the Second Amendment because it was not connected with militia activity.[190]

The Eighth Circuit has said that membership in an unorganized militia (as opposed to a well-regulated militia) will not cloak a defendant with Second Amendment protection.[191]

The Tenth Circuit rejected the individual rights view of the Second Amendment and failed to apply Second Amendment protection to a man who possessed a machine gun, rejecting his claim that he was technically a standby member of the Kansas' militia because he was in the statutory age range to be called up.[192]

Similarly, the Eleventh Circuit rejected a man's claim to Second Amendment protection of his possession of machine guns and pipe bombs, notwithstanding his claim to membership in Georgia's "unorganized militia" (a standby group of able-bodied males of a certain age).[193]

One case stands alone in announcing that the Second Amendment protects an individual's right to keep and bear arms. That is the Fifth Circuit's case of *United States v. Emerson*.[194] In this case, the criminally accused defendant, Timothy Joe Emerson, was charged with, among other things, violating a federal statute[195] that makes it a crime to possess a firearm while subject to a restraining order during a divorce. Emerson moved to dismiss the charges, claiming that the statute violates the Second Amendment (and other constitutional provisions not relevant here).

The federal trial court had recognized the Second Amendment constitutional right of an individual to own and possess firearms, and it had declared the applicable portion of the federal statute unconstitutional, because it would disarm a citizen merely because he is subject to a boilerplate injunction in a restraining order.

On appeal, the Fifth Circuit held that the trial court was correct that the Second Amendment protects the rights of individuals to keep and bear firearms that are suitable as individual, personal weapons, regardless of whether the individual is a militia member. But the court did not declare that this particular federal statute violated the Second Amendment. Therefore, the trial court's dismissal was reversed and the appellate court ordered the trial court to continue with Emerson's criminal prosecution.

Note that this case upheld as constitutional the specific deprivation of Emerson's firearms rights, and thus left his criminal conviction standing. In other words, the court was saying, yes, the individual has a constitutional right to keep and bear arms but there are circumstances in which constitutional rights may be lawfully restricted, and this was one of them.

The court in *Emerson* pointed out ambiguities in the 1939 Supreme Court case of *United States v. Miller* and concluded that *Miller* did not clearly support either side. Because *Miller* did not adopt an individual rights view of the Second Amendment nor a states rights or collective rights view, *Miller* did not resolve the question. Because the *Emerson* court did not feel bound by any Supreme Court precedent, it took a fresh look at the issue by delving into the history and wording of the Second Amendment for guidance.

The *Emerson* court dissected the text of the Second Amendment and concluded that "people" refers to individual Americans, not members of a militia, that "bear arms" refers generally to carrying arms in both military and non-military contexts, and that "keep ... arms" does not command a military connotation. The Second Amendment's preamble, "a well regulated Militia is necessary to the security of a free State" refers to the object of arming ordinary citizens so that they can participate in the defense of their communities and state by assuring that the federal government may not disarm them.

The *Emerson* opinion continues with an epic historical analysis of the debates that led to the Second Amendment. A summary of that analysis follows.

The *Emerson* court contrasts the views of the Federalists, who thought the fledgling Union would benefit from a strong, central government, with those of the Anti-Federalists, who feared that a powerful central government would strip the states of their power and strip individual citizens of their hard-won liberties. After shaking off one tyrant, the Anti-Federalists were not anxious to fall prey to another.

On May 25, 1787, the Federal Convention met in Philadelphia and began crafting the U.S. Constitution. Anti-Federalists lobbied for three things relevant to the Second Amendment.

First, they wanted a Bill of Rights incorporated within the Constitution to assure that the federal government would act only within its limited and enumerated powers and to prevent it from infringing people's fundamental rights. They did not succeed, but their subsequent dissatisfaction sufficiently threatened the stability and security of the new Union that, in a spirit of compromise and reconciliation, the Bill of Rights was later enacted in the form of the first ten amendments to the Constitution. The Second Amendment was one of these.

Second, the Constitution had given the federal government powers over the militia. The federal government could call up the state militias to help enforce federal laws, and the federal government could organize, arm, and discipline the militia, leaving the states to appoint militia officers and to train the militia members. The Anti-Federalists had argued for state authority over their militias, and they considered that they had lost ground on this point.

Third, the Anti-Federalists feared a central standing army. They wanted military force to remain in the hands of the people who formed the state militias, and only wanted Congress to call up armed forces in emergencies.

The Federalists tried to quell fears by responding that, because the American people were armed, they could successfully resist any standing army that chose to oppress them, and that, because the federal government could call on the state militias, it would not need a standing army.

On September 27, 1787, the Congress submitted the proposed Constitution to the states for ratification. The Anti-Federalists, who felt they'd lost ground at the Constitutional Convention, caused a number of the states to propose changes to the Constitution, including a number of proposals that would guarantee the right of citizens to keep and bear arms.

In 1788, enough states (nine) had ratified the Constitution without change, and the Federalists had won. But the disaffected Anti-Federalists had persuaded many that a Bill of Rights was still necessary. Now that the federal government was in place, the Federalists softened on the subject of a Bill of Rights, feeling that it could be added on without affecting the basic design of government that had been constructed in the Constitution. Therefore, on June 8, 1789, James Madison proposed the first of the changes that were to become the Bill of Rights.

The *Emerson* case continues with a description of the political wrangling and the historical backdrop that eventually led to the final version of the Second Amendment. The *Emerson* court concludes that the Federalists, who wanted to appease the Anti-Federalists if they could do so without altering the carefully crafted federal-state balance of power, "had no qualms with recognizing the right of individual Americans to keep and bear arms,"[196] but they held firm on the subject of leaving leeway for the federal government to maintain a standing army and on the subject of maintaining federal power over the militias. One reason the preamble states that a well-regulated militia is necessary to the security of a free state is that such a militia would greatly reduce the need for a standing army. The preamble reassures the Anti-Federalists on this point while making no explicit guarantees. So, while the Anti-Federalists did not succeed in getting the federal government to cede all control over state militias, they got a guarantee that individuals could keep and bear arms, and they got assurances that a standing army would not become necessary.

The *Emerson* case concludes unequivocally that "The Second Amendment protects the right of individuals to privately keep and bear their own firearms that are suitable as individual, personal weapons [not including certain out-lawed weapons], regardless of whether the particular individual is then actu-ally a member of the militia."[197]

After the Fifth Circuit Court of Appeals issued this ruling, the defendant appealed the case to the U.S. Supreme Court. Then an astonishing turnabout took place. Keep in mind that the prosecutor was a deputy U.S. attorney rep-resenting the people against the defendant, Dr. Emerson. The prosecutor had raised all the arguments in support of the "militia rights" theory, while Dr. Emerson's lawyer had argued that the defendant had a personal Second Amendment right to keep and bear arms. The Court of Appeals agreed with the criminal defendant on that point, but ruled against him on other matters, so the defendant appealed.

The briefs that were filed in the U.S. Supreme Court show that the prose-cutor suddenly reversed position on this hard-fought issue. Here is the prose-cutor's changed position as it appears in a footnote in the *Emerson* brief:

In its brief to the court of appeals, the government argued that the Second Amend-ment protects only such acts of firearm possession as are reasonably related to the preservation or efficiency of the militia. . . . The current position of the United States, however, is that the Second Amendment more broadly protects the rights of individ-uals, including persons who are not members of any militia or engaged in active mil-itary service or training, to possess and bear their own firearms, subject to reasonable restrictions designed to prevent possession by unfit persons or to restrict the posses-sion of types of firearms that are particularly suited to criminal misuse. [A reference appears here to an Attorney General's memorandum which is attached as an appen-dix to the brief.][198]

Why did the prosecutor throw in the towel on this point after such a hard-fought battle? There can only be one answer: politics.

On May 17, 2001, Attorney General John Ashcroft, the *Emerson* prose-cutor's boss, had written a letter to James Baker, executive director of the National Rifle Association. In it, Ashcroft told Baker that "the Second Amendment protects an individual right to keep and bear arms."[199] He also said, "I believe it is clear that the Constitution protects the private ownership of firearms for lawful purposes."[200]

Despite the fact that gun crime prosecutions across the country have long been bolstered by the government's consistent assertion that the Second Amendment does not guarantee individual rights, and despite the fact that this turnabout in prosecutorial policy could harm the government's pending prosecutions of gun crimes, John Ashcroft tried to make his turnabout look like a moral imperative, and not political pandering to the NRA. He wrote, "When I was sworn as Attorney General of the United States, I took an oath to uphold the Constitution. That responsibility applies to all parts of the Constitution, including the Second Amendment."

What he fails to mention is that, as a lawyer, he is also obligated to argue in his client's best interests if there is any favorable law that supports his client's position. There is a wealth of law, in the form of Circuit Court opinions, which limit application of the Second Amendment to militia-related conduct, and which benefits the people of the United States whom he represents. How he, as the nation's top lawyer, can choose to stand by his personal interpretation of the law over the law that best serves his client is a mystery only he can explain.

Then on November 9, 2001, Ashcroft wrote a memorandum to all U.S. attorneys in which he advised them that the Fifth Circuit was correct in the *Emerson* case when it ruled in favor of the criminal defendant on the issue of the individual right to bear arms. He wrote, "[T]he Fifth Circuit...affirmed that the Second Amendment 'protects the right of *individuals,* including those not then actually a member of any militia or engaged in active military service or training, to privately possess and bear their own firearms....'...In my view, the *Emerson* opinion...[reflects] the correct understanding of the Second Amendment."[201]

Although this explains the government's reversal of position in the *Emerson* case, it does not explain why John Ashcroft has done this. A lawyer could ruin his own career by failing to vigorously represent his client's best interests. In this case, Mr. Ashcroft appears to be acting more like a political candidate than like a lawyer. His motives might become clear if he decides to throw his hat in the ring for an elected office.

SECOND AMENDMENT CONCLUSION

The U.S. Supreme Court, on June 10, 2002, refused to hear the *Emerson* case. This is not surprising, because the Supreme Court agrees to review only disputed issues, not issues on which the parties agree.

Even so, the Second Amendment landscape has changed and is now tilted significantly in favor of the criminal defendant in gun cases. If the federal government continues to concede Second Amendment rights, criminal defendants stand to win if they can prove that the law under which they are being prosecuted impermissibly infringes on their rights. This brings up the question of the standard of review.

In the *Emerson* case, the Fifth Circuit held that, even though Dr. Emerson enjoyed Second Amendment protection, the law under which he was being prosecuted did not overstep that constitutional limit, and his criminal conviction was allowed to stand. How the court reached that conclusion remains a murky part of that case, because the Court did not clarify what standard of review it was applying. In post-*Emerson* prosecutions, the legal arguments should now switch from the Second Amendment to the question of the standard of review.

WHAT STANDARD OF REVIEW SHOULD APPLY?

There are many local, state, and federal gun control laws on the books now. In light of Ashcroft's Second Amendment concession, the question becomes, which gun control laws will stand as lawful exercises of government authority and which ones will be found to overreach the protections afforded by the Second Amendment?

Constitutional rights are not always absolute. For example, we have a first amendment free speech right, but if our false words harm another's reputation, we may be held accountable for libel or slander. Scholars of constitutional law have identified different degrees to which a law may restrict our constitutional rights, depending on the nature of the right and on the nature of society's interest in curbing that right.

There are three degrees of protection. If a constitutional right is a fundamental right, any law that restricts that right is subject to the strict scrutiny of the appellate courts. Seldom can a law that restricts a fundamental constitutional right pass the stringent judicial "strict scrutiny" standard. Such laws are usually declared unconstitutional.

If the constitutional right does not rise to the level of a fundamental right, a law that restricts that right must have a rational relation to an important government interest in order to survive. Because there are numerous important governmental interests, many laws that must meet this "rational basis" test will pass constitutional muster.

There is an intermediate standard of judicial review. It falls halfway between the nearly impossible standard of "strict scrutiny" and the relatively easy "rational basis" standard. Some laws must be said to foster a "compelling state interest" before those laws are allowed to trump constitutional rights.

The question is, what standard of review should the courts apply to determine whether a gun control law unconstitutionally tramples on Second Amendment rights? This question has not been at the heart of Second Amendment jurisprudence, probably because, in the vast majority of cases heard so far, individuals have not yet qualified for Second Amendment protection. Therefore, the courts have not needed to take the next analytical step.

Now that Ashcroft has conceded Second Amendment rights, the question of the standard of review should begin to come into focus in gun prosecutions. When a court reviews the constitutionality of a given firearms regulation, should it apply the "strict scrutiny" test, the "rational basis" test, or the intermediate, "compelling state interest" test?

Gun control proponents argue for the rational basis test.[202] This would give any gun regulation under consideration a better chance of being upheld by the courts.

The gun rights advocates, on the other hand, usually argue that the right to bear arms is a fundamental right, so strict scrutiny should apply. Most incursions of constitutional rights fail to meet the strict scrutiny standard, and gun control laws would be easily struck down, if this becomes the standard of review.

The National Rifle Association has argued in a way that mixes the strict standard with the intermediate standard. Perhaps that is its fallback position. It has argued that laws regulating weapons' possession "must be narrowly tailored to serve compelling public purposes [the intermediate standard], and all such laws must be subject to strict scrutiny by the courts [the most strict standard]."[203] They also argue that any gun control regulation should be written so that it is the least restrictive means to further the articulated government interest.[204]

John Ashcroft himself seems to have landed in the middle. In his controversial letter to the National Rifle Association[205] he did not give away the entire farm when he acknowledged Second Amendment individual rights. He said in a footnote that those rights could be restricted in certain instances. He wrote, "Of course, the individual rights view of the Second Amendment does not prohibit the Congress from enacting laws restricting firearms ownership for compelling state interests, such as prohibiting firearms ownership by convicted felons...."[206] Notice that he did not choose the term "strict scrutiny," nor did he use the term "rational basis." He used language that would allow for some governmental intrusion on the Second Amendment right, but only when the government has a "compelling state interest."

Now that gun rights advocates (and criminal defendants) have a friend in John Ashcroft, what is the extent of their victory? It may turn out that the courts will still uphold our myriad gun control laws as reasonable and necessary infringements on personal rights. The courts have yet to decide on the standard of review to be applied. Even this 180-degree shift in prosecutorial policy might not make a dent in how the courts treat gun control laws if the rational basis test wins out. But if the strict scrutiny test wins, it could keep many lawyers employed for many years to come, challenging all the gun laws on the books.

5

The Commerce Clause: Federal Jurisdiction over Firearms

Our federal Constitution springs from the principle that the people are the natural repository of all rights and powers, and the government may only exercise such powers as the people grant. The Constitution and the Bill of Rights state which powers are delegated by the people to the federal government, and which rights and powers are reserved to the people. So, whenever Congress passes a law, it must assure itself that it is acting under the authority of the powers delegated to it.

When Congress passed its first major firearms regulations, it relied on its power to tax.[1] The National Firearms Act of 1934, which was meant to control proliferation of the infamous tommy guns used by Chicago gangsters, was an intricate regulatory tax scheme designed to price the weapons out of the market.

It was not until passage of the 1968 Gun Control Act that Congress began to invoke instead its power to regulate interstate commerce in order to legitimize its regulation of firearms. The Commerce Clause of the U.S. Constitution provides, "The Congress shall have the Power...To regulate Commerce...among the several States...."[2]

The general idea is that Congress should have no power to regulate commerce that takes place completely within one state's borders, but that it may do so if the transaction reaches across state lines.[3] When it comes to firearms, almost any gun has, at some point in its history, either crossed a state line or had one of its parts cross a state line. So, according to the courts, even a gun that has come to rest within one state can be subject to congressional authority under the Commerce Clause. For example, a felon who is found with a very old gun, perhaps one that has not been out of the particular state since before he was born, can be prosecuted for the federal crime of unlawful possession of a firearm if the government alleges that the weapon was possessed "in or affecting commerce."[4] In order to prove this, the government need not prove that the felon caused the gun to move across state lines, but only that the gun, at some point in its history, crossed a state line. This is fairly easy to prove in cases where the state of its manufacture differs from the state in which the gun is found.

To highlight this point, notice the language of this typical court case describing the effect of the Commerce Clause in relation to federal gun regulations:

Without question, Congress has the power to regulate the interstate trade in firearms. Pursuant to that authority, it may act to stem the flow of guns to those whom it rationally believes may use them irresponsibly [including those convicted of certain crimes]. The possibility that a particular individual might possess his gun solely within one state...is irrelevant. So long as that gun has moved across state lines at least once, it is subject to the exercise of congressional Commerce Clause authority.[5]

This view is still the prevailing one in the courts in spite of the fact that the Supreme Court has said that, in order for a federal law to meet constitutional muster under the Commerce Clause, the activity that Congress regulates must substantially affect interstate commerce.[6] Although it is counterintuitive that an object that has long ago come to rest within a state's borders should still be subject to Congress' Commerce Clause powers even when the object is used in a purely private, noncommercial way, there have been no successful legal challenges to Congress' broad reach under the Commerce Clause, at least as to firearms possession.

A notable exception is found in one of the rare Supreme Court cases that has disapproved of the way Congress exercised its Commerce Clause power. Generally, the Congress can count on the Supreme Court to uphold its claim of authority under its power to regulate commerce. But when Congress criminalized possession of a firearm within a certain distance of schools, the Supreme Court failed to find a sufficient connection to the Commerce Clause, and the high court struck down the federal Gun Free School Zones Act of 1990.[7] According to the Supreme Court, the problem with the Gun Free School Zones Act was that, unlike other federal criminal gun laws, which require that the firearm must have some nexus with interstate commerce, this law criminalized possession of *any* gun near a school, whether or not there was proof of the gun's connection with interstate commerce.

Shortly after the high court declared the law unconstitutional, President Bill Clinton proposed an amended version to cure the Commerce Clause problem. On May 10, 1995, Clinton sent Congress the Gun Free School Zones Amendments Act of 1995 and urged Congress to add language that would require proof that the firearm has either moved in interstate commerce or that its possession affects interstate commerce.[8] Congress did so. The original law made it unlawful "knowingly to possess a firearm" in a school zone. The amended version makes it unlawful "knowingly to possess a firearm that has moved in or that otherwise affects interstate or foreign commerce" in a school zone.[9] This version of the law still stands, and illustrates the point that a person accused of any of the Commerce Clause sanctioned gun crimes need not personally engage in a commercial transaction nor personally move a firearm across state lines in order for the Commerce Clause to give authority to Congress to criminalize his conduct.

HISTORY OF THE BUREAU OF ALCOHOL, TOBACCO, AND FIREARMS

The Bureau of Alcohol, Tobacco, and Firearms (BATF) is a relatively new federal bureau within the U.S. Treasury Department. It officially came into its own as a separate bureau on July 1, 1972, but its roots go back to the founding of the nation.

In 1789, the first Congress taxed imported alcohol in order to pay some of its Revolutionary War debt. The Treasury Department was given responsibility for administering the alcohol tax. From then until the mid-1930s, the responsibility for collecting tax on alcohol and for enforcing alcohol tax laws stayed with the Treasury Department, although the name of the responsible agency changed several times.

The era of national alcohol prohibition, which ran from 1919 to 1933, gave rise to notorious organized crime figures famous for their public shootouts with automatic weapons, nicknamed "tommy guns." Public outrage over their dangerous antics led to passage of the National Firearms Act of 1934, which taxed and regulated such weapons. Tax collection and enforcement under the new gun law fell to the Internal Revenue Service (IRS), and within that agency to the Alcohol and Tobacco Tax Division. This made some sense because the Firearms Act was part of the tax code, not part of the criminal code. Although the word "firearms" was not in the unit's name, the unlikely linkage of the three bedfellows—alcohol, tobacco, and firearms—was cemented during this era.

Unlike the 1934 National Firearms Act, the Gun Control Act of 1968 went beyond the tax code, and criminalized certain gun-related conduct. It relied for its jurisdiction, not on the congressional power to tax, but on Congress' power to regulate interstate commerce, in this case the movement of firearms. The Alcohol, Tobacco, and Firearms Division of the IRS would now be doing more than imposing and enforcing tax laws. It would assume a broad responsibility for investigating criminal law violations as well. In recognition of this new role, a Treasury Department order of July 1, 1972, severed the BATF from the IRS. From then until November 26, 2002, it was an independent bureau, still within the Treasury Department, and still responsible for tax collection, but no longer part of the IRS.[10]

With the proliferation of federal firearms laws after 1968, the BATF evolved into a hybrid agency that both taxed goods and, in conjunction with agencies like the FBI, enforced criminal firearms laws. Specifically, the BATF used mandatory and enhanced sentencing laws to "target, investigate and recommend prosecution" of certain armed criminals.[11] It also helped law-enforcement agencies "to identify and apprehend criminals who illegally purchase firearms."[12] Although its mission was to aid other law enforcers by investigating violations of firearms laws, in reality, it went far beyond this investigatory function when it participated, fully armed, in searches, seizures, and arrests of suspects.

The BATF acted as a regulatory agency as well. To deal in firearms, one needs a federal firearms license. BATF issued these licenses after determining the applicant's qualifications and it conducted compliance inspections of firearms dealers to make sure they were keeping to the many restrictions imposed by federal law. As of September 30, 1995, there were 191,495 federal firearms licensees.[13]

Licensees can easily run afoul of the law without a roadmap, so the BATF published a 153-page handbook for distribution to licensees. It is called the "Federal Firearms Regulations Reference Guide."[14] It consists of more than ninety pages of federal gun laws, single-spaced in small print. It contains twelve pages of additional rules and regulations, more than ten pages of "general information" and, finally, one section of more- or less-readable questions and answers. With so many difficult to decipher laws and regulations, one wonders how the thousands of licensees stay on the sunny side of the law without a lawyer-in-residence.

BATF compliance inspections have gone beyond mere regulation of an industry. They have lapped over into criminal conspiracy investigations. The bureau has targeted licensees "likely to divert firearms from legitimate trade to criminal use."[15] The agency has also handled a wide array of gun-related matters such as forensic examinations of firearms, development of gun-tracing systems to track the sales history of guns seized in crimes, and involvement with community and youth groups to reduce gun-related violence.

Gun rights groups, such as the National Rifle Association have often blasted the BATF for, in their view, overstepping their bounds and targeting law abiding gun owners and dealers instead of the real criminals. When the NRA referred in a well-known fundraising letter to jack-booted government thugs, it was referring to BATF agents.

The BATF was already unpopular with these groups when it got tangled up in two controversial incidents that now loom large in the literature and on the Web sites of gun rights groups. The details are so familiar to those who dwell on these incidents, that they refer to them simply as "Ruby Ridge" and "Waco."

On February 28, 1992, at Waco, Texas, David Koresh, who is usually described by the government as a cult leader of a religious group called the Branch/Davidians, was inside his compound with his followers while government agents, including agents from the BATF, conducted a raid while serving a search warrant that authorized them to look for weapons and drugs. The dramatic raid triggered a shootout in which four agents and six Branch/Davidians died. This escalated into a fifty-one-day standoff that ended when government agents stormed the compound. A huge fire engulfed the compound, killing Koresh and about eighty of his followers, including more than twenty children. To this day, the cause of the fire is disputed. The government claims the Davidians started it, while critics blame government agents. Eleven of the surviving Davidians were tried for murder of the BATF agents, but none were convicted, although some were convicted of lesser charges including abetting manslaughter.[16]

Here follows a sample of the kind of commentary this incident aroused. The writer identifies himself as a businessman and Vietnam veteran, not as a gun advocate, but the tone will sound familiar to gun rights advocates:

Like Ruby Ridge it was the ATF (Department of Alcohol, Tobacco and Firearms) that dreamed up these operations for no better reason than it needed to do something to justify its existence. Down here we used to call the ATF "revenuers," who at one time tramped around in the woods looking for stills. Like other law enforcement agencies, ATF has its heavily armed SWAT teams with few missions. These are really no more than paramilitary units operating like combat units within the United States. Thus are born the seeds of disaster. When we have poorly trained wannabe commando cops running with machine guns, tanks and armed helicopters, expect more Wacos.[17]

Similarly, Ruby Ridge has prompted the same kind of critical response. Randy Weaver was, according to the government, a white separatist of the Aryan Nation variety. He allegedly sold two impermissibly short-barreled shotguns to an undercover agent who had asked Weaver to shorten the guns for him. Then the BATF allegedly offered to go light on Weaver if he would help them penetrate a local white separatist group, but he refused. They charged him with firearms offenses, and he failed to appear for his trial.

On August 21, 1992, federal agents, while conducting a secret surveillance of Weaver's cabin, wound up in a firefight with his son. When it was over, Weaver's son, Weaver's dog, and one agent lay dead. This began a week-long standoff, during which government sniper fire hit Weaver in the arm and killed his wife. Weaver finally surrendered, went on trial, and was found not guilty of the murder of the agent and of all other charges except failure to appear at his original trial.[18]

This prompted Joe Waldron, special activities director for the Second Amendment Foundation, a gun rights group, to say this about the Bureau of Alcohol, Tobacco, and Firearms:

[T]he BATF represents an agency out of control. On a daily basis, the BATF routinely and consistently violates the civil rights of law abiding citizens. The typical BATF "case" involves catching the villain committing some unscrupulous deed such as a procedural violation of Federal firearms code, followed by threats of felony prosecution and long prison terms. In a classic "bait and switch" sales presentation, the threats are followed by an offer to place a hold on the charges if the miscreant will turn informant for the agency. This is almost exactly what happened in the Randy Weaver case, with a strong dose of entrapment added.[19]

As to the Ruby Ridge and the Waco incidents, even gun control proponents stay mostly mute while critics of the BATF dominate the discussion. Perhaps this is because nobody warms to the image of our law enforcers sneaking around in full military getup, pushing so hard on people that, regardless of fault, people die who might otherwise have lived. This is especially true when citizen jurors end up acquitting those accused.

The National Rifle Association had been on the back of the BATF from well before these notorious incidents and almost succeeded in getting President Ronald Reagan to abolish the agency. In 1981, under relentless NRA pressure, Reagan unveiled plans to abolish the BATF, but law-enforcement agencies rose up in protest. A compromise was struck. It was proposed that the BATF would still be abolished, but its agents and their mission would move under the umbrella of the Secret Service.

Now it was time for the NRA to take a second look at their supposed victory. If they'd thought the BATF was improperly playing superspy before, now gun owners were really in for some trouble. The low-prestige, underfunded BATF would be getting a boost instead of getting the boot. The NRA backed off, and the BATF stayed put, with some reduced funding.[20]

Then, in response to the notorious acts of terrorism of September 11, 2001, President George W. Bush pushed for creation of a new federal agency called the Department of Homeland Security. On November 26, 2002, he signed into law the Homeland Security Act of 2002. One of its provisions split the Bureau of Alcohol, Tobacco, and Firearms into two new agencies.

One agency is the Alcohol and Tobacco Tax and Trade Bureau, which remains in the Treasury Department, and which regulates the federal firearms and ammunition excise tax. The other, the Bureau of Alcohol, Tobacco, Firearms, and Explosives was moved under the umbrella of the Department of Justice, the agency that prosecutes federal crimes.[21] So, except for some residual taxing power, it appears that the BATF has completed an evolution from toothless "revenuer" to "top cop" status.

6

History of Federal Gun Control Laws

Since the beginning of America's history as a nation, tension has existed between the government's interest in keeping weapons out of the hands of those it considers potentially dangerous, and the interests of private individuals in self-defense, hunting, and target shooting. Whenever gun laws have been passed at the federal level, they have been in response to the perceived threat *du jour.* Whether the threat be newly freed slaves of the nineteenth century, tommy-gun-toting gangsters of the 1930s, political assassins of the 1960s, drug running gangs of the 1980s, or schoolhouse snipers of the 1990s, law makers have tried to keep the rabble at bay with gun control, while gun owners have pushed back, fearing that gun control laws will punish the law-abiding along with the criminal.

Gun laws are passed at many levels of government, and create a dizzying maze of regulations that are difficult for even the experts to comprehend. To understand the entire field, one would need to know all the relevant provisions of the U.S. Constitution, the federal statutes (laws passed by both houses of Congress), the Code of Federal Regulations (regulations passed by federal agencies that have the force of law), all the state, county, and local gun laws, and all of the appellate court cases in which judges interpret the meaning of these laws. In other words, even most lawyers do not stay current in this area unless they specialize in firearms law. To explain all these laws in detail would take many volumes.

Therefore, for purposes of this book, the focus is on the U.S. Constitution and on federal gun control statutes, because, in recent years, the battle over gun rights and gun control has been fought most visibly in our nation's Capitol.

During America's first century as a nation, federal control of firearms was not an issue. There could be many reasons for this. In the nineteenth century, distrust of a strong central government plus a slim national budget generally kept federal legislation in check, and left states free to dominate most legislative fields.

Furthermore, according to one theory, America's gun culture had not yet grown to the stage where there arose a need for gun regulations. Until the post–Civil War period of mass production of handguns and technical advances in the accuracy of hunting rifles, perhaps a scarcity of reliable firearms meant a low rate of gun violence, and thus, a lack of legislative concern.[1] On the other hand, Second Amendment enthusiasts would argue that there were plenty of firearms in early America, but perhaps there was no federal interest in gun regulation because legislators back then respected what the enthusiasts view as the individual's right to bear arms.

Whatever the cause, the first major federal gun regulation came, as did regulations that followed, in response to gun violence that shocked the nation. Before describing its key provisions, it is important to point out that this law is applicable throughout the United States, but each state can also regulate firearms by way of state statutes. Counties, cities, and towns may also pass firearms laws. These local laws might be more restrictive than federal law, but they cannot trump federal law with less restrictive standards. For example, federal law prohibits felons from possessing firearms, so states cannot make it legal for felons to possess them.

Although we have ended up with a bewildering patchwork of federal, state, and local laws,[2] the federal laws, being uniformly applicable, are paramount. For that reason, and because the war of words between gun rights and gun regulation proponents has been fought most vigorously in the halls of Congress, this book focuses primarily on federal firearms laws.

As a preliminary matter, it is important to note that laws may not end up meaning what they seem to mean. When a judge applies a law in a specific case, the law means whatever the judge decides it means. When judges interpret laws at the appellate court level, their written opinions are binding in later cases in the same jurisdiction. Therefore, if an appellate judge rules that the statutory definition of a "cow" includes a two-legged, feathered animal that quacks, you must think "duck" whenever you read "cow" in the statute. Although this example is exaggerated for the sake of illustration, the point is, the meaning of statutory language can be profoundly affected by subsequent court decisions. Therefore, individual legal research is always required when applying a law to a given set of facts because a legal term can sometimes leak outside the confines of its dictionary definition.

THE NATIONAL FIREARMS ACT OF 1934

During the days of Prohibition, the gangs who fought over control of illegal liquor distribution shot it out in public with their infamous tommy guns. The tommy gun was a fully automatic, handheld gun, also called a machine gun. The public wanted them gone.

Clarification of terminology is important, because the word "automatic" means more than one thing. There are fully automatic and semiautomatic weapons. Some revolvers are also referred to as automatic.

A fully automatic weapon is one that fires multiple rounds of ammunition with one pull of the trigger. This is also referred to as a machine gun. A fully automatic gun can stand alone, as do military-style machine guns that stand on tripods and shoot long distances, or it can be of a smaller, handheld design. Because a fully automatic gun is capable of spraying multiple rounds in quick blasts, it can take out groups of people.

A semiautomatic weapon needs a pull of the trigger for each shot fired, so it does not fire quite as rapidly as a fully automatic. Multiple rounds of ammunition are fed rapidly into the chamber, so the shooter need not pause to reload. The number of rounds available depends on the design of the clip. Some hold up to fifty rounds, with ten to twenty being average.

An automatic revolver is a handgun that stores ammunition in a built-in cylinder and that automatically feeds the next round into the barrel after a shot is fired. The number of rounds available depends on the design, but six to ten are common.

When the gangsters of the Prohibition era began to spray each other in public with tommy guns, the risk to the urban populace became intolerable. The public outcry resulted in the National Firearms Act of 1934, also called the NFA. Contrary to common perception, the law did not ban machine guns. It taxed and regulated them to such a degree that they would, hopefully, become undesirable.

The law is still found in Title 26 of the United States Code, along with other Internal Revenue Service laws. As originally written, it covered machine guns, silencers, short-barreled ("sawed-off") shotguns or rifles, and certain other weapons. In the wake of advancing technology, it was expanded in 1968 to include explosives, poisonous gas, bombs, grenades, rockets, missiles, and mines.[3]

The definition of a machine gun is broad and includes certain of its parts. The definition also includes any parts designed to convert a gun into a machine gun, and any combination of parts that, when put together, could be used to assemble a machine gun. The law also restricts antique or inoperable machine guns, and inoperable items appearing on the 1968 list of destructive devices.[4] Collectively, for convenience, all restricted devices will be referred to as National Firearms Act weapons.

The restrictions work this way. To transfer any NFA weapon (except to the military), the U.S. Treasury Department must approve the transfer before the weapon changes hands. The transferor files a form with the Treasury Department with a tax stamp showing that the $200 transfer tax has been paid. (Note that this amount has not changed since 1934 when $200 was a significant sum.) The person to receive the weapon must send in fingerprints and a photograph, and the weapon must be specifically identified so it can always be tracked by the government.[5] Such transfers are not impossible, but criminals would be reluctant to send prints and photos to the government, and the tax adds to the cost of the weapon, so the transfers would presumably be rare.

The National Firearms Act also restricts and regulates the importation, interstate transportation, manufacture, and sale of NFA weapons, and prohibits the alteration of their serial numbers.[6]

These regulations of long-standing were originally opposed by the National Rifle Association, but over the many decades the NFA has been in effect, there have been no serious legislative battles over its key provisions. It is still the law.

THE FEDERAL FIREARMS ACT OF 1938

This law marked the first time gun dealers were required to obtain a federal firearms license, for an annual fee of $1. They were also required to maintain records of the names and addresses of the people who bought firearms, although they were not, and are still not required to turn over lists of gun purchasers to the government. The law also barred them from selling guns to people convicted of violent felonies.[7] Dealers still must be licensed and must keep sales records, as well as complying with the new criminal background check requirements of the Brady law.

THE GUN CONTROL ACT OF 1968

The next major step in federal gun regulation came in response to assassinations in the 1960s. Lee Harvey Oswald called himself "A. Hidell" when he ordered a rifle by mail. It was an Italian army surplus rifle with a telescopic sight, which he ordered from the pages of the National Rifle Association's *American Rifleman*. It cost him only $19.95. With that rifle he allegedly killed President John F. Kennedy.[8]

That and two other assassinations in the 1960s stirred a clamor for new gun regulations. John F. Kennedy's brother, Robert, was killed by a gunman during the Democratic National Convention of 1968, and the influential civil rights leader, the Reverend Martin Luther King, Jr. was killed by sniper fire that same year. Legislators responded by banning the mail order sale of guns and ammunition in the federal Gun Control Act of 1968.[9] The law included other important provisions and has been amended many times since its passage. It is the heart of federal firearms law.

Unlike the National Firearms Act of 1934, which was grounded in the federal government's taxing authority, when Congress passed the Gun Control Act, it invoked its constitutional right to regulate interstate commerce.[10] The Gun Control Act regulates and prohibits interstate firearms transactions, whereas it presumably does not regulate behavior that takes place entirely in a single state. But, because almost any firearm may have once crossed a state line from its place of manufacture, or may be made from parts manufactured in different states, the federal government has successfully claimed an interstate commerce interest in regulating conduct that otherwise appears to take place in only one state. For more on this subject see the Commerce Clause discussion in Chapter 5.

The Gun Control Act of 1968, as originally enacted, prohibited federally licensed gun dealers from sending firearms through the mails or across state lines to anyone except another licensed dealer. The law also barred the possession of guns by high risk individuals such as felons, minors, and addicts. This section will describe some of the highlights of the Gun Control Act, as it exists today.

Although amended many times, the original emphasis was to stop anonymous, interstate movement of firearms by mail order or otherwise. Gun transactions must generally be face to face with licensed firearms dealers who must record the transaction. Sales of firearms are restricted to people who live in the same state as the seller. In order to ship firearms across state lines, firearms dealers, manufacturers, and importers must have a federal firearms license, and then, they can generally only ship to each other, not to individuals.[11]

The law restricts interstate movement of firearms by private persons. With some exceptions, a licensed dealer may not sell to an individual who does not live in the same state as the dealer,[12] and an individual may not purchase or receive a firearm in one state and transport it back to his home state, unless the firearm is a rifle or shotgun that he receives in a face-to-face transaction that complies with the laws of both states, or unless he inherited the firearm.[13] Also, it is illegal to in any way transfer a firearm to somebody you know does not reside in your state.[14] There are exceptions for temporarily loaning or renting firearms to out-of-state persons for "lawful sporting purposes."[15]

Gun display at J&D Guns, Avon, Montana. (Photo by Constance Crooker.)

A person must not make false statements or use falsified documents to acquire firearms or ammunition from a federally licensed firearms provider.[16]

The law includes age restrictions. Federally licensed firearms dealers may
not sell or deliver handguns or handgun ammunition to anyone under
twenty-one. Rifles, shotguns, and their ammunition may be sold only to
those who are eighteen or over.[17] In 1994, the law was expanded to prohibit
juveniles (persons under eighteen) from possessing a handgun or handgun
ammunition, but the exceptions are so broad that juveniles are still permitted
much legitimate handgun use.[18]

The law prohibits certain people, considered dangerous, from possessing
firearms and prohibits dealers from selling to them. The list includes felons,
fugitives, illegal drug users, adjudicated mental defectives, illegal aliens, those
dishonorably discharged from the armed forces and those who have re-
nounced U.S. citizenship. These people may not possess firearms or ammunition[19] and dealers may not lawfully sell or transfer firearms or ammunition
to them.[20] In 1996, people subject to domestic-violence restraining orders
and people convicted of misdemeanor crimes of domestic violence were
added to this list.[21] Along the same lines, a person who is under indictment
for a felony may not ship or receive firearms or ammunition that have been,
at any time, in interstate commerce.[22]

There are many other provisions that regulate gun manufacturers, dealers, noncitizens, and others. Some provisions were passed in 1968 and others were grafted on later, but the general thrust of volume 18 of the United States Code, Sections 921–922 is that interstate commerce in firearms be tightly regulated.

1986: RESTRICTIONS ON ARMOR-PIERCING BULLETS

The details of the controversy that erupted between the NRA and the law-enforcement community over the restrictions on certain bullets capable of boring through a police officer's bulletproof vest has been described in Chapter 3 under the heading "Law Enforcement Veers toward Gun Control."

In 1986, the Law Enforcement Officers Protection Act was passed. This law did not actually ban the bullets, but it made it illegal to manufacture or import them,[23] and made it illegal for manufacturers or importers to sell or deliver them.[24] The definition of "armor piercing" is technical,[25] but the idea is that people should not have access to handgun ammunition that is designed, either by the type of metal used in its core, or by its heavily weighted jacket, to pierce Kevlar or other bulletproof garments commonly worn by police officers. Certain prohibited bullets are listed in the BATF's "Federal Firearms Regulations Reference Guide" on page 125.

It is interesting to note that it is not a federal crime to possess these bullets. But it is a crime to knowingly receive any unlawfully imported ammunition.[26] Also, if armor-piercing bullets are possessed along with a gun while a person is committing certain felonies, the judge must impose an additional minimum sentence of five years on top of the sentence for the underlying felony.[27] This is referred to as a "mandatory minimum" sentence because the judge has no discretion. The sentence must be imposed.

Also, note that a licensed firearm dealer is not prohibited from selling armor-piercing ammunition as long as he fills out the same forms required for the sale of a firearm.[28] But if the ammunition can't be legally manufactured or imported, how the dealer would have it for sale is unknown.

1986: FIREARM OWNERS PROTECTION ACT, OR McCLURE-VOLKMER

The National Rifle Association, feeling that gun owners had lost too much ground under the provisions of the Gun Control Act of 1968, spent much time and energy in the 1980s trying to shift federal gun law in favor of gun owners. By this time, the gun control lobby had started to assert itself, so it was an uphill battle for the NRA. In 1986, after a long struggle, the NRA scored a victory when the McClure-Volkmer Act passed. Two of its key provisions are described here.

Interstate Transport under McClure-Volkmer

As mentioned previously, all local, state, and federal jurisdictions may pass gun laws. Needless to say, this can create headaches for the gun owner who wishes to stay in compliance with all of them. Particularly, when a gun owner travels from state to state and even from town to town within some states, the varying laws on how a gun may be carried in a vehicle can make a law-abiding gun owner's head spin. Must the gun be unloaded? Must it be locked up? Must it be out of reach of driver and passengers? When is it considered illegally "concealed" and when is it considered properly "stored"? Are the rules different for rifles and handguns?

The McClure-Volkmer Act of 1986[29] was meant to remedy this. It is an amendment to the Gun Control Act of 1968 and is designed to smooth out the problems involved with interstate transport of a personal firearm. By its terms, it trumps state and local laws if they conflict with it, and it permits a traveler to follow one rule. Any traveler who may legally possess a firearm at a given departure point and who may legally possess that firearm at the point of destination may transport the firearm between those points under certain conditions. The firearm must be unloaded. Neither it nor any ammunition can be readily accessible from the passenger compartment. The firearm and any ammunition may not be carried in a glove compartment, but may be placed in the trunk or in a locked container in a vehicle that has no trunk.

Although this law is intended to smooth out the legal wrinkles in interstate transport, it applies only to travelers going directly from one point to another. So, when traveling with a firearm from New York to California, a weekend stay with cousin Vinnie in Iowa might necessitate a close look at Iowa's gun laws.[30]

Note that this law regarding transport is not the same as laws permitting qualified individuals to carry concealed weapons. Gun rights proponents have pointed out that McClure-Volkmer Act does not solve the problem of the right to self-defense while on the road, because the weapon and the ammunition must be kept out of reach of the driver and passengers.[31] And a traveler with a concealed weapons permit issued by one state still needs to check other state laws to see whether the permit will be honored elsewhere.

McClure-Volkmer Prohibits Gun Registration

A long-time concern of gun rights advocates is that they not only be free to keep and bear arms, but that they be free from government snooping as to

what arms they own. The gun rights literature frequently warns about totalitarian regimes that force people to register their guns, then, knowing who
owns the guns, goes out and confiscates them. The NRA leadership believes
that the right to keep and bear arms includes the right to keep information
about gun ownership out of government hands. The NRA scored a huge victory when it won passage of a provision of the McClure-Volkmer Act that
prohibits any branch of government from gathering gun ownership data.

Remember that federally licensed dealers are required to keep records of all
gun sales. If needed in any particular criminal investigation, a dealer may give
information about a gun sale to investigators. But McClure-Volkmer prevents
government agencies from requiring licensed dealers to turn over lists of their
sales records to the government. It also prohibits the government from estab-
lishing "any system of registration of firearms, firearms owners, or firearms
transactions."[32]

THE UNDETECTABLE FIREARMS ACT OF 1988

With advances in technology, some guns are no longer made entirely of
metal. Specifically, the Glock 17, a handgun now popular among police officers, has a frame and grip made from lightweight, high-tech plastic polymers,
although its internal parts and its barrel are still metal. Police officers like
Glocks because, among other things, they are relatively light to carry. But the
concern has arisen that as guns are made with less metal and more plastic,
they are more likely to slip undetected through airport metal detectors.

When the Glock first appeared in the mid-1980s, a controversy erupted
over whether or not they were "terrorist weapons" designed specifically for the
purpose of getting past metal detectors.[33] Columnist Jack Anderson of the
Washington Post wrote that the new Glock 17 was easy to get through detectors and that the Libyan dictator, Muamar Qadaffi, was buying up hundreds
of them.[34] Alarmed by the news, the police, who were as yet unfamiliar with
Glocks, joined in calling for a ban on the guns.

The NRA took its familiar "make-no-inroads" stance, while Handgun
Control, Inc. (since renamed the Brady Campaign to Prevent Gun Violence
and described in Chapter 7) was all for the ban. The controversy turned on
whether the guns were really so undetectable after all. The metal portions did
show up on metal detectors, and, according to some studies, so did the plastic gun shape.[35] Perhaps the Glock was not such a threat to security after all.

Back and forth legislative haggling ensued. Gun rights advocates wanted
the law to require that the government prove that the gun was "undetectable."
Their opponents wanted guns like the Glock banned.

Eventually legislators were convinced that it was a question of how much
metal a "plastic" gun still contained. A gun with about half the amount of

metal as a Glock might indeed be undetectable, but more metal than that and the gun probably posed no security risk.

An interesting compromise was struck whereby both sides claimed victory. A ban would be passed, which pleased the gun control camp, because it meant they'd made inroads on the NRA's longstanding stranglehold on Congress.[36] But the amount of metal a "plastic" gun could contain and still be legal was so minimal that no real guns were affected, which suited the NRA just fine.

The law as it stands[37] bans firearms that are less detectable than a government "security exemplar," which sets the minimum standard. This security exemplar is a gun-shaped object that contains only 3.7 ounces of stainless steel. Author David Kopel noted the irony that the bill "had no effect on any existing gun, and as far as I can tell, no effect on any gun that anyone has ever wanted to build."[38] Still, gun control proponents claim victory, calling the bill a "proactive measure" that can solve "a serious potential problem."[39]

1990: THE GUN FREE SCHOOL ZONES ACT

In 1990, Congress made it a violation of federal law for a person "knowingly to possess a firearm at a place he knows is a school zone."[40] This was called the Gun Free School Zones Act of 1990. Passage of this law did not stir up as much public debate as other federal gun control laws. After all, who wants to be seen recommending that our children be exposed to the dangers of firearms? But there was a flaw in this law that surfaced after it passed. It made a federal crime out of what had traditionally fallen within the jurisdiction of local and state authorities—regulation of conduct on and around school grounds. How could federal authorities possibly claim a legitimate interest in regulating such conduct?

The U.S. Supreme Court, in *United States v. Lopez*,[41] asked the same question. Chief Justice W. H. Rehnquist said that congressional power under the Commerce Clause may not be extended to cover effects on commerce that are so indirect and remote that it would obliterate the "distinction between what is national and what is local and create a completely centralized government."[42] On April 26, 1995, the Supreme Court held that the Act exceeded the authority of Congress because it "neither regulates a commercial activity nor contains a requirement that the [gun] possession be connected in any way to interstate commerce."[43]

After the Court declared the law unconstitutional, President Clinton proposed an amended version to cure the Commerce Clause problem. On May 10, 1995, Clinton sent Congress the Gun Free School Zones Amendments Act of 1995, which Congress passed.[44]

The unconstitutional version made it unlawful to possess any firearm in a school zone. The reworded version added the requirement that the gun possession be connected to interstate commerce:

It shall be unlawful for any individual knowingly to possess a firearm *that has moved in or that otherwise affects interstate or foreign commerce* at a place that the individual knows, or has reasonable cause to believe, is a school zone.[45] (Emphasis added.)

Also, in what was probably a case of legislative overkill, Congress added a nine-paragraph preamble in which it specified all the ways that gun possession in a school zone might impact interstate commerce. This version of the law is still in effect.

The law contains exceptions for law-enforcement officers, security guards, people with legitimate concealed weapons permits, or for guns that are unloaded and locked up.[46] The law also makes it a crime to knowingly or recklessly shoot a gun—sufficiently connected to interstate commerce—on school grounds.[47]

The amendment of the law was clearly cosmetic, but enough so to save it from Commerce Clause defects. Although lawyers frequently point out the tenuous connection between a gun that has, at some point in its history crossed a state line, and interstate commerce, judges are quick to uphold any Commerce Clause connection when it comes to guns.

The practical effect on a person charged with a gun crime is that most federal crimes carry more severe penalties than equivalent state laws. And schools with policies of zero tolerance for firearms on school grounds can now seek the backing of the federal government to enforce their policies.

1994: ASSAULT-WEAPONS BAN

One year after the Brady Bill (discussed in the next section) was first introduced in Congress, another gun control proposal arose that eventually captured as much attention and spurred as much acrimony as the Brady Bill. The idea of a ban on assault weapons had been floating around the halls of Congress, and on March 14, 1988, the secretary of education sent a memo to the attorney general in which he urged such a ban. Congress took this as a green light to move on the issue.[48]

The public took notice when, in January 1989, Patrick Edward Purdy walked onto a school playground in Stockton, California, and opened fire with a Chinese version of a Soviet AK-47. This is a weapon that looks like the type of handheld automatic weapons with banana-shaped clips that American soldiers used in Vietnam, but it had been modified for the American market from fully automatic to semiautomatic, meaning the shooter needs to pull the trigger for each shot, after which the next round loads automatically. Although this weapon did not fire as rapidly as an automatic, Purdy managed to spew 105 rounds in a matter of minutes. The body count was five students dead, thirty-three students injured, one teacher injured, and Purdy himself dead.[49]

The Chinese had dumped more than 80,000 of these weapons onto the U.S. market between 1985 and 1988,[50] and people were starting to take notice that these were not designed for hunting squirrels. When cries went out for assault weapons to be banned, the NRA took its usual position: guns don't kill people, people do. Punish the criminal not the tool. Purdy was a repeat criminal who shouldn't have been on the streets.

Senator Howard Metzenbaum had a different view. He said, "Assault weapons are designed for one purpose, and one purpose alone, for killing human beings."[51]

The NRA began to lose supporters over its intransigence on this issue. Former senator Barry Goldwater, a lifelong NRA member, said that assault weapons "have no place in anybody's arsenal. If any SOB can't hit a deer with one shot, then he ought to quit shooting."[52]

On March 14, 1989, the (first) Bush administration, which up until then had avoided the ire of the NRA, caved in and issued an executive-level import ban on certain semiautomatic assault weapons. The ban listed the weapons by make and by country of origin. They included, among others, the AK-47 and the Israeli-made Uzi.[53] This first executive order blocked 80 percent of the imports on guns of this type, and a second executive order on April 5, 1989, blocked twenty-four more models, the remaining 20 percent.[54] (In 1997, the list of barred imports was again expanded to include even modified semi-automatics that had previously been permitted.)[55]

That left the problem of domestically manufactured weapons. This executive order did not stop their production, nor did it make their possession illegal. Of the estimated 3 million assault weapons already in circulation, at least three quarters were made in the United States.[56] One American manufacturer, the Colt Firearms Company, made a big show of stopping production of its AR-15 semiautomatic to bolster its image as the sportsman's friend, but reintroduced it under a new name one year later without the bayonet mount and the flash suppressor.[57]

During debates over the bill, the NRA argued that banning all guns that fire in a semiautomatic fashion would be overinclusive, because some hunting rifles and pistols of long-standing use are designed to fire this way. They argued that referring to semiautomatics as "assault weapons" was itself misleading. The terms are not synonymous.

Wayne LaPierre, chief executive officer of the NRA, argued that a semiautomatic weapon should not be banned merely because it is "readily convertible" to a fully automatic weapon. He pointed out, correctly, that it is already against federal law to convert a semiautomatic to a fully automatic. He wrote, "Apparently it is easier to propose a new law than to enforce an existing one."[58]

On the other hand, some semiautomatics such as the Ingram Mac-10 look-alike are so easily convertible to automatic that the Bureau of Alcohol, Tobacco, and Firearms classifies them as fully automatic, because it takes only seconds to file down a small, metal catch and leave the bolt free to fire machine-gun style.[59]

Finally, after much political wrangling and much handwringing in both camps, the Violent Crime Control and Law Enforcement Act of 1994 imposed what has been popularly but inaccurately referred to as the federal assault-weapons ban,[60] which makes it a crime to manufacture, transfer, or possess a semiautomatic assault weapon. The name "assault-weapons ban" is inaccurate because the ban is not complete, as explained below. The law was a victory for gun control proponents, but it has the NRA's fingerprints all over it in that a number of compromises were made before the law passed.

First, the NRA was correct that a semiautomatic is not the same thing as an assault weapon. In Congress' attempt to ban only the type of semiautomatics that have enough military characteristics that they can be classed as assault weapons, the list of what is and is not a prohibited "semiautomatic assault weapon" goes on for pages.

The term "semiautomatic assault weapon" includes a list of specific brands and models that are prohibited. The definition also includes semiautomatic rifles, pistols and shotguns if they have at least two listed features. The list of features differs depending on whether the weapon is a rifle, a pistol, or a shotgun, and the features include things like folding or telescoping stocks, flash suppressors, grenade launchers, and the gun's ability to accept a detachable magazine.[61]

Excluded from the definition of prohibited weapons are hundreds of firearms listed in Appendix A by make and model. Also excluded (meaning it would be lawful to transfer or possess them) are any semiautomatic assault weapons that a person lawfully possessed when the law went into effect on September 13, 1994. In other words, millions of such weapons already in existence were grandfathered in. Also legal are firearms that are manually operated by bolt, pump, lever, or slide action, antique firearms, permanently inoperable firearms, and rifles and shotguns that can't accept magazines that hold more than five rounds.[62]

This law also makes it a crime to transfer or possess a large-capacity feeding device.[63] This is defined as a device that can accept more than ten rounds of ammunition, but only if it was manufactured after the date of this law.[64] In other words, such devices as already existed were grandfathered in.

Although the NRA won many concessions, it still complains bitterly about this law, while gun control proponents count it as a victory.

1994: BRADY HANDGUN VIOLENCE PREVENTION ACT

While it was pending in Congress it was called the Brady Bill. After it passed, it was called the Brady Handgun Violence Prevention Act. Now that it applies to long guns as well as handguns, it is called simply the Brady law.

This law engendered more debate, more amendments piled onto amendments, and more acrimony than any of the other gun laws of the last several decades. In a nutshell, the storm raged for seven years as gun rights groups and gun control groups faced off in a legislative battle that ended with the gun control camp claiming victory, but with the gun rights camp holding significant ground on key issues.

The idea behind the law is that people known to be disqualified from possessing guns should not be able to buy them. This includes convicted felons, those who have been adjudicated mentally defective, and others disqualified by federal law. How to stop them from buying guns?

First, require federally licensed dealers to request the police to run background checks on all gun purchasers. This is referred to as the background check requirement of the Brady law.

Second, require purchasers to wait five days for two reasons: one, to give law enforcement time to run the checks, and two, to provide a cooling-off period so a consumer cannot buy a gun and use it in the heat of passion.

When these proposals first surfaced, the gun rights camp geared up for a fight. It objected that the background check was a subterfuge for the government to set up a registration system whereby it could track lawful gun owners along with those who would be disqualified. Why such strong feelings on this point? After all, the government knows who owns which automobile. What's so bad about tracking dangerous items like guns? Gun rights advocates point to totalitarian regimes that have turned gun registration systems into gun confiscation systems once they know who has the guns. They argue that because, in their view, the Second Amendment grants citizens the fundamental right to keep and bear arms, that the government should not be permitted to know who has the guns.

Second, once a gun purchaser passes the background check, there is no longer a reason to keep a government record of that gun transaction, because it was a lawful one. Therefore, say gun rights proponents, if a background check is run, no record of it should be retained by the government.

As for the waiting period, gun rights proponents have argued that there is no proof that fewer crimes will be committed if purchasers are required to

President Clinton gestures toward former White House press secretary James Brady in the Rose Garden of the White House, Thursday, August 6, 1998, where he called on Congress to extend the Brady Gun Law, which was named after Brady. The president said he would reject any bill that weakens law enforcement's ability to keep weapons out of the hands of criminals. (AP/ Wide World Photos.)

wait. They say that a person angry enough to kill will probably still be angry in five days.

The CATO Institute said that many states had already instituted waiting periods, and, according to the Institute, one study showed that in cities with populations over 100,000 that waiting periods had no statistically significant effect on the murder and robbery rates, and that another study showed that waiting periods had no influence on either gun homicides or gun suicides.[65]

Gun rights activists were also concerned about potential danger to a gun buyer from being forced to wait. What if a person suddenly needs protection from a violent spouse or abuser? Must the person wait five days to earn the right to self-defense? Gun rights proponents also view waiting periods as "social conditioning" claiming that it "sends the message that citizens do not have the right to bear arms, but merely a privilege dependent on police permission."[66]

Therefore, the gun rights camp said there should be no waiting period. If you are going to run a background check, they argued, why not run it instantly on law-enforcement computers? They claimed that states that require instant background checks at the time of a gun purchase, with no waiting period, stop the same number of unqualified gun buyers as those states with waiting periods.

Gun control advocates noted that the difficulty with running an instant criminal background check at the federal level was that the federal government does not keep records of all criminal convictions. Many disqualifying convictions appear in state records only, and there is no supercomputer that tracks all the needed information in one place. Therefore, law enforcement needs time to run the requested checks.

Out of this dispute was born the National Instant Criminal Background Check System (NICS) now run by the FBI. The upshot was that the five-day waiting period would become the law for the first several years, from the time of passage of the Brady law in 1994 until November 30, 1998. After that time the records checks would go through a yet-to-be-established FBI computer system called NICS. The lag time was to give the government time to set up the system. It is comprised of all federal criminal records and of all records that states voluntarily provide to it.[67] Once NICS was established, the record checks could be processed at the time of the gun purchase, and the five-day waiting period would be abolished, at least as a national requirement. (Some states still require waiting periods for gun purchases.)

In the interim, the state and local agencies were called on to run the background checks. This requirement, however, ran afoul of the Constitution. In 1997, the U.S. Supreme Court, in the case of *Printz v. United States*,[68] said that the federal government cannot conscript the state's officers to administer a federal regulatory program because that is fundamentally incompatible with our constitutional system of duel sovereignty.

So, between the 1997 date of the *Printz* decision and the 1998 effective date of the FBI's NICS computerized system, most state and local jurisdictions acted voluntarily in continuing to run the Brady background checks. And today, in some states, such as Oregon for example, states still administer the background checks, running whatever state or local record checks they deem necessary. Then, acting as "point of contact" agencies responsible for handling gun dealers' requests for national background checks, the state agencies perform the NICS check in fulfillment of federal requirements, killing two jurisdictional birds with one stone.[69] Of course the states that do this do so voluntarily in cooperation with the federal government, because the federal government cannot order them to run these records checks. In states that do not administer the background checks, the firearms dealers contact the FBI directly to run the NICS check.[70]

There has been concern over the fact that NICS has information gaps based on the inability to track all criminal information nationwide from one source. The Americans for Gun Safety Foundation reported that, due to flaws in record keeping, during a thirty-month period, 202 prohibited buyers purchased guns in Oregon and 343 purchased guns in Washington. While states should ideally report felony convictions and mental disability and domestic violence records to the FBI's National Instant Criminal Background Check System, more than half have not yet fully complied. The Americans for Gun Safety Foundation concludes that better gun laws and better enforcement of existing laws are needed, while the National Rifle Association says the fault lies with the criminal justice bureaucracy, and that the rights of law-abiding citizens should not be restricted.[71]

One final concern of gun rights advocates is, will the government keep records of these background checks, and thus establish a national registry of gun owners in violation of the "no gun registry" provisions of the 1986 Firearm Owners Protection Act? The Brady law[72] and the Code of Federal Regulations[73] are explicit on this point. A number is to be assigned to each record request, and if a gun purchaser is not disqualified, the record of the request for information must be destroyed within six months.[74] The law prohibits the FBI from using the system's information to establish any kind of gun owner's registry.

These limitations took an unexpected twist after the September 11, 2001, attack on New York's World Trade Center. When the FBI was asked whether any of the suspects in the attack had ever purchased firearms, the FBI reported that an assistant attorney general had advised them that the FBI could not use gun-purchase records to find that out. The Brady law forbids it.

As a practical matter, how does the system work? A licensed gun dealer calls the NICS administrator and provides the name, sex, race, date of birth, and state of residence of the gun buyer over the telephone. The administrator runs the computer check and responds in one of three ways. "Proceed" means the gun sale is authorized, "denied" means something came up on the computer that would disqualify the purchaser, and "delayed" means the agency needs more time to investigate. If the response is "delayed," the agency must come back with a final decision within three business days. If it does not, the gun sale may proceed.[75]

If the response is "denied," the gun dealer may not sell the firearm to the purchaser. The dealer is not told the reason for the denial, but gives the purchaser a pamphlet that tells the purchaser about the right to appeal the denial. The purchaser may then contact the NICS agency directly to find the reason for the denial and to start any appeal of the denial.[76]

A former U.S. prosecutor, Eric Holder, Jr., has pointed out what he calls two "terrorist loopholes" in the Brady Act, and has urged Congress to pass laws to close those loopholes.[77]

First, the criminal background checks required by Brady only apply to transactions between federally licensed firearms dealers and gun purchasers. Private parties may sell their guns at gun shows, flea markets, or through advertisements, and the private seller is not required to first check the criminal background of the buyer. (Some states, such as Oregon, have closed the gun show loophole. Private parties must have their gun show sales approved through the state system.)

Second, the background check itself now requires only a search for criminal convictions. If the potential buyer has never been convicted, but is on an FBI watch list of *suspected* terrorists, the gun sale could legally go through under Brady.

In support of his call for new laws, Holder cites specific cases in which a suspected Hezbollah terrorist and a suspected Irish Republican Army member purchased weapons at gun shows without being screened through background checks, although he does not make clear whether background checks would have revealed criminal convictions nor whether these people were on any FBI watch list.[78]

It seems that Holder may not have thought his proposal through to the end. What would his proposal require of a firearms dealer who checks and finds that the potential buyer is on some government "suspect" list? Remember, it is only unlawful for convicted felons to possess firearms.[79] Must the dealer notify the government or refuse to sell to a "suspect" who wishes to engage in an otherwise lawful transaction? And which law-enforcement agency gets to name the suspects?

The CATO Institute claims that it is a myth that private sales at gun shows are responsible for a large number of firearms falling into the hands of criminals. It claims that the "small number of non-commercial sellers" who do not have to run background checks are not enough to create a "gun show loophole."[80] The Institute does not quantify how small is small, but claims that U.S. Department of Justice figures show that "at most 2 percent of guns used by criminals are purchased at gun shows, and most of those were purchased legally by people who passed background checks."[81]

Although gun rights proponents vigorously fought the Brady Bill requirement that gun purchasers undergo criminal background checks, gun dealers have acquiesced in its provisions. Gun industry spokesman Richard J. Feldman has said, "Even if we think philosophically that a background check is not exactly right, we've been able to direct this to a livable compromise."[82] He explained that gun dealers do not want to unwittingly transfer firearms to felons or other prohibited people, and the background check helps dealers know if a customer has a criminal background. One gun dealer at a Portland, Oregon, gun show said he was glad of the background check requirement. He used to feel nervous about selling guns to suspicious people but he had no excuse to refuse the sale. Now, if a customer has a bad record he is justified in turning him down.

How effective are background checks in preventing violence? The Justice Department reported that in 1997 69,000, or 3 percent, of attempted purchases were blocked as a result of criminal background checks.[83] The Bureau of Alcohol, Tobacco, and Firearms has reported that between 1994 to 1998 that Brady law background checks prevented 320,000 firearms sales, mostly to individuals with prior criminal histories. This means that people whose records disqualified them from legally buying a gun made 320,000 attempts to get them anyway. What they would have done with those guns, and whether they later got guns on the black market are open to question, but in four years, 320,000 fewer guns passed from licensed dealers into the hands of disqualified people as a result of background checks.

1994: JUVENILES CAN'T POSSESS HANDGUNS

Federal law bars persons under twenty-one from purchasing handguns and those under eighteen from purchasing rifles or shotguns, but a ban on minors possessing handguns was added in 1994.[84] Now a person under eighteen may not possess a handgun or ammunition that is suitable only for a handgun. The law, however, contains many exceptions for legitimate use of a handgun by a minor.

For example, a person may "temporarily transfer" a handgun to a minor for use in employment, farming, ranching, target practice, hunting, firearms training, with prior written parental consent, and in accordance with state and local law. Also excepted are juveniles who are members of the armed forces, and juveniles who use a handgun against an intruder into the residence.

1996: DOMESTIC VIOLENCE GUN-OFFENDER BAN

In 1996, a little-noticed amendment, called the Lautenburg amendment, was tacked onto other federal legislation, and thus slipped under the radar screen of gun rights groups.[85] The law passed without much fanfare, but subsequently raised the ire of those groups.

The Domestic Violence Gun-Offender Ban[86] prohibits a person who has been convicted of a misdemeanor crime of domestic violence from possessing

or purchasing firearms or ammunition. The law had long applied to convicted felons—persons convicted of crimes where the sentence can exceed
one year. The difference is that a person convicted of a crime carrying a sentence of one year or less can now be barred from possessing firearms if that
crime involved domestic violence.

As it turns out, this law began to be applied to some law-enforcement officers who had been convicted of domestic violence. No exceptions for them
had been written into the law, as is often the case with gun control laws. Police began losing their jobs because they could no longer carry firearms on the
job. They have not yet successfully challenged the law. It remains on the
books.

Gun control advocates do not believe police officers should be exempt. If
they have committed crimes of domestic violence and they are armed,
couldn't they be just as dangerous to their spouses as other citizens?

A similar law, already on the books when this passed, is the law that bars
people subject to domestic-violence restraining orders from possessing or re-
ceiving firearms or ammunition.[87] This is also controversial, because the person need not be convicted of a crime to be barred from possessing firearms. If
a judge, after the person had opportunity for a hearing, restrains a person
from harassing, stalking, or threatening an intimate partner or child, the
firearms ban applies to the person restrained. This is the law that applied to
Dr. Emerson in the case described in the section on the Second Amendment
in Chapter 4. It also applies to some police officers, so it has stirred similar
complaints as the misdemeanor section of the law.

7

Gun Control and Gun Rights Organizations

There are a multitude of organizations lobbying on all sides of the question of gun control. Some have other agendas also, such as sport shooting competitions, but include lobbying as one activity of the organization. Others are purely political tools. Still others, such as the militia groups are their own subcategory in that membership in a militia is generally a political statement in itself. This section describes some of the key groups and the positions they have taken on major issues, but does not purport to be exhaustive.

Note how recently some of these groups came into existence. Of course, the National Rifle Association has a long history stretching back to the nineteenth century, but even that organization did not reach full political sophistication as a lobbying force until after its so-called Cincinnati Revolt of 1977.

Note also that it took all of human history for the world population to reach 1 billion in 1804. The population tripled to 3 billion by 1960. Then in the next mere forty years, the human population doubled again to 6 billion.[1] It may not be coincidental that the surge in population growth has gone hand in hand with our alarm over an increase in gun deaths and injuries. We live closer together and feel less safe. Perhaps overcrowding itself creates pressures that contribute to violence. Whatever the cause, in a single generation many of us have gone from living in homes without locks to barricading ourselves in homes protected by deadbolts and burglar alarms while we wonder how to stem lawlessness and violence. It is not surprising that people have banded together to try to come up with solutions.

One disturbing aspect of the controversy over gun rights and gun control is that members of the opposing groups tend to vilify each other as enemies rather than recognizing their mutual interest in keeping society safe from violence. Many gun rights supporters see gun control proponents as "gun grabbers" with a hidden agenda: disarm the people so they will become malleable puppets in a totalitarian state. They do not acknowledge the genuineness of the gun control proponents' desire to make this land safer for all of us.

On the other hand, gun control proponents tend to see gun rights advocates as motivated only by greed and lust for the kind of macho power that deadly weapons can bestow on an otherwise insecure person. They do not acknowledge that law-abiding persons who wish to retain control over their fate in life-or-death struggles genuinely believe that their possession of firearms helps improve public safety.

And so the battle between opposing groups makes it look like the other group is the enemy when the truth is that each side is looking for answers to the same question. How can we be safe again? The answers differ. Some say, disarm everybody. Others say, be realistic. We should arm ourselves against threat. Still others strike a middle ground, where arms would be permitted but within limits in terms of type and safety features of arms.

THE BRADY CAMPAIGN TO PREVENT GUN VIOLENCE AND THE BRADY CENTER TO PREVENT GUN VIOLENCE

This gun control group has changed names several times, and even now is an amalgam of two groups. The Brady Campaign to Prevent Gun Violence and the Brady Center to Prevent Gun Violence emerged from former groups in June 2001. The history, however, begins much earlier.

In 1974, the National Council to Control Handguns (NCCH) was started by Dr. Mark Borinsky, a victim of gun violence. That organization was renamed Handgun Control, Inc. (HCI) in 1980. Its sister organization, the Center to Prevent Handgun Violence (CPHV) was founded in 1983 as an educational outreach group.[2] During the 1980s and 1990s, these two groups were able to sway opinion away from the take-no-prisoners stance of the NRA and to influence a number of gun control laws. They did not win all battles, nor did they win complete victories in those they did win, but they chipped away at what had been previously thought to be the invincible gun lobby.

In 1981, President Ronald Reagan's press secretary, Jim Brady, was shot and wounded for life in an assassination attempt on the president. Three years later, his wife, Sarah Brady, joined the gun control battle. In 1989 she became Chair of Handgun Control, Inc., and in 1991 she chaired the Center to Prevent Handgun Violence. Although the gun lobby has accused her of becoming a paid mouthpiece for gun control, their accusations ring hollow because she speaks from such harsh personal experience. She has written a book titled *A Good Fight*,[3] which chronicles her lobbying efforts on behalf of gun control. In it, she describes her personal growth from shy wife of a White House press secretary to persuasive lobbyist whose life was transformed by the tragedy that left her husband brain damaged and partially paralyzed.

Not long after Sarah Brady joined the fight for gun control, the membership and the budget of Handgun Control, Inc. doubled.[4] Handgun Control, Inc. and the Center to Prevent Handgun Violence have supported many changes in state gun laws, and have had great impact going head to head with the gun lobby in the area of federal gun laws. For example, in 1986, Handgun Control, Inc. successfully lobbied Congress to restrict distribution of armor-piercing "cop killer" bullets that puncture the vests worn by the police. In 1988, it supported a successful ban on so-called "plastic" handguns that cannot be detected by airport x-ray machines.

Its biggest win was the Brady Bill. After seven long years of political wrangling, the bill went into effect on November 30, 1993. In its original form it required a five-day waiting period and a criminal background check on handgun purchases. (As of November 1998, the background checks became instantaneous so there is no longer any waiting period. The background checks have been extended to rifles and shotguns.)

During the time the Brady Bill has been in effect, gun deaths in the United States have dropped 27 percent from 39,595 in 1993 to 28,874 in 1999. The Brady Campaign claims that a significant reason is that the background checks have prevented many criminals from buying guns.[5]

The organization also celebrated when, in 1994, President Clinton signed the Violent Crime Control and Law Enforcement Act, which banned the future manufacture and importation of certain military-style assault weapons.

Felons had long been barred from possessing firearms, but in 1996 gun control groups celebrated another victory when Congress passed a law prohibiting anybody convicted of a domestic violence misdemeanor or anybody subject to a domestic violence restraining order from buying or owning a gun.

In 1998, the Center to Prevent Handgun Violence began to support negligence lawsuits against the gun manufacturing industry and to encourage state laws aimed at child safety, such as gun-lock and parental-responsibility laws.

On June 14, 2001, in honor of Jim and Sarah Brady, the two organizations changed their names to the Brady Campaign to Prevent Gun Violence and the Brady Center to Prevent Gun Violence.

VIOLENCE POLICY CENTER

The home page of the Violence Policy Center's (VPC) Web site[6] reads: "Ban handguns now." While some gun control groups have little quarrel with the type of guns that are lawfully used and enjoyed by many, the Violence Policy Center makes no bones about the fact that it would like to accomplish what gun rights proponents most fear. A total ban on handguns.

The Violence Policy Center's Web site describes the group as "a national non-profit organization working to fight firearms violence through research, education, and advocacy. As a gun control think tank, the VPC analyzes a wide range of current firearm issues and provides information to policymakers, journalists, public health professionals, grassroots activists, and members of the general public."

The Violence Policy Center has proved to be an influential voice on gun control issues, and a favorite target of criticism of gun rights groups. Its Web site is a sophisticated compendium of articles and links on a wide array of gun control topics.

THE HELP NETWORK

Gun control groups have been rankled by the fact that, throughout the 1980s, the gun rights groups got to define the gun debate as a criminal justice issue. As health care professionals witnessed more senseless gun injuries, they began to enter the fray of public discourse. Groups such as the Handgun Epidemic Lowering Plan (HELP) Network have tried to steer the focus away from criminal justice to "enhance public health efforts to prevent firearm injury and death."[7]

The HELP Network began in 1993 and says it serves "as a clearinghouse for information on the modern epidemic caused by firearms—especially handguns—emphasizing prevention and policy solutions based on research."[8] Among its goals are to reduce minors' access to firearms and to reduce "civilian access to most lethal handguns."[9]

While gun rights groups believe that HELP members are really gun banners masquerading as protectors of public health, HELP's membership list includes over 125 groups including the American Medical Association, the American Academy of Pediatrics, the National Association of Children's Hospitals, and the Emergency Nurses Association.[10]

THE COALITION TO STOP GUN VIOLENCE

The Coalition to Stop Gun Violence claims that its membership roll contains more than forty religious, labor, medical, educational, and civic organi-

Hilary Clinton speaking at the Million Mom March, Washington, May 14, 2000. (News-Com/BlackStar.)

zations plus more than 100,000 individual members.[11] It was formerly called the National Coalition to Ban Handguns.[12]

The organization's mission is "to stop gun violence by fostering effective community and national action."[13] More specifically, it would ban personal handguns. It supports a ban on "the importation, manufacture, sale and transfer of handguns [not shotguns or rifles] and assault weapons, with reasonable exceptions for police, military, security personnel, gun clubs, and antique and collectible firearms stored in inoperable condition."[14]

It also supports the handgun licensing and registration that gun rights groups fear will lead to outright government confiscation once the government is allowed to know who owns what weapons. It supports regulating handguns as consumer products, banning assault weapons and so-called Saturday night specials and a one-a-month handgun purchase limit.

THE MILLION MOM MARCH

On Mother's Day of 2000, more than 750,000 people marched on the National Mall in Washington, D.C., to demonstrate their support for "sensible gun laws," according to the Web site of the Million Mom March.[15] The organization's purpose was to pass national laws that "prevent gun violence in this country, rather than legislation to placate the gun lobby."[16] The motto of the group: "We love our children more than the gun lobby loves its guns."[17]

The Million Mom March merged in October of 2001 with the Brady Campaign and the Brady Center to Prevent Gun Violence.

STATE GUN GROUPS

Some gun control and gun rights groups function primarily at the state level. Because gun laws may differ depending on the jurisdiction—federal, state, county, or local municipality—some groups have found it expedient to focus their energies on gun laws at the state and local level. For example, gun rights groups have worked hard to get "shall issue" concealed-carry laws passed in many states, while at the same time, gun control groups have won passage of gun safety laws or gun bans that are more restrictive than federal laws.

Gun control groups that operate primarily at the state level include Ceasefire Oregon, Ceasefire New Jersey, New Hampshire Ceasefire, Washington Ceasefire, and others. For a list of more gun control groups by state, see http://www.bradycampaign.org/activism/groups/list.asp?query=all.

As an example, Ceasefire Oregon has been in existence for more than ten years, and has supported successful state legislation that closes the "gun show loophole" of the Brady Bill. At gun shows, federal law requires federally licensed firearms dealers to run instant criminal background checks on gun purchasers, but private parties may also sell firearms at gun shows, and federal law does not require them to run the same checks. Under Oregon law, such private parties must request the state police to run criminal background checks.[18] Gun control groups operating at the state level have spearheaded these types of state laws.

Similarly, there are gun rights organizations that function primarily at the level of the state. For example, in Massachusetts, the Gun Owners Action League[19] purports to be the second-largest dues-paying membership organization in the state. It is an education and lobbying group that holds that "an unarmed public lies prostrate at the feet of criminals and thugs."[20] It cites the failure of Washington, D.C.'s twenty-year-old gun ban to stem crime and violence in our nation's capital, and urges people to join, saying "Every intrusion on our gun rights is an intrusion on all rights."[21]

8

Gun Rights Groups

The National Rifle Association is perhaps the best-known and is certainly the oldest of the groups that loudly resist any imposition of legal restrictions on gun ownership. Others formed more recently, and, in some ways, are more radical. The members of the National Rifle Association, because they are so many (the group claims millions of members), are not monolithic in their political views. Although the NRA's legislative lobbying branch sounds uncompromising, the NRA's rank and file is not always the hotbed of hard-liners the group's public line portrays. Other groups have sprung up that seem to speak with even more strident voices. Some of the most prominent are described here.

MODERN MILITIA GROUPS

The Nature of Modern Militia Groups

The new militia movement in America appears to be of fairly recent origin. The historical militias are discussed in the context of the history of the Second Amendment in Chapter 4. The modern militia movement arose within the last several decades and flourished in the mid-1990s. It has quieted some after Timothy McVeigh acted out principles espoused by some of these groups when he bombed the federal building in Oklahoma City, killing 168 American citizens. Since then, these groups have either lost some of their luster or have become more secretive. Although militia groups do not seem so prominent in recent years, they still exist.

In fairness to these groups, it should be noted that McVeigh did not claim to be acting as a militia member, and most militia groups have publicly voiced their condemnation of his crimes. That, however, does not diminish the eerie resemblance of his belief system to theirs, including their extreme distrust of a centralized federal government.

Some of the still-active groups include the Militia of Montana,[1] the Missouri 51st Militia,[2] the Southern Michigan Regional Militia,[3] and the Marietta, Pennsylvania, Militia,[4] to name a few of the groups that keep updated Web sites. (Many militia Web sites went dormant around the time of the McVeigh bombing.) These Web sites tend to sport over-the-top patriotic designs. For example, the Marietta, Pennsylvania, Militia site opens to a colorful home page that plays the "Battle Hymn of the Republic."

Most of these groups classify themselves as "unorganized" militias; a result of the U.S. Constitution placing the authority for militias under federal control, but leaving their supervision to the states. Congress may call forth the militia to enforce federal law, suppress insurrections and repel invasions, but the states retain the authority for training the militia and for appointing officers.[5]

Federal statutes further describe the nature of the militia.[6] It is made up of all able-bodied male citizens between seventeen and forty-five years of age. It is two-tiered. The organized militia "consists of the National Guard and the Naval Militia."[7] It is important to note that this classification is made by way of federal statute. Some militia group members claim that it is a mistake to think the militia has anything to do with the National Guard. As a matter of federal law, they are incorrect. The National Guard is the "organized militia."

The next tier is the "unorganized militia," which consists of the remaining able-bodied male citizens, ages seventeen to forty-five, who are not already members of the National Guard or the Naval Militia.[8] In other words, these men make up a pool of citizens from which troops can be called up in time of need.

Members of the modern militia movement sometimes claim that they have the constitutional authority, and even the duty, to organize themselves into "unorganized" militia groups in order to best be prepared for service. But nothing in the militia law directs them nor authorizes them to do so. And historically, militia groups mustered only at the call of state or local authorities, but did not band together on their own initiative.

The Second Amendment says that a "well regulated Militia" is necessary for the "security of a free State," so the Second Amendment contemplates that militia duty will be under state regulation, which mirrors the requirements of Article I, Section 8, Clause 16 of the Constitution. In spite of this, most modern militia groups have no connection to a government body. They are self-proclaimed "unorganized" militias. They sometimes also describe their makeup as "leaderless resistance."

What Do They Believe?

Although not all groups and not all members of such groups believe in the same things, there are certain clusters of beliefs that seem to be common to many of these organizations. One core belief pertinent to this text is, of course, the belief that any form of gun control violates the Second Amendment right to keep and bear arms. This is usually coupled with an assertion that the central government is eroding cherished constitutional rights as a first step toward tyrannizing us.

According to one watchdog group, they also tend toward a cluster of beliefs that reflect a deep mistrust of the federal government's involvement in other areas such as education, abortion, and the environment.[9] This is typified by a bumper sticker for sale at a Portland, Oregon, gun show. It said, "I love my country, but I fear my government." Another bumper sticker displayed an ironic twist on the abortion issue, proclaiming, "I'm pro-choice. I choose to own firearms."

An example of the cluster of views prevalent in these groups is seen in this title from the 7th Missouri Militia's Web site. It reads, "How Our Enemy Views Us: A Marxist Abortionist's Views on Christian Identity & Leaderless Resistance."[10] This hits communism, abortion, those who are not nonfundamentalist Christians, and those who are foes of militia groups all in one title.

Militia groups claim they are not antigovernment because the power to govern resides in people like them, but they do fear the potential for abuse of power by a centralized government. The statement of purpose of the Southern Michigan Regional Militia claims that it is "increasingly obvious" that the Constitution is being "ignored, violated, and trampled on." Therefore, the group puts all levels of government on notice that it will defend violations of the Constitution "with a fierce and determined resistance."[11]

Similarly, the North Carolina Citizen Militia says that the "potential for governmental tyranny" makes it "essential that citizen soldiers, as part of the unorganized militia, organize early to ensure their security and efficiency."[12] Note the call to organize the "unorganized" militia, an oxymoron at best.

The Missouri 51st Militia says that it is "deeply concerned over the apparent trend in our country towards a police state," that it is "deeply concerned over the blatant attempt to disarm the citizenry" and that it is "determined" to meet those who "oppose the constitutional principles of this land at the ballot box, at protest demonstrations, in the media, and if necessary...*on the battlefield of freedom*."[13] (Emphasis added.)

Notice that, even if you agree with the principle that the people have the right to overthrow a tyrannical government by force, it appears these militia groups reserve to themselves the right to decide whether constitutional rights have been infringed such that armed intervention is needed. The problem is obvious. These are groups of unelected, armed men, acting under no authority, yet they would take it on themselves to decide for the rest of us when protection of our constitutional rights needs their armed intervention.

Populists or Extremists?

Fear of federal government has a long and respected tradition in America. It began in the early days of our nation with the Anti-Federalists, described more thoroughly in the Second Amendment discussion in Chapter 4. Having just rebelled from one oppressive government, they feared that too much centralized power would again give rise to governmental abuse. The distrust of centralized power survived in America in one form or another throughout our history. For example, it characterized the populist movement, made up primarily of farmers in the 1890s, who noticed that the banks, the railroads, and the central government seemed to have stacked the deck against their agricultural interests.[14]

People who follow these traditions, by whatever name they adopt, fear that a strong central government could snatch all local control from individuals, their communities, and their states. Such groups have usually provided a healthy check on centralized power in that they treat the government as a necessary evil that needs constant watching, which, in a democracy, of course it does.

The modern militia groups, on the one hand, mirror this long populist tradition of keeping a watchful eye on a centralized government. To the extent that they participate in political debate within the bounds of law, they contribute as good Americans always have to our robust public life.

On the other hand, some militia members exhibit the kind of extreme distrust of government that looks to the rest of the world like paranoia. This is exemplified by a book title spotted in January 2001 at a Portland, Oregon, gun show that read, *The Policeman Is Your Friend and Other Lies.* This degree of distrust may reflect nothing more than unwillingness to acknowledge the complexities of our populous, multifaceted nation in which laws are supposed to account for competing interests and thus forego simplistic, bumper-sticker solutions to vexing problems. An individual who clings to a bumper-sticker view of reality may feel enraged when laws do not march in lockstep with that view, especially the take-no-prisoners view that any gun control law is intolerable. One regional militia commander who is also a gun shop owner has been quoted as saying, "We're talking about a situation where armed conflict may be inevitable if the country doesn't turn around."[15] Thus, these groups may stockpile military-style weapons in preparation for a showdown with their own government.[16]

In the defense of these groups, when the word "paranoia" comes up, Jim Goad, the author of *The Redneck Manifesto,* goes on a literary rampage, excoriating the "militia chasers" and listing notorious moments in recent history when the federal government has been caught red-handed in flat-out lies. He concludes, "Maybe we wouldn't be so FUCKING PARANOID if they hadn't FUCKING LIED to us so many times."[17] This author hammers on the power imbalance between government and citizen that fuels the fears behind the militia movement. He says:

When people get weepy about one hundred sixty-eight dead bodies in OK City—not that they shouldn't—it might be wise to put things in perspective. Government-sponsored death, whether through war or the murder of its own citizens, is estimated to have killed one hundred sixty-nine million people in this century alone. [Footnote omitted.] That's almost exactly a MILLION times the casualties of Oklahoma City.[18]

Understanding the frustration that fuels these groups is one thing, but the public fear is that they are not merely ready to defend, but that they will take the offensive. Factor in that racism and white supremacism motivates some of their members, and the threat to law-abiding citizens cannot be ignored. A watchdog group, which has studied militia groups that have surfaced in thirteen states, reports that "we find militia leaders with backgrounds in the Aryan Nations movement and . . . other erstwhile neo Nazis and Ku Kluxers."[19]

For example, the Florida State Militia's handbook contains a "Patriot List" of periodicals, which includes such anti-Semitic propaganda as *The Truth at Last,*[20] containing articles with titles such as, "Did Six Million Really Die?" A quick scan of the book stalls at any gun show will reveal the extent to which hate literature goes hand in hand with the other products marketed there. At a Portland, Oregon, gun show, titles such as *Mein Kampf* by Adolf Hitler and *Anthology of Racist Issues* by Charles Weisman were displayed in a booth decorated with signs that said, "We sell politically incorrect books," "Something to offend everyone," and "This Ain't Barnes & Noble."

The fact that hate literature is marketed alongside military style semiautomatics, many of which convert easily to fully automatic machine guns, raises an interesting question about the economic motives of gun manufacturers and dealers to stir the passions of gun buyers. Aside from technical and historical books about guns, much of the literature at gun shows falls into one of two categories: fear and hate.

The "fear" books, such as *Armed and Female*[21] by Paxton Quigley, promote handguns as the great equalizer between the otherwise defenseless and her worst nightmare, be it rapist, mugger, or burglar. One entire chapter of Quigley's book never mentions firearms, while it details the brutal specifics of one humiliating rape after another.[22] The message? The unarmed woman always loses. It has been noted that Quigley is not only a well-publicized author on women and guns, but she is also a firearms instructor who (at least as of 1995) received a monthly stipend from the gun manufacturer, Smith & Wesson, for giving talks to gun groups and advising women on the guns they ought to buy.[23] Surely Smith & Wesson has not missed the connection. Quigley sells fear and fear sells handguns.

If fear sells handguns, then hate sells high-powered, military-style weapons. If you are going to arm your militia in preparation for warfare against groups of people who represent a hated threat, you need more than a pistol in your night stand. You need to stockpile military weapons and enough survival gear for the duration.

So, the question becomes, does the literature that stirs fear and hate come directly or indirectly from those who engage in the all-American business of marketing goods to consumers, or did a culture of fear and hate arise on its own, with entrepreneurs ready to jump in to meet a perceived need? In other words, which came first, gun consumers or inflammatory literature designed to create gun consumers?

This leads to another interesting question. If the literature came first, then who is really manipulating the average citizen? Perhaps militia members should ask themselves, does the feared group *du jour* (fill in the blank: Jews, liberals, government, Communists, the United Nations, the New World Order) really conspire to run their lives, or could it be that the beloved gun manufacturers themselves in tandem with the money-hungry National Rifle Association purposely fan the fires of fear and hate in order to reach into these peoples' pockets?

Are Militia Groups Legal?

The final question regarding militia groups is, are they legal? Although they claim to be acting under constitutional mandate, this stems from a misunderstanding of federal law. But in America, the constitutional right to freedom of assembly and the right to free speech allows for gatherings of people to express even unpopular opinions. Whether these gatherings are legal or not depends on what goes on there.

Inciting people to unlawful violence can constitute criminal conspiracy, aiding or abetting a crime, or even more specifically in the state of Oregon, the crime of unlawful paramilitary activity.[24] In Oregon, it is a felony to conduct or participate in any kind of firearms or explosives training knowing the firearm or explosive will be unlawfully used in a "civil disorder." A civil disorder is an assemblage of three or more people who inflict or create a danger of inflicting damage to property or injury to a person. This statute has been on the books, with some amendments, since 1983, which is about the time that militia groups began to surface. Militia members present themselves as law-abiding patriots and enforcers of the Constitution, but some walk perilously close to the line that separates criminals from law-abiding citizens.

SECOND AMENDMENT FOUNDATION AND THE CITIZENS COMMITTEE FOR THE RIGHT TO KEEP AND BEAR ARMS

These two organizations are so closely linked that, except for the logo at the top of the page, their Web sites look nearly identical and were obviously crafted by the same hand.[25] These groups are the brainchildren of one of the more prolific writers on the subject of gun rights, Alan Gottlieb.

Alan Gottlieb has been active in the gun rights movement since at least the 1970s. His books (mostly self-published by his company, Merril Press) include titles such as *The Gun Grabbers, The Gun Rights Fact Book, Politically Correct Guns, The Rights of Gun Owners,* and others.[26] He also writes about guns for magazines and newspapers, and he is president of several talk radio stations. He is the founder of and an officer in the Second Amendment Foundation, and he chairs the Citizens Committee for the Right to Keep and Bear Arms (CCRKBA). Although he claims to have helped "create a grassroots army from the bottom up,"[27] a single tone of sneering irony pervades his publications such that one wonders whether he is in reality a one-man gun rights industry.

Note, for example, Gottlieb's characteristic tone of condescension when he writes, "The rocket scientists in our government haven't figured out a lot of things, but they should have noticed by now that the first thing people do when a new gun ban is announced is to run out and buy a lot of guns before it goes into effect."[28] He takes pride in the label "gun nut," and is sometimes perceived by others in the movement as a "loose cannon."[29]

In spite of this, the CCRKBA alone claims 650,000 members and supporters.[30] Although Gottlieb is, himself, a member of the National Rifle Association and says they do "a great job of defending gun rights," he also says that "they do not have a monopoly on the best way of doing it," and that his organizations were needed in order to create a gun rights movement. "You can't have a movement with only one organization."[31]

SECOND AMENDMENT SISTERS

Although gun rights activists have tended to be predominantly male, women have also entered the fray. When the Million Mom March organized

750,000 people to march in Washington, D.C., for gun control on Mother's Day of 2000, a group of women formed to rally in opposition. After the rally, they began accepting paid memberships in July 2000, and they claim that they continue "to grow in leaps and bounds."[32]

The Second Amendment Sisters say that for "increasing numbers of women [an estimated 17 million], ownership of a gun, and knowing how to use it properly, are significant steps toward peace of mind and security."[33] They say we do not need more laws because criminals will not obey them. "Self-defense is everyone's right. Vigorous prosecution of and stiff sentences for violent criminals need to be the order of the day."[34] They also promote teaching children "firearms safety."[35]

MORE GUN RIGHTS GROUPS

For a list of more pro-gun groups with links to their Web sites, see http://www.guntruths.com/Resource/links_to_other_pro.htm#Pro-Firearms %20Sites.

The National Rifle Association

The largest, oldest, and most politically influential of the gun rights groups is the National Rifle Association. It began in 1871 to encourage the art of rifle shooting at targets. Prior to that time, in part due to the inability to accurately aim some of the older models of firearms, even the military did not have its soldiers engage in systematic target practice. In addition, post–Civil War military experts believed that target practice was actually harmful because it might encourage individualism among enlisted men, a characteristic reserved to officers. However, with improved technology at the beginning of the industrial age, sharpshooting became more accessible.[36]

The two veterans who founded the NRA, Colonel William C. Church and General George Wingate, were distressed over the lack of marksmanship in their own troops, so they began to promote "rifle shooting on a scientific basis."[37] As originally formed, the NRA focused on military marksmanship, although it was technically independent of the armed forces.[38]

The NRA's first project was to construct a modern rifle range on Long Island. It did so by convincing the New York legislature to appropriate $25,000 for the purchase of the land needed for the range. Although Church, like many NRA members since, was a staunch opponent of socialism and a fierce defender of private enterprise, this first government subsidy began a long history of hand-in-glove relationships between the NRA and public funding bodies.[39]

Emily McGonigal, of Fort Washington, Maryland, holds protest signs as she attends a rally by the Second Amendment Sisters on the grounds of the Washington Monument, Sunday, May 14, 2000 in Washington, D.C. The rally was staged in opposition to the Million Mom March. (AP/Wide World Photos.)

After a brief period, New York pulled the plug on funding and the NRA collapsed. It rose again in 1901 when a new clamor for military preparedness coincided with renewed government aid, partly in the form of free surplus military rifles for the NRA's annual shooting matches.[40]

The NRA also began its long history of "promoting the shooting sports among America's youth" when, in the early 1900s, it established rifle clubs at colleges, universities, and military academies. It still sponsors youth shooting events through the Boy Scouts, the American Legion, and other groups.[41]

Its political activity was slower to evolve. Not until 1934 did it form the Legislative Affairs Division. The Division did not lobby directly, but did stir its members to take action on proposed firearms laws.[42]

In the 1930s, for the first time in U.S. history, sweeping legislation was proposed to tighten gun policy by banning or regulating a wide variety of firearms. The NRA's letter-writing campaign resulted in passage of a pared-down version of the National Firearms Act of 1934. The law, still in existence, regulates and taxes the sale of machine guns and sawed-off shotguns. Soon after, the NRA's legislative arm fell dormant while the organization evolved into what, by the 1950s, was primarily a hunter's and sportsman's club.[43]

In the mid-1950s, the NRA began its involvement in firearms training for law-enforcement officers.[44] This made police officers its natural ally for many years until the NRA began to oppose laws supported by the police, such as the banning of armor-piercing bullets that could rip through a police officer's bulletproof vest.

The NRA has long played a major role in civilian firearms training. Its 50,000 certified instructors train more than 750,000 gun owners a year, and its 1,000 certified coaches work with competitive shooters.[45] Over the course of its history the NRA claims to have trained more than 1.5 million police, 17 million hunters, and "millions upon millions" of others.[46]

The NRA has also established the Eddie Eagle Gun Safety Program, which teaches young schoolchildren that if they see a gun they must, "Stop. Don't touch. Leave the area. Tell an adult."

In spite of all this, in recent years, legislative lobbying became the organization's main focus. The NRA describes itself as "a major political force and as America's foremost defender of Second Amendment Rights."[47] How did this come about?

The assassination of President John F. Kennedy triggered the Gun Control Act of 1968, which imposed major changes in gun laws. The assassin, Lee Harvey Oswald, had purchased his fateful Italian army surplus rifle, complete with four-power telescopic sight, by mail order from an advertisement in the NRA's magazine, the *American Rifleman*.[48] As a result, the Gun Control Act of 1968 banned mail order sales of guns and ammunition.

Rankled by the new gun restrictions, the NRA began to reawaken to legislative action. In 1975, recognizing what it called the need for "political defense of the Second Amendment," the NRA formed the soon-to-be-powerful Institute for Legislative Action, or ILA. This is the branch of the NRA that people now think of as the "gun lobby."[49]

The ILA's strength and singleness of purpose came about through a split in NRA members' priorities after passage of the Gun Control Act. One group in the NRA was uninterested in legislative lobbying, and was talking about expanding the NRA's mission from shooting to include camping, wilderness survival training, conservation education, and environmental awareness. The hard-liners reared up in protest. They were led by the notorious Harlon Carter (notorious because he'd once been convicted of murder for shooting a fifteen-year-old Mexican when Carter was seventeen—the conviction was reversed on appeal on a legal point).[50]

In November 1976, the first group, those with broadening outdoor interests, fired seventy-four NRA employees in one weekend. Most of those fired

The National Rifle Association's Whittington Center in Raton, New Mexico, comprised of 52 square miles, is the world's largest shooting and training facility. (Photo by Constance Crooker.)

were hard-liners who followed Harlon Carter. This incident became known as the "Weekend Massacre."[51]

Carter got his revenge at the NRA's annual meeting in Cincinnati in 1977. He and his hard-liners manipulated the parliamentary procedure, and when the dust settled after the voting, the would-be conservationists were out and Carter and his crowd, including Neal Knox, who later headed the ILA, were in. This became known as the Cincinnati Revolt. From that day on, as author Osha Gray Davidson put it, "the NRA became more than a rifle club. It became the Gun Lobby."[52]

From the time of the 1968 Gun Control Act through the mid-1980s, the NRA successfully blocked every major attempt at federal gun control legislation. It not only blocked what it considered bad gun laws, but it engineered passage of a major federal law that favored its interests, the McClure-Volkmer Act. It did this by a combination of smart lobbying on the part of the ILA and by the so-called "hassle factor." This involved the NRA membership bombarding their legislators with their strongly held views in letters or in testimony at public meetings.[53] In spite of vigorous opposition from Handgun Control, Inc., the NRA cleverly maneuvered the passage of the McClure-Volkmer Act, which smoothed out some of the interstate transportation problems in carrying a personal weapon across state lines.[54]

But at the peak of its glory, the NRA began to discover that it could not always stomp its foot and have its own way. Gun control groups began to become more sophisticated in their own lobbying while the NRA began to alienate one of its strongest allies—the law-enforcement community.

Law enforcement and the NRA had been natural friends for years. The NRA had been training law-enforcement officers since the 1950s. That and their mutual interest in firearms technology sealed the alliance. Then a dispute over the legality of Teflon-tipped KTW bullets (called "apple greens" for the color of the Teflon) broke up the relationship. Apple greens were also dubbed "cop-killer" bullets because they could pierce the lightweight body armor worn by cops, and could rip through the metal doors of police cars. The majority of police officers wanted them banned. The NRA said that bullets are neither good nor bad, and that "the so-called 'cop killer' bullet issue is a Trojan Horse waiting outside gun owners' doors."[55]

The NRA also began to personally condemn the leaders of law-enforcement groups who supported this legislation, thus stirring the ire of cops everywhere. Although the NRA, which was simultaneously fighting for passage of McClure-Volkmer, ended up not opposing the final version of the armor-piercing-bullet-bill, the damage had been done. President Reagan signed the bill into law on August 28, 1986, and the law-enforcement community ceased to automatically dance to the NRA tune.[56]

Then came the NRA's long, head-to-head battle with Handgun Control, Inc. over the Brady Bill. Although the NRA of the 1970s had supported an earlier proposal for a waiting period before a person could receive a newly purchased gun, by the latter half of the 1980s, the NRA viewed waiting periods as a major threat to gun rights.[57]

The NRA eventually lost this fight, although it did gain a modification to the original five-day waiting period provision. The Brady Bill's five-day period was designed to give law enforcement sufficient time to respond to requests for criminal background checks of gun purchasers while, at the same time, assuring a cooling-off period for anybody rushing in to buy a gun in the heat of passion. The NRA successfully lobbied to have that changed to an instantaneous criminal background check that is done over the telephone while the customer waits to complete the gun purchase. Under the amended version of the Brady Bill, the five-day period would go into effect on passage of the bill, and, after sufficient time for the system to get up and running, the instantaneous check would later replace it. At the same time, the NRA lost ground in that this Brady amendment extended the background checks from handguns to rifles and shotguns also.

In February 1994, this amended version of the Brady Bill passed into law. Although the U.S. Supreme Court, in 1997, said that one of its provisions violated the separation of powers doctrine in that it required state law-enforcement officers to run federally mandated background checks, the states voluntarily complied until such time as the instant federal background check system went into effect.[58]

The NRA lost another round when semiautomatic weapons were barred. This was first done by an executive-level import ban in 1989 during the first of the Bush administrations.[59] Although the NRA went to great lengths to point out that these were not rapid-fire machine guns as the name "assault weapon" implies (a semiautomatic requires that you pull the trigger for each shot—then the next round chambers automatically) and that the threatening, military appearance of most of these weapons was only a cosmetic feature that did not add to their dangerousness, the decision makers were persuaded that these were not the weapons of choice of the fun-loving sportsman, and that their easy convertibility into fully automatic machine guns made them too dangerous for public consumption. Thus, imports were barred by executive order.

The NRA fared no better when a bar to possession of semiautomatic assault weapons passed through Congress in 1994. Although previously owned assault weapons were grandfathered in as legal, federal law banned the manufacture, transfer, or possession of certain semiautomatic firearms possessing "military" features such as flash suppressors, bayonet mounts, and folding stocks. The law also banned large capacity feeding devices holding more than ten rounds.[60]

Another federal law that passed in 1996 was little noticed at the time, but now has great impact. It had long been a federal crime for convicted felons to possess firearms that have passed in interstate commerce (as essentially all guns have). This law extended that prohibition to those convicted of misdemeanors involving domestic violence, and to those subject to domestic violence restraining orders.[61]

Now, in a twist that must taste like sweet revenge to the NRA, one Dr. Emerson, a man charged with illegally possessing a firearm while subject to a domestic restraining order, has convinced the Fifth Circuit Court of Appeals to hold that, indeed, the Second Amendment does guarantee an individual's right to keep and bear arms, regardless of a person's membership in any militia. Not only that, the government, after having vigorously argued in the Emerson appeal that the Second Amendment protects only militia-related activity, reversed that position in its U.S. Supreme Court brief. It came about this way.

Attorney General Ashcroft surprised the world with, first, a letter to the NRA in which he conceded that the Second Amendment protects individual rights, followed by a memorandum to the U.S. Attorney offices across the nation in which (although his own assistant U.S. attorneys had vigorously argued to the contrary in *Emerson*) Ashcroft conceded that Dr. Emerson's side of the argument was the correct one, and that individuals do enjoy Second Amendment protection of their gun rights. Following the dictates of that controversial memorandum, the government has uncharacteristically conceded to the U.S. Supreme Court that such an individual Second Amendment right exists. The repercussions of this astonishing reversal of prosecutorial policy, in which the country's top prosecutor sides with a criminally accused defendant, remain to be seen.

While the NRA has lost ground in the area of federal gun control laws, during the same period, it has been successful in convincing many state and local jurisdictions to pass so-called "concealed-carry" laws. These laws allow qualified individuals to carry concealed firearms on their persons in public places, with exceptions for public buildings, airports, jails, and other places where security is mandated.

The concealed-carry laws come in two versions. In the "discretionary" jurisdictions, the administrator of the concealed-carry permit program can exercise discretion as to whether or not an applicant should receive the permit. In "shall issue" jurisdictions, the administrator must issue the permit if the applicant meets all the criteria. The NRA can boast that it has helped convince many jurisdictions to adopt "shall issue" concealed-carry laws.

During the period that the NRA lost ground to the gun rights groups, it was also badly leaking members. Its huge budget needed a boost to feed its large bureaucracy. The NRA accomplished a public relations coup when it elected one of the manliest of all movie actors, Charlton Heston, as president of the NRA. This seems to have worked well for them as Heston is now serving an unprecedented fourth term as NRA president.[62] The NRA is proud of Heston's outspoken support of the Second Amendment, even when he goes over the top. Heston says things like, "We have to pass on to America in the 21st century the same Bill of Rights that those wise, old, dead white guys that invented the country passed on to us...."[63]

To boost itself from its slump, the NRA ran aggressive membership drives and sent out urgent fundraising letters, but the tone of its urgent appeals caused some backlash. It used the tactic of draping the organization in the American flag while it warned that tyranny will triumph unless people act now.

Author Osha Gray Davidson, an expert on NRA history, has said that the NRA produced a climate of "pseudo-patriotic paranoia that easily gets out of hand," and that "an organization that still red-baits its opposition after the collapse of communism appears foolish and not a little delusional."[64] Davidson has said, "The NRA attempts to portray itself as a uniquely patriotic organization dedicated only to the common good of all Americans—instead of the typical consumer/manufacturing special interest group that it actually is."[65]

Author Erik Larson, a gun control proponent, has noted the interplay between the National Rifle Association and the gun manufacturers' economic interests. He wrote:

The domestic gun industry, despite its privileged status as the least regulated of consumer-product industries, sold so many guns in America that it saturated the market and now must scramble for ways to open new markets. The industry relies on Paxton Quigley, and other outspoken sales promoters, including gun writers and the leadership of the National Rifle Association, to make guns more palatable to a society that reads daily of gunshot death and injury.[66]

The National Rifle Association is famous for its strident fundraising letters designed to move its members to make their wishes known to lawmakers while filling NRA coffers. Of course, fundraising letters are designed as urgent calls to action, but the dangerously polarizing message of some NRA missives can be seen in this controversial reference to BATF agents as "jack-booted government thugs":

It doesn't matter to them [gun control advocates in Congress] that the semi-auto ban gives jack-booted government thugs more power to take away our Constitutional rights, break in our doors, seize our guns, destroy our property, and even injure or kill us....[67]

The NRA responded to criticism of the impassioned tone of this letter by reemphasizing its concern over the "seriousness of the alleged federal law enforcement abuses to which the letter refers."[68] These guys don't back down.

But as ardently as the NRA supports gun rights, even it admits that some restrictions are permissible for the sake of the safety of society. Wayne LaPierre, CEO of the National Rifle Association, has written, "Neither felons nor children under eighteen, of course, have the right to own arms—any more than they have the right to vote. The National Rifle Association, moreover, has for over seventy years supported laws to prohibit gun ownership by those who have been convicted of violent felonies."[69] The NRA also does not claim constitutional protection for possession of artillery pieces, tanks, nuclear devices, heavy ordinances, grenades, bombs, bazookas or other devices that have never been commonly possessed for self-defense. They claim that "the right to arms does protect ordinary small arms—handguns, rifles, and shotguns—including 'assault weapons.' "[70]

Recently, the flurry of debate over controversial gun laws has settled down to some extent, with no major federal gun issues looming at present. But the NRA, still a powerful voice for gun rights, stands ready to take action whenever needed.

9

The Debate Continues

The dust has settled on major federal gun legislation, but the debate still goes on at state and local levels. The most active areas of controversy at present are over so-called "smart guns," which can only be fired by their owners, and over the liability of gun manufacturers. A controversy over restoration of gun rights to convicted felons has recently been resolved.

SMART GUNS

It has been reported that one in six police officers killed by a gun has been killed with his or her own gun.[1] This prompted the Justice Department to help fund a study by Sandia National Laboratories to design a gun that would only shoot while in the hands of its authorized user. The idea was to come up with a gun that would not fire if grabbed from a cop or toyed with by a child or accidentally dropped.[2]

The result is the Colt Manufacturing Company's Smart Gun. The shooter wears a wrist transponder that sends a radio signal to an electronic system built into the gun's magazine. If the transponder is close enough to the gun, and both codes match, the gun will fire.[3] Another idea for personalizing handguns would be to develop a weapon that recognizes the owner's fingerprint or hand size.[4] Other suggestions include combination trigger locks and bar code scanning.

Gun rights advocates, fearing that smart-gun technology might come to be required on all new guns, have criticized the feasibility of such weapons. Regarding the Colt Smart Gun, they explain that a police officer is trained to shoot with either hand, in case one hand becomes injured, yet the Colt transponder is only worn on one wrist, so the gun is inoperable in the other hand. And if the assailant who grabs the gun is near enough to the officer's hand, the gun could still fire. An injured officer could not hand off the gun for his partner to use. Plus, criminals could figure out ways to jam the transponder signals. In addition, the proposed cost of the Smart Gun, which could cost one third more than a conventional gun, would be hard on budget-strapped police departments.[5]

Most gun control groups see smart guns as a solution for keeping children from firing their parents' guns. Dennis Hennigan, attorney for Handgun Control, Inc., has argued, "We believe it's shameful that the industry has not marketed guns that are personalized. It's as absurd as if the auto industry marketed automobiles without a unique key. Imagine if you could just get in a car and push a button. That would be completely irresponsible."[6]

Interestingly, one prominent gun control organization has also criticized the smart gun, but from different motives. The Violence Policy Center fears that so-called "safer handguns" would only increase the market for guns, and that even more households would end up with firearms, even though smart guns are not truly safe. The Center argues that homicides would not be reduced, because most killers use their own guns, whether personalized or not. Furthermore, most unintentional gun injuries occur while the owner is cleaning a gun thought to be empty or while hunting, and personalization would not prevent these injuries. And because the personalization can be changed as the gun changes owners, the guns could still end up in the hands of criminals.[7]

The Violence Policy Center opines that personalization technology is the gun industry's response to a saturated handgun market—that the industry wants old customers to return for a so-called safer gun, and wants new customers to buy their first weapon. The Center's idea for a better solution? "[T]he real key to reducing firearm death and injury in America," it claims, would be to cease to exempt firearms from the health and safety laws that apply to all other consumer products. If consumer safety standards were applied, "handguns would be banned because of their high risk and low utility."[8]

GUN MANUFACTURER LIABILITY

Gun manufacturers enjoy a unique position in that guns are specifically excluded from the oversight of the Consumer Product Safety Commission.[9] This has caused critics to note the irony that, in America, the safety of children's Teddy Bears is more closely regulated than gun safety. In spite of this, gun control groups have tried suing gun manufacturers in products liability cases, claiming that firearms are so dangerous that gun makers should help foot the bill for firearms injuries.

Gun manufacturers deny that they are responsible for gun deaths when their products work as designed.[10] Under our legal system, product liability is imposed on the manufacturer only when a defective product causes damage. Guns are designed to kill and injure. When they perform as designed, there is generally no liability because there are no defects. Only if a design flaw causes disabling misfires might the manufacturer be held accountable. As a result, when people attempt to hold gun manufacturers liable for the injuries caused by guns, they seldom win.

Gun control advocates are now trying a new twist. They are filing cases against gun manufacturers claiming that guns that do not "recognize" their owners are so unreasonably dangerous, that, if, for example, a child gets hold of one and injures himself, the manufacturer should be liable for not having built recognition technology into the weapon. The results of such suits remain to be seen. Gun manufacturers and dealers are making an end run around this one in that manufacturers, in 1997, voluntarily agreed to include child safety trigger devices on all new handguns.[11] By doing so, they managed to forestall legislation requiring them to manufacture all handguns with trigger locks. Such a bill was defeated in the Senate in July 1988, although it did require dealers to offer trigger locks or gun lock boxes for sale.[12]

RESTORATION OF RIGHTS

One last battle that was recently resolved involves a law favorable to gun owners that has been on the books, but which Congress refuses to fund, so it is effectively dormant. Although it is a federal crime for convicted felons to possess firearms,[13] another law exists that purports to give felons the right to apply to have their gun privileges restored if they can show that they are no longer dangerous to public safety.[14] But, since 1992, without amending the law, Congress has instead specifically barred the Bureau of Alcohol, Tobacco, and Firearms from using any of its funding to implement the law. So the law, although it remains on the books, is effectively dormant.[15] In other words, a felon who asks the Bureau of Alcohol, Tobacco, and Firearms to restore his firearms rights is told that the application can't be processed due to lack of funding. Because the Bureau refuses to process these requests, some felons have turned to the courts to request restoration of their gun privileges. One such controversial Texas case went all the way to the U.S. Supreme Court.[16]

Thomas Lamar Bean, a federally licensed firearms dealer, was attending a gun show in Texas when he decided to cross the border into Mexico for dinner, and, although he had told his assistants to remove weapons and ammunition from his car, some ammunition inadvertently remained, as a result of which Mr. Bean was convicted of a felony by the Mexican courts for importing ammunition illegally. This (arguably)[17] caused him to be barred by federal law from possessing firearms, which, in his case, would cost him his livelihood. He asked the Bureau of Alcohol, Tobacco, and Firearms to restore his rights, and the Bureau refused for lack of funding. Bean then petitioned the federal district court to restore his rights, which it did.

The government appealed, and the Fifth Circuit Court of Appeals also agreed to the restoration. The appellate court noted that the record was full of testimony from legislators, BATF agents, and law-enforcement officers as to Bean's upright character, and the court, while acknowledging serious concerns about returning gun rights to felons, called Mr. Bean's predicament an "almost incredible plight."[18]

On December 10, 2002, Justice Clarence Thomas, writing for a unanimous U.S. Supreme Court, disappointed the gun rights camp.[19] He ruled that the federal district court acted without legal authority in restoring Mr. Bean's firearms rights. An actual decision by the BATF on the felon's petition is a prerequisite to judicial review. The BATF's mere inaction due to lack of funding does not give the court jurisdiction to decide to restore firearms rights to a convicted felon. So the restoration of gun rights to qualifying convicted felons, though theoretically available, is in practice impossible to achieve unless Congress authorizes the necessary funding, which it never has and probably never will.

On the other side of this issue is the Violence Policy Center. It urges legislation to permanently bar convicted felons from possessing firearms, and it has dubbed this NRA-supported "relief from disability" program as the "guns-for-felons" program.[20]

10

Conclusion

The dust has settled on the most controversial gun legislation. Bob Walker, president of Handgun Control, Inc. recently said, "At the present time, there is no major piece of legislation on the front burner and there may not be for another four or five years. Remember, it took seven years to pass the Brady Bill and four years to pass the assault weapons ban."[1] Except for the ongoing debates over products liability and personalizing handguns for reasons of child safety, life appears to go on as before.

The commercial and recreational life of gun aficionados continues. On the other hand, there can be no doubt that lives have been saved by gun control laws that keep guns out of the hands of criminals and by strict sentencing laws that keep criminals out of circulation.

The Bureau of Alcohol, Tobacco, and Firearms reported that from 1994 to 1998 the Brady law background checks prevented 320,000 firearms sales, mostly to individuals with prior criminal histories. BATF says the Brady law "prevented countless crimes and, indeed saved many lives."[2]

During the same two decades, many mandatory minimum sentencing laws and enhanced sentencing laws have proliferated. These laws, which were encouraged by gun rights groups, have certainly kept people behind bars who might otherwise have been out committing gun crimes. So, in a way, both sides have prevailed.

The challenge now is not to pass new laws. The burden has shifted to law enforcement to enforce the many laws we already have. Law enforcement seems to be stepping up to the plate with new programs such as Project Safe

Men practicing on the "black powder" range at the NRA's Whittington Center. (Photo by Constance Crooker.)

Neighborhoods. One of the problems with gun law enforcement has been that the complex mix of federal, state, and local laws has tended to leave each level of the law-enforcement community paying attention to its own laws only. As one lawyer argued in a legal brief, "We have now arrived at a point where federal firearms regulations are so arcane and incomprehensible that even those responsible for enforcing them find them difficult to comprehend."[3] Until recently, it would have been hard to find, for example, a local sheriff or a county district attorney who knew much about the more obscure corners of federal firearms law.

Now, with Project Safe Neighborhoods, the U.S. Attorney's office has a federal mandate to join with local district attorneys, chiefs of police, community groups, and others to come up with strategies to reduce gun violence by enforcing gun laws. This means, in part, cross-training of officers and prosecutors in the complexities of gun laws. This national strategy is modeled on local strategies such as Project Exile in Richmond, Virginia, and Operation Ceasefire in Boston, Massachusetts, which are said to have proven successful in reducing gun crime.[4]

This type of super task force with its mission to slow the rate of gun crimes could become problematic. If it does what the NRA claims the BATF has done, which is to overstep its bounds and target law-abiding folks as well as criminals, such a powerful combination of forces could make Project Safe

Neighborhoods the next target of gun rights groups. If it functions within the bounds of the law and the Constitution, this approach could achieve what gun rights groups have always asked for—that is, to enforce the laws we have, rather than pass new ones. How Project Safe Neighborhoods will work out in practice remains to be seen.

Notes

INTRODUCTION

1. Osha Gray Davidson, *Under Fire: The NRA and the Battle for Gun Control* (Iowa City: University of Iowa Press, 1998), 147.

2. Ibid., 65.

3. Ibid., 147.

4. Ibid., 64–65.

5. Marjolijn Bijlefeld, *People for and against Gun Control: A Biographical Reference* (Westport, Conn.: Greenwood Press, 1999), 84–85.

6. Davidson, *Under Fire,* 296.

7. Ibid., 46.

8. Ibid., 45.

9. Charley Reese, "Gun Control Isn't about Crime—It's an Elitist Way to Control People," *Orlando Sentinel* (March 31, 1994).

10. Davidson, *Under Fire,* 280.

CHAPTER I

1. Osha Gray Davidson, *Under Fire: The NRA and the Battle for Gun Control,* expanded ed. (Iowa City: University of Iowa Press, 1998), 121.

2. Ibid., 121.

3. Ibid.

4. Violence Policy Center Web site at http://www.vpc.org/nrainfo/index.html. (Accessed March 10, 2003.)

5. Davidson, *Under Fire,* 122.

6. 18 U.S. Code, sec. 922(g)(8).

7. House of Representatives Conference Report 103–711 (1994).

8. Arthur L. Kellerman, Frederick P. Rivara, Norman B. Rushforth, Joyce G. Banton, Donald T. Reay, Jerry T. Francisco, Ana B. Locci, Jancice Prodzinzki, Bela B. Hackman, and Grant Somes, "Gun Ownership as a Risk Factor for Homicide in the Home," *New England Journal of Medicine* 329, no. 15 (1993): 1084–1091.

9. Violence Policy Center, *When Men Murder Women: An Analysis of 1996 Homicide Data.* http://www.vpc.org/studies/dvconc.htm. (Accessed February 24, 2003.)

10. Judith Bonderman, "Firearms and Domestic Violence," in *The Impact of Domestic Violence on Your Legal Practice: A Lawyer's Handbook.* American Bar Association Commission on Domestic Violence. http://www.abanet.org/cle/clenow/dv/intersta.html. (Accessed February 24, 2003.)

11. Kellerman et al., "Gun Ownership as a Risk Factor," 1097.

12. James E. Bailey, "Risk Factors for Violent Death of Women in the Home," *Archives of Internal Medicine,* 157 (1997): 777–782.

13. Arthur L. Kellerman, F. P. Rivara, G. Somes, D. T. Reay, J. Francisco, J. G. Banton, J. Prodzinzky, C. Flinger, and B. B. Hackman, "Suicide in the Home in Relation to Gun Ownership," *New England Journal of Medicine* 327, no. 7 (August 13, 1992): 467–472.

14. Arthur Kellerman and Donald Reay, "Protection or Peril? An Analysis of Firearm Related Deaths in the Home," *New England Journal of Medicine,* 314, no. 24 (June 1986): 1557–1560.

15. L. Saltzman, J. Mercy, P. O'Carroll, M. Rosenberg, and P. Rhodes, "Weapon Involvement and Injury Outcomes in Family and Intimate Assaults," *Journal of the American Medical Association* 267, no. 22 (1992): 3043–3047.

16. Albert J. Reiss Jr. and Jeffrey A. Roth, eds., "Chapter Six: Firearms and Violence," in *Understanding and Preventing Violence* (National Research Center, National Academy Press: Washington, D.C., 1993). Also found at http://sun.soci.niu.edu/~critcrim/guns/gun.viol. (Accessed February 24, 2003.)

17. Ibid.

18. Ibid.

19. Wayne LaPierre, *Guns, Crime and Freedom* (New York: HarperPerennial, 1995), 69.

20. David Lampo, "Gun Control: Myths and Realities," CATO Today's Commentary, at http://www.cato.org/dailys/05-13-00.html. (Accessed February 24, 2003.)

21. John R. Lott Jr., *More Guns, Less Crime: Understanding Crime and Gun Control Laws* (Chicago: University of Chicago Press, 1998), 8–9.

22. See, *About the Brady Campaign* at http://www.bradycampaign.org/about/index.asp. (Accessed February 24, 2003.)

23. Davidson, *Under Fire,* 121.

24. David Lampo, "Gun Control: Myths and Realities."

25. See discussion of Lott, *More Guns, Less Crime* in Chapter 2, "Deterrence to Crime."

26. See discussion of Reiss and Roth, *Firearms and Violence* in *Understanding and Preventing Violence* (National Research Center, National Academy Press: Washington, D.C., 1993). Also found at http://sun.soci.niu.edu/~critcrim/guns/gun.viol. (Accessed February 24, 2003.)

27. Marjolijn Bijlefeld, *People For and Against Gun Control: A Biographical Reference* (Westport, Conn.: Greenwood Press, 1999), 246.

28. Reiss and Roth, *Firearms and Violence.*

CHAPTER 2

1. Alan Korwin, "The Noble Uses of Firearms," at http://www.gunlaws.com/noble.htm. (Accessed March 6, 2003.)

2. See discussion in John R. Lott, Jr., *More Guns, Less Crime: Understanding Crime and Gun Control Laws* (Chicago: University of Chicago Press, 2000).

3. Korwin, "The Noble Uses of Firearms."

4. A fact disputed in Michael A. Bellesiles, *Arming America: The Origins of a National Gun Culture* (New York: Vintage Books, 2001).

5. Davidson, *Under Fire,* 65.

6. Note that the right to self-defense referred to in Mr. Korwin's quotation does not include the right to possess a given weapon. For example, if you are charged with the crime of assault for shooting an intruder, you might be found not guilty if you prove you shot in self-defense. This does not preclude the government from also prosecuting you for a separate crime if, in lawfully defending yourself, you used a weapon which it was illegal for you to possess.

7. Alan Korwin, "Gun Law Updates," at http://www.gunlaws.com. (Accessed March 4, 2002.)

8. Paxton Quigley, *Armed and Female* (New York: St. Martin's, 1989).

9. Ibid., 5.

10. Ibid., 13.

11. Albert J. Reiss Jr. and Jeffrey A. Roth, eds., "Chapter Six: Firearms and Violence," in *Understanding and Preventing Violence* (National Research Center, National Academy Press: Washington, D.C., 1993). Also found at http://sun.soci.niu.edu/~critcrim/guns/gun.viol. (Accessed February 24, 2003.)

12. David Lampo, "Gun Control: Myths and Realities," CATO Today's Commentary, at http://www.cato.org/dailys/05-13-00.html. (Accessed March 6, 2003.)

13. Lott, *More Guns, Less Crime,* 6.

14. Quigley, *Armed and Female,* 25–27.

15. Ibid., 28–32.

16. Wayne LaPierre, *Guns, Crime and Freedom* (New York: HarperPerrenial, 1995), 27.

17. George Flynn and Alan Gottlieb, *Guns for Women* (Bellevue, Wash.: Merril Press, 1988), 69–78.

18. Ibid., citing Gary Kleck, "Crime Control through the Private Use of Armed Force," *Social Forces* 35 (1988): 1–22. See Table 4, p. 8.

19. Quigley, *Armed and Female,* 139.

20. Ibid., 154.

21. Marjolijn Bijlefeld, *People For and Against Gun Control: A Biographical Reference* (Westport, Conn.: Greenwood Press, 1999), 189.

22. Ibid., 173.

23. Ibid.

24. Ibid., 176.

25. Oregon Revised Statutes, sec. 161.219, Limitations on Use of Deadly Physical Force in Defense of a Person.

26. Oregon Revised Statutes, sec. 161.225, Use of Physical Force in Defense of Premises; Oregon Revised Statutes, sec. 161.229, Use of Physical Force in Defense of Property.

27. Franklin E. Zimring, "Firearms, Violence and Public Policy," *Scientific American* (November 1991): 21.

28. Lott, *More Guns, Less Crime.*

29. Ibid., 90.

30. Ibid., 75.

31. Ibid., 81.

32. Ibid., 92.

33. Ibid., 5.

34. Stephen Teret, "Critical Commentary on a Paper by Lott and Mustard," The Johns Hopkins Center for Gun Policy and Research at http://www.asahinet.or.jp/~zj5j-gttl/teret.htm. (Accessed March 6, 2003.)

35. Lott, *More Guns, Less Crime,* 133.

36. Ibid.

37. Ibid., citing Franklin Zimring and Gordon Hawkins, "The Counterfeit Deterrent," *The Responsive Community* (Spring 1997).

38. Maxine Bernstein, *The Oregonian* (March 9, 2001): 1.

39. Lott, *More Guns, Less Crime,* 153.

40. Teret, "Critical Commentary on a Paper by Lott and Mustard."

41. Ibid.

42. Ibid.

43. Ibid.

44. Marianne W. Zawitz, "Guns Used in Crime," *FirearmsID.com* (September 2000), at http://www.firearmsid.com/Feature%20Articles/0900GUIC/Guns%20Used%20in%20Crime.htm. (Accessed March 6, 2003.)

45. Ibid.

46. Michael A. Bellesiles, *Arming America: The Origins of a National Gun Culture* (New York: Vintage Books, 2001), 4.

47. Erik Larson, *Lethal Passage* (New York: Vintage Books, 1995), 19.

48. Davidson, *Under Fire,* 123.

49. Larson, *Lethal Passage,* 21.

50. Ibid., 22.

51. Bijlefeld, *People For and Against Gun Control,* 66.

CHAPTER 3

1. Presidential debate at Wake Forest University, October 11, 2000. http://www.debates.org/pages/trans2000b.html. (Accessed February 25, 2003.)

2. "Hillary Clinton Offers Support for Gun Licensing Bill," *CNN.com* (June 20, 2000).   http://www.cnn.com/2000/ALLPOLITICS/Stories/06/02/lazio.bustour/. (Accessed February 25, 2003.)

3. *Boston Globe* (March 21, 2000): A4.

4. Jesse Ventura, *Ain't Got Time to Bleed* (New York: Villard Books, 1999), 41–42.

5. "Issues: Right to Keep and Bear Arms," www.GoPatGo.org/ (June 5, 1999).

6. Quotable Quotes from Chuck Heston, NRA President. http://nrawinningteam.com/hestquot.html. (Accessed March 8, 2003.)

7. Osha Gray Davidson, *Under Fire: The NRA and the Battle for Gun Control* (Iowa City: University of Iowa Press, 1998), 44.

8. Domestic Violence Firearm Protection Amendment to 18 U.S. Code, sec. 922(g)(8).

9. 139 Cong. Rec. sec. 7884–01 (1994).

10. *Amicus Curiae* brief of the State of Alabama, in *United States v. Emerson*, no. 99–10331 (5th Cir., 1999), at http://www.ccrkba.org/ALABAMAbrief.htm. (Accessed February 25, 2003.)

11. Ibid., at Section I.

12. Hubert Humphrey, "Know Your Law Makers," *Guns* (February 1960): 4.

13. "Rogue of the Week," *Willamette Week* (June 13, 2001). http://wweek.com/flatfiles/allstories.lasso?xxin=1754. (Accessed February 25, 2003.)

14. Tom Robbins, *Fierce Invalids Home from Hot Climates* (New York: Bantam Books, 2000), 301.

15. Wayne LaPierre, *Guns, Crime and Freedom* (New York: HarperPerrenial, 1995), 86, citing the Associated Press (December 12, 1993) and ABC's *Good Morning America* (December 10, 1993).

16. Paxton Quigley, *Armed and Female* (New York: St. Martin's, 1989).

17. Ibid., 105.

18. LaPierre, *Guns, Crime and Freedom,* 60.

19. Ibid., 91.

20. Erik Larson, *Lethal Passage* (New York: Vintage Books, 1995).

21. Ibid., 16.

22. Ibid., 228–229.

23. Marjolijn Bijlefeld, *People for and against Gun Control: A Biographical Reference* (Westport, Conn.: Greenwood Press, 1999), 61.

24. Ibid., 118.

25. Ibid., 124.

26. Ibid., 138.

27. Ibid., 141.

28. Ibid., 162.

29. Ibid., 163.

30. Ibid., 157–166.

31. "Attorney General Nominee Ashcroft Member of National Rifle Association," Violence Policy Center Web site at http://vpc.org/press/0101ash3.htm. (Accessed February 25, 2003.)

32. "Shot Full of Holes," Violence Policy Center Web site at http://vpc.org/studies/ashapa.htm. (Accessed February 25, 2003.)

33. A gun control advocacy group's spokeswoman, Kristen Rand, legislative director of the Violence Policy Center, said, "The practical effect of what he's done with this letter is to produce a 180-degree shift in policy on the Second Amendment. If Ashcroft's view prevails, the NRA will go back and challenge every gun law on the books. It would be a massive shift in how federal gun laws might be implemented and enforced." Kristen Rand as quoted in Dan Eggen, "Ashcroft: Gun Ownership an Individual Right," The Washington Post Online (May 23, 2001), at http://www.washingtonpost.com/wp-dyn/articles/A66898-2001May23.html. (Accessed February 25, 2003.)

34. *United States v. Emerson*, 46 F.Supp.2d 598 (5th Cir. 2001), *cert. denied*, 122 S.Ct. 2362 (2002).

35. *Silveira v. Lockyer*, 312 F.3d 1052 (9th Cir. 2002).

36. Alan M. Gottlieb, Second Amendment Foundation fundraising letter of March, 2003.

37. Alan Gottlieb, *Politically Correct Guns* (Bellevue, Wash.: Merril Press, 2000), 57.

38. Ibid., 69.

39. Celeste Freemon, *Father Greg and the Homeboys* (New York: Hyperion, 1995), 44.

40. Ibid., 48–50.

41. Ibid., 70–71.

42. Ibid., 151–152.

43. Larry P. Goodson, *Afghanistan's Endless War* (Seattle: University of Washington Press, 2001), 144–145.

44. Ibid., 97.

45. Ibid., 99.

46. Ibid., 100.

47. Ibid.

48. MSNBC, *Explorer*, December 21, 2001.

49. CNN News, December 12, 2001.

50. Mark Landler, "Kabul Takes Steps toward Disarming Afghan Population," *New York Times*, at http://www.nytimes.com/2002/01/14/international/asia/14AFGH.html (January 14, 2002). (Accessed February 25, 2003.)

51. Ibid.

52. Davidson, *Under Fire*, 89.

53. Ibid., 85–87.

54. Ibid., 88.

55. Ibid., 95. See also 18 U.S. Code, sec. 922 (a)(7) and (a)(8).

56. Davidson, *Under Fire*, 98.

57. Ibid., 96–114.

58. *Amicus Curiae* brief of Center to Prevent Handgun Violence, in *United States v. Emerson*, no. 99–10331 (5th Cir. 1999), at http://www.ccrkba.org/CenterToPreventHandgunViolencebrief.htm. (Accessed February 25, 2003.)

59. Larson, *Lethal Passage*, 58.

60. Ibid.

61. Ibid., 83.

62. Lieutenant Colonel Dave Grossman and Gloria DeGaetano, *Stop Teaching Our Kids to Kill* (New York: Crown Publishers, 1999), 72 et seq.

63. Ibid., 74.

64. Ibid., 4.

65. Ibid., 75–76.

66. Ibid., 4.

67. Ibid., 77.

68. Ibid., 78.

69. Ibid., 78–81.

70. Ibid., 132–136.

71. Ibid., 134.

72. Thomas N. Robinson, Marta L. Wilde, Lisa C. Navracruz, K. Farish Haydel, and Ann Vardy, "Effects of Reducing Children's Television and Video Game Use on Aggressive Behavior: A Randomized Controlled Trial," *Archives of Pediatrics and Adolescent Medicine* 155, (January 2001): 17–23.

73. *The Washington Post*, May 19, 1999.

74. LaPierre, *Guns, Crime and Freedom*, 77.

75. Trey Walker, "Violent Media May Not Be to Blame," *Game Spot PC* (February 8, 2001), at http://gamespot.com/gamespot/stories/news/0,10870,2683948,00.html.

76. Lewis Cole, "Violence and the Media: The Wrong Controversy?" at http://www.columbia.edu/cu/21stC/issue-1.2/Media.htm. (Accessed February 25, 2003.)

77. The First Amendment to the U.S. Constitution provides that Congress shall make no law abridging the freedom of speech, or of the press.

78. Lieutenant Colonel Dave Grossman, *On Killing* (Boston: Back Bay Books, 1996), 327.

79. Ibid., 330.

80. Ibid., 326.

81. Grossman and DeGaetano, *Stop Teaching Our Kids to Kill*, 117.

82. 18 U.S. Code, sec. 922(b)(1).

83. 18 U.S. Code, sec. 922(x)(2).

84. 18 U.S. Code, sec. 922(x)(3).

85. Alan Gottlieb, *Politically Correct Guns* (Bellevue, Wash.: Merril Press, 2000), 100.

86. Ibid.

87. Richard Poe, "What's Wrong with Toy Guns?" FrontPageMagazine.com (October 5, 2000), at http://frontpagemag.com/Articles/ReadArticle.asp?ID=3634. (Accessed February 25, 2003.)

88. Oxnard Police, "Toy Guns: A Deadly Game" (December 20, 2001), at http://www.oxnardpd.org/toyguns.htm. (Accessed February 25, 2003.)

89. On January 3, 2001, Congressman Ed Towns (NY, Brooklyn, District 10) introduced bill HR215, a measure which would ban "toys which in size, shape or over-

all appearance resemble real handguns." Similarly, in October 1999, New York City Mayor Rudolph Giuliani signed a law prohibiting "realistic looking" toy guns.

90. In an attempt to curb violent behavior, Maryland alderwoman Cynthia Carter proposed a buy-back program for toy guns. Lance Jonn Romanoff, "Somebody Call the National Toy Rifle Association," Liberzine.com (February 19, 2001), at http://www.liberzine.com/lanceromanoff/010219toyguns.htm.

91. Americans for Gun Safety Foundation, "Parents Guide to Firearm Safety" (no date), at http://w3.agsfoundation.com/safety/parents.html#facts. (Accessed February 25, 2003.)

92. LaPierre, *Guns, Crime and Freedom,* 79.

93. The National Rifle Association Headquarters, https://www.nrahq.org/history.asp. (Accessed February 25, 2003.)

94. Quigley, *Armed and Female,* 144–145.

95. Kellerman quoted in Larson, *Lethal Passage,* 34.

CHAPTER 4

1. *Marbury v. Madison,* 1 Cranch. 137 (1803)(Marshall, C.J.).

2. U.S. Const. amend. II.

3. *United States v. Cruikshank,* 92 U.S. 542, 553 (1875).

4. *Presser v. Illinois,* 116 U.S. 252, 264–265 (1886). *Presser* also held that the Second Amendment applied only to the federal government, and not to the states, as did *Miller v. Texas,* 153 U.S. 535, 538 (1894). Although the Supreme Court has subsequently held that some parts of the Bill of Rights also constrain state governments through the Fourteenth Amendment's Due Process clause, the Supreme Court has never ruled that the Second Amendment applies to the states. See discussion in Section II, Brief Supporting Appellee of Amicus Curiae, National Rifle Association, in *United States v. Emerson,* no. 99–10331 (5th Cir. 1999), at http://www.ccrkba.org/NRAbrief.htm. (Accessed February 28, 2003.) Also see Senator Jacob Howard, Cong. Globe, 39th Cong., 1st Sess. 2765 (May 23, 1866), who explained, when introducing the Fourteenth Amendment, that its purpose was to protect "personal rights" such as "the right to keep and bear arms." See also Halbrook, "Personal Security, Personal Liberty, and 'the Constitutional Right to Bear Arms': Visions of the Framers of the Fourteenth Amendment," 5 *Seton Hall Constitutional Law Journal* 341 (Spring 1995).

5. *United States v. Miller,* 307 U.S. 174 (1939).

6. 18 U.S.C. sec. 1132–1132(q).

7. *United States v. Miller,* 307 U.S. 174 (1939).

8. *Miller,* at 178.

9. *Miller,* at 178, citing U.S. Const. art. I, sec. 8.

10. *Miller,* at 178.

11. *Konigsberg v. State Bar,* 366 U.S. 36, at 49–50, footnote 10 (1961).

12. *Lewis v. United States,* 445 U.S. 55 (1980).

13. Title VII of the Omnibus Crime Control and Safe Streets Act of 1968.

14. *Lewis,* at 65–66.

15. In a dissenting opinion, Justice Douglas slams the "powerful lobby that dins in the ear of our citizenry that these gun purchases are constitutional rights protected by the Second Amendment," and concludes that, under the rule in *Miller,* "[t]here is no reason why all pistols should not be barred to everyone except the police." *Adams v. Williams,* 407 U.S. 143 (1972).

More recently, Justice Thomas, in a concurring opinion, suggests that he is open to the argument that the Second Amendment might confer a personal right to keep and bear arms. *Printz, Sheriff/Coroner, Ravalli County, Montana, v. United States,* 521 U.S. 898, concurring at para. 2 and footnotes 1 and 2 (1997).

A concurring opinion in *Atlanta Motel v. United States,* 397 U.S. 241, footnote 11 (1964), cites *Miller* with approval for its use of the commerce clause to support restrictions not entirely commercial (i.e., firearms regulations).

16. *See* Section I (C) of *Amicus Curiae* brief of Center to Prevent Handgun Violence, in *United States v. Emerson,* no. 99–10331 (5th Cir. 1999), at http://www.ccrkba.org/CenterToPreventHandgunViolencebrief.htm. (Accessed February 28, 2003.) See also Section I(D) of Government's Brief in *United States v. Emerson,* no. 99–10331 (5th Cir. 1999), at http://www.ccrkba.org/EmersonAppealGovt1.html. (Accessed February 28, 2003.)

17. *Silveira v. Lockyer,* 312 F. 3d 1052 (2002).

18. *Printz, Sheriff/Coroner, Ravalli County, Montana, v. United States,* 521 U.S. 898, concurring opinion, footnote 2 (1997).

19. Michael A. Bellesiles, *Arming America: The Origins of a National Gun Culture* (New York: Vintage Books, 2001), 21–34.

20. Joyce Lee Malcolm, *To Keep and Bear Arms: The Origins of an Anglo-American Right* (Cambridge, Mass.: Harvard University Press, 1994), 84–85.

21. Bellesiles, *Arming America,* 35–39.

22. Michael A. Bellesiles, "Gun Laws in Early America: The Regulation of Firearms Ownership, 1607–1794," *Law & History Review* 16 (1998): 567, 587.

23. Bellesiles, *Arming America,* 72, 76.

24. Ibid., 75.

25. Ibid., 72.

26. Ibid., 74.

27. Ibid., 79.

28. Ibid., 97.

29. Act of May 8, 1792, 1 Stat. 271. *See also,* Act of May 2, 1792, 1 Stat. 264 (president may call state militia to suppress insurrection); Act of April 2, 1794, 1 Stat. 352 (federal arsenals and magazines authorized); Act of May 22, 1794, 1 Stat. 369 (providing for a uniform militia throughout the United States).

30. U.S. Const. amend. II.

31. *The Compact Oxford English Dictionary,* 2d ed., s.v. "militia."

32. Ibid.

33. Jonathan Elliot, ed., "Luther Martin's Letter to the Maryland Legislature," 1: *The Debates in the Several State Conventions on the Adoption of the Federal Constitution* (1836, reprint 1941): 371–372.

34. *United States v. Miller,* at 180.

35. The General Court of Massachusetts, January Session 1784 (Laws and Resolves 1784, c. 55, pp. 140–142).

36. 12 Hening's Statutes, c. 1, p. 9 et seq. (Virginia, 1785).

37. Ibid.

38. Act of April 4, 1786, N.Y. Laws 1786, c. 25.

39. Jonathan Elliot, ed., "Debates in the Several State Conventions" 3, no. 45 (2d ed., 1836).

40. Jonathan Elliot, ed., "The Debates in the Several State Conventions on the Adoption of the Federal Constitution" 3, no. 386 (1836, reprint 1941).

41. Bellesiles, *Arming America.*

42. Michael A. Bellesiles, "Exploring America's Gun Culture," *The William and Mary Quarterly* 3d Ser., vol. LIX, no. 1, (January 2002): 241, 244.

43. Bellesiles, *Arming America,* 103.

44. Ibid., 136.

45. Ibid., Table Three, 447.

46. Ibid., 140–153.

47. Ibid., 172–173.

48. Ibid., 174.

49. Bellesiles, "Exploring America's Gun Culture," 241.

50. Bellesiles, *Arming America,* 106–107.

51. Ibid., 377–381.

52. Ibid., 381–387.

53. Ibid., Chapter 10.

54. Robert A. Gross, "Forum: Historians and Guns," *The William and Mary Quarterly* 3d Ser., vol. LIX, no. 1, (January 2002): 203.

55. Stephen P. Halbrook, "Deconstructing the Second Amendment," NewsMax.com at http://www.newsmax.com/archives/articles/2000/11/3/220439.shtml. (Accessed March 1, 2003.)

56. Gross, "Forum: Historians and Guns," p. 203.

57. Gloria L. Main, "Many Things Forgotten: The Use of Probate Records in *Arming America,*" *The William and Mary Quarterly* 3d Ser., vol. LIX, no. 1, (January 2002): 211.

58. Ibid., p. 213.

59. Ibid., pp. 213, 215.

60. Ibid., p. 215.

61. Ira D. Gruber, "Of Arms and Men: *Arming America* and Military History," *The William and Mary Quarterly* 3d Ser., vol. LIX, no. 1, (January 2002): 217.

62. Ibid., p. 218.

63. Ibid., p. 219.

64. Ibid., p. 221.

65. Randolph Roth, "Guns, Gun Culture, and Homicide: The Relationship between Firearms, the Uses of Firearms, and Interpersonal Violence," *The William and Mary Quarterly* 3d Ser., vol. LIX, no. 1, (January 2002): 223.

66. Michael A. Bellesiles, "Exploring America's Gun Culture," *The William and Mary Quarterly* 3d Ser., vol. LIX, no. 1, (January 2002): 241, 248.

67. Ibid., p. 253.

68. Roth, "Guns, Gun Culture, and Homicide," pp. 231–232.

69. Jack N. Rakove, "Words, Deeds and Guns: *Arming America* and the Second Amendment," *The William and Mary Quarterly* 3d Ser., vol. LIX, no. 1, (January 2002): 205.

70. Ibid., pp. 206, 210.

71. Ibid.

72. Bellesiles, "Exploring America's Gun Culture," p. 241.

73. Ibid., p. 243.

74. Ibid., p. 244.

75. Ibid., p. 251.

76. Ibid., p. 263.

77. Ibid.

78. Ibid., p. 264.

79. Ibid., p. 266.

80. Ibid., p. 267.

81. Ibid., p. 268.

82. David Young, "Emerson Case Letter," at http://www.ccrkba.org/Young.html, citing Benjamin Franklin, *Benjamin Franklin Papers*, Vol. III, p. 202. (Accessed March 1, 2003.)

83. Bellesiles, *Arming America*, 178.

84. *See*, James J. Baker, "In the News: Americans for Gun Safety Is a True Anti-Gun Group," at http://www.nraila.newscenter.asp?FormMode=Detail&ID=683. (Accessed March 1, 2003.)

85. Akhil Reed Amar, "Second Thoughts," *The New Republic*, (July 12, 1999): 24.

86. Ibid.

87. Section I, Brief Supporting Appellee of *Amicus Curiae*, National Rifle Association, in *United States v. Emerson*, No. 99–10331 (5th Cir. 1999), at http://www.ccrkba.org/NRAbrief.htm. (Accessed March 1, 2003.)

88. *See*, Section I, Brief of *Amicus Curiae*, Texas Justice Foundation in Support of Timothy Joe Emerson, in *United States v. Emerson*, no. 99–10331 (5th Cir. 1999), at http://www.ccrkba.org/TXJusticeBrief.htm. (Accessed March 1, 2003.)

89. *Independent Gazetteer* (August 20, 1789): 2.

90. Carl T. Bogus, "The Hidden History of the Second Amendment," *University of California Davis Law Review* 31 (1998): 309, 357.

91. *The Compact Oxford English Dictionary*, 2d ed., s.v. "bear": "to bear arms against: to be engaged in hostilities with.... 1568 ... apt to bear arms.... 1609 ... he bure armes, and made weir against the King.... 1679 ... an ample ... pardon to all who had born arms against him."

92. Helen E. Veit, Kenneth R. Bowling and Charlene Bangs Bickford, eds., *Creating the Bill of Rights: The Documentary Record from the First Federal Congress,* (The George Washington University, Washington, D.C.: The First Federal Congress Project, 1991): 12.

93. *The Compact Oxford English Dictionary,* 2d ed., s.v. "arms."

94. *Aymette v. State,* 21 Tenn. 154, 161 (1840), (The phrase "bear arms" in the Tennessee Constitution has a military sense and no other).

Hill v. Georgia, 53 Ga. 472, 475 (1874), (The constitutions of Georgia and of the United States guarantee the right to keep and bear the arms necessary for a militiaman.)

English v. State, 35 Tex. 473, 476 (1872), (In the United States Constitution, the word "arms" is used in its military sense.)

State v. Workman, 35 W.Va. 367, 373 (1891), ("Arms" must be held to refer to weapons of warfare to be used by the militia.)

Ex Parte Thomas, 21 Okla. 770 (1908), (In the Oklahoma Constitution, "arms" are such as are usually employed in civilized warfare.)

Joel Prentice Bishop, *Commentaries on the Law of Statutory Crimes,* 497 (1873), ("Arms" are those used for purposes of war, since such, only, are properly known by the name of "arms.")

Lucilius Emery, "The Constitutional Right to Keep and Bear Arms," *Harvard Law Review* 28 (1915): 473, 476. (The single individual or the unorganized crowd, in carrying weapons, is not spoken of or thought of as "bearing arms.")

95. *Amicus Curiae* brief of David Yassky in *United States v. Emerson,* no. 99–10331 (5th Cir. 1999), at http://www.potomac-inc.org/yass.html. (Accessed March 1, 2003.)

96. The Pennsylvania Declaration of Rights, Article XIII (1776), and The Vermont Constitution, Article I, section 15 (1777).

97. *See,* Section III, Brief of *Amicus Curiae* Texas Justice Foundation in Support of Timothy Joe Emerson, in *United States v. Emerson,* no. 99–10331 (5th Cir. 1999), at http://www.ccrkba.org/TXJusticeBrief.htm. (Accessed March 1, 2003.)

98. Section III, Amended Brief of Second Amendment Foundation as *Amicus Curiae* in Support of Defendant Appellee, in *United States v. Emerson,* no. 99–10331 (5th Cir. 1999), at http://www.ccrkba.org/EmersonSAF.htm. (Accessed March 1, 2003.)

99. Section II (b), *Amicus Curiae* Brief of Center to Prevent Handgun Violence, in *United States v. Emerson,* no. 99–10331 (5th Cir. 1999), at http://www.ccrkba.org/CenterToPreventHandgunViolencebrief.htm. (Accessed February 25, 2003.)

100. *See,* Section I, Brief of *Amicus Curiae* Texas Justice Foundation in Support of Timothy Joe Emerson, in *United States v. Emerson,* no. 99–10331 (5th Cir. 1999), at http://www.ccrkba.org/TXJusticeBrief.htm. (Accessed March 1, 2003.)

101. C. Adams, ed., *Works of John Adams* 6, (1851): 197.

102. Section II(B), Brief of Appellee, in *United States v. Emerson,* no. 99–10331 (5th Cir. 1999), at http://www.saf.org/EmersonMainBrief.html. (Accessed May 6, 2003.)

103. *See,* Section I, Brief Supporting Appellee of *Amicus Curiae* Academics for the Second Amendment, in *United States v. Emerson,* no. 99–10331 (5th Cir. 1999), at http://www.ccrkba.org/EMERSONacadsecd.html. (Accessed March 1, 2003.)

104. *See,* Section I, brief of *Amicus Curiae* Texas Justice Foundation in Support of Timothy Joe Emerson, in *United States v. Emerson,* no. 99–10331 (5th Cir. 1999), at http://www.ccrkba.org/TXJusticeBrief.htm. (Accessed March 1, 2003.)

105. Michael A. Bellesiles, "Gun Laws in Early America: The Regulation of Firearms Ownership, 1607–1794, *Law & History Review* 16 (1998): 567, 568.

106. Lucilius A. Emery, Note in "The Constitutional Right to Keep and Bear Arms," *Harvard Law Review* 28 (1915): 473, 474.

107. Carl Stephenson and Frederick George Marcham, eds., *Sources of English Constitutional History* (New York: Harper Row, 1937): 600–601.

108. Ibid., pp. 486, 541.

109. Bellisiles, "Gun Laws in Early America," pp. 571–573.

110. Ibid., pp. 580, 585.

111. James Madison, *Federalist Paper No. 46,* and *1st Annals of Congress* (June 8, 1789).

112. Madison, "Federalist Paper No. 46," *The Federalist,* ed. Edward Mead Earle (Washington: R.B. Luce, 1976): 311.

113. Ibid., pp. 305, 310, 311.

114. David P. Szatmary, *Shay's Rebellion: The Making of an Agrarian Insurrection* (Amherst: University of Massachusetts Press, 1980), 129; Richard B. Morris, *The Forging of the Union* (New York: Harper Row, 1987), 265.

115. Szatmary, *Shay's Rebellion.*

116. Bogus, Carl T. "The Hidden History of the Second Amendment." *University of California Davis Law Review* 31 (1998): 309, 394–395 (quoting Washington, Hamilton, Franklin, Marshall, Jay, Samuel Adams, Rufus King, Hancock, and Anti-Federalist Elbridge Gerry, who expressed shock over Shay's Rebellion).

117. Szatmary, *Shay's Rebellion,* generally.

118. Michael Bellesiles, "Suicide Pact: New Readings of the Second Amendment," *Constitutional Commentary* 16, (1999): 247, 256; Thomas Slaughter, *The Whiskey Rebellion* (Oxford, NY: Oxford University Press, 1986), 190–204.

119. U.S. Const. art I, sec. 8.

120. "[The] organized militia [of the United States]...consists of the National Guard and the Naval Militia," 10 U.S. Code, sec. 311(b)(1). See also *Perpich v. Dept. of Defense,* 496 U.S. 334 (1990).

121. For example, Texas Government Code Annotated sec. 431.051 authorizes a volunteer force known as the "Texas State Guard." See also, Tennessee State Guard, http://home.att.net/~dcannon.tenn/TNSG.html; Vermont State Guard, www.vt. guard.com/VSG/index_main.htm. (Accessed March 4, 2003.)

122. Texas Government Code Annotated sec. 431.010. See also *Vietnamese Fisherman's Association v. Ku Klux Klan,* 543 F.Supp. 198, 210 (S.D. Tex. 1982), holding that Texas' Ku Klux Klan is not a protected militia under the Second Amendment.

123. Oregon Revised Statutes sec. 166.660.

124. Bogus, "Hidden History," 351.

125. Ibid., 369.

126. Veit, *Creating the Bill of Rights,* 12.

127. U.S. Const. amend. II.

128. Jonathan Elliot, ed., "The Debates in the Several State Conventions on the Adoption of the Federal Constitution as Recommended by the General Convention at Philadelphia in 1787," vol. 1 (2d ed., 1891, photo reprint, William S. Hein & Co., 1996): 244, 328, 335, 659.

129. Ibid., 326.

130. Ibid., 88, 371–372; Elliot, "The Debates in the Several State Conventions," vol. 2, 96–99, 406, 520–522, 531, 536–537; Elliot, "The Debates in the Several State Conventions," vol. 3, 378–394, 400–403, 405–431, 440–441; Elliot, "The Debates in the Several State Conventions," vol. 4, 97–100, 214–215, 260–262; Elliot, "The Debates in the Several State Conventions," vol. 5, 127, 440, 443–444, 451, 464–467, 480.

131. Herbert J. Storing, ed., *The Complete Anti-Federalist,* vol. 7 (Chicago: University of Chicago Press, 1981): 9, 94–95.

132. U.S. Const. art. I, sec. 8.

133. Elliot, "The Debates in the Several State Conventions," vol. 4, 424; Marguerite Driessen, "Private Organizations and the Militia Status," *Brigham Young University Law Review* (1998): 7–8.

134. U.S. Const., art. I, sec. 8.

135. *United States v. Miller,* 307 U.S. 174 (1939).

136. *See,* Gun Rights Advocates and the Second Amendment, in Chapter 4.

137. *See* Section III(A), Reply Brief for Appellant, in *United States v. Emerson,* no. 99–10331 (5th Cir. 1999), at http://www.ccrkba.org/EMERSONgovtrepl.html. (Accessed March 1, 2003.)

138. *United States v. Hale,* 978 F.2d 1016, 1019 (8th Cir., 1992), *cert. denied,* 507 U.S. 997 (1993).

139. The Potomac Institute, Maryland, at http://www.potomac-inc.org/emeramic.html. (Accessed March 1, 2003.)

140. Laurence H. Tribe, *American Constitutional Law* 1:902, n. 221 (3d ed., 2000).

141. Leonard W. Levy, *Origins of the Bill of Rights* 134 (New Haven, Conn.: Yale University Press, 1999).

142. Section IV(A), Brief Supporting Appellee of *Amicus Curiae,* National Rifle Association, in *United States v. Emerson,* no. 99–10331 (5th Cir. 1999), at http://www.ccrkba.org/NRAbrief.htm. (Accessed March 1, 2003.)

143. *See* footnote 160, this chapter, for full quotation.

144. Elliot, "The Debates in the Several State Conventions," vol. 3 (2d ed., 1836): 45.

145. *See,* Section III, Brief of *Amicus Curiae* Texas Justice Foundation in Support of Timothy Joe Emerson, in *United States v. Emerson,* no. 99–10331 (5th Cir. 1999), at http://www.ccrkba.org/TXJusticeBrief.htm. (Accessed March 1, 2003.)

146. Ibid., I(A).

147. Ibid., I(A).

148. Ibid. citing Section I, Brief Supporting Appellee of *Amicus Curiae,* National Rifle Association in *United States v. Emerson,* no. 99–10331 (5th Cir. 1999), at http://www.ccrkba.org/NRAbrief.htm. (Accessed March 1, 2003.)

149. Ibid., Section I(A).

150. 10 U.S. Code, sec. 311(b)(1); Twenty-four states and the District of Columbia once had naval militias, but only New York and Alaska still retain them.

151. Act of May 8, 1792, chapter 33, 1 Stat. 271.

152. 10 U.S. Code, sec. 311(b)(2).

153. Federal Public Defender, David Guinn, in Richard Willing, "Case Could Shape Future of Gun Control," *USA Today* (August 27, 1999), at http://www.ccrkba.org/EmersonUSA1.html. (Accessed March 1, 2003.)

154. Section I(A), Brief Supporting Appellee of *Amicus Curiae*, National Rifle Association, in *United States v. Emerson*, no. 99–10331 (5th Cir. 1999), at http://www.ccrkba.org/NRAbrief.htm. (Accessed March 1, 2003.)

155. Ibid.

156. Section I(B), Brief of Texas State Rifle Association as *Amicus Curiae in Support of Appellee*, in *United States v. Emerson*, no. 99–10331 (5th Cir. 1999), at http://www.ccrkba.org/TXRifleBrief.htm. (Accessed March 2, 2003.)

157. Ibid., citing S. Halbrook, "Encroachments of the Crown on the Liberty of the Subject: Pre-Revolutionary Origins of the Second Amendment," *University of Dayton Law Review* 15 (Fall 1989): 91.

158. U.S. Const. art. I, sec. 8.

159. Luther Martin, "The Genuine Information, Delivered to the Legislature of the State of Maryland, Relative to the Proceedings of the General Convention, Held at Philadelphia, in 1787," in Max Farrand, *Records of the Federal Convention* 3 (New Haven, Conn.: Yale University Press, 1911): 208, note 14.

160. "Besides the advantage of being armed, which the Americans possess over the people of almost every other nation, the existence of subordinate governments, to which the people are attached and by which the militia officers are appointed, forms a barrier against the enterprises of ambition, more insurmountable than any which a simple government of any form can admit of. Notwithstanding the military establishments in the several kingdoms of Europe, which are carried as far as the public resources will bear, the governments are afraid to trust the people with arms. And it is not certain that with this aid alone they would not be able to shake off their yokes." James Madison, *The Federalist No. 46*, ed. C. Rossiter (1961), 299.

161. Section I(C), Brief Supporting Appellee of *Amicus Curiae* Academics for the Second Amendment, in *United States v. Emerson*, no. 99–10331 (5th Cir. 1999), at http://www.ccrkba.org/EMERSONacadsecd.html. (Accessed March 6, 2003.)

162. Ibid., Section I(C)–Section II.

163. Ibid., Section III. See also Glenn Harlan Reynolds and Don B. Kates, "The Second Amendment and States' Rights: A Thought Experiment," *William and Mary Law Review* 36 (1995): 1737.

164. Thomas Jefferson, *Papers of Thomas Jefferson*, vol. 1, 344, and James Madison, *Federalist No. 46* (Heritage Press, 1945): 321.

165. Harry Alonzo Cushing, ed., *The Writings of Samuel Adams,* vol. 1 (New York: G.P. Putnam's Sons, 1904–1908): 317, 318, quoting with approval, Blackstone, *Commentaries,* vol. 1: 144.

166. Federalist Tench Coxe in *Federal Gazette,* June 18, 1789.

167. Justice Joseph Story, *Commentaries on the Constitution* 2 (5th ed., 1891): 646.

168. Justice Joseph Story, *A Familiar Exposition of the Constitution of the United States* (1893): 264.

169. Section V, Brief Supporting Appellee of *Amicus Curiae* Academics for the Second Amendment, in *United States v. Emerson,* no. 99–10331 (5th Cir. 1999), at http://www.ccrkba.org/EMERSONacadsecd.html. (Accessed March 6, 2003.)

170. Wayne LaPierre, *Guns, Crime and Freedom* (HarperPerrenial, 1995), 19.

171. Ibid., 20.

172. Ibid., Chapter 2.

173. Ibid., 8.

174. Bellesiles, *Exploring America's Gun Culture,* 264.

175. Section II, Brief *Amici Curiae* of the Independent Women's Forum and Doctors for Responsible Gun Ownership, in *United States v. Emerson,* no. 99–10331 (5th Cir. 1999), at http://adnetsolfp2.adnetsol.com/ssl_claremont/doc/drgoamicusbrief 000107.cfm. (Accessed March 6, 2003.) Citing William Meyerhofer, "Statutory Restrictions on Weapons Possession: Must the Right to Self-Defense Fall Victim?" *Annual Survey of American Law* vol. 1996 (1996): 219, 226.

176. Section I(B), Brief Supporting Appellee of *Amicus Curiae,* National Rifle Association, in *United States v. Emerson,* no. 99–10331 (5th Cir. 1999), at http:// www.ccrkba.org/NRAbrief.htm. (Accessed March 6, 2003.)

177. *United States v. Miller,* 307 U.S. 174 (1939).

178. Ibid., 178.

179. Section II(C), Brief Supporting Appellee of *Amicus Curiae,* National Rifle Association, in *United States v. Emerson,* No. 99–10331 (5th Cir. 1999), at http://www.ccrkba.org/NRAbrief.htm. (Accessed March 6, 2003.)

180. Ibid., Section IV(B).

181. Section II(B), Brief of *Amicus Curiae,* Law Enforcement Alliance of America, Inc., in *United States v. Emerson,* no. 99–10331 (5th Cir. 1999), at http://www. ccrkba.org/LEAAbrief.htm. (Accessed March 6, 2003.)

182. *United States v. Miller,* 179.

183. Section I(A), Brief of *Amici Curiae* Ethan Allen Institute, Heartland Institute, in *United States v. Emerson,* no. 99–10331 (5th Cir. 1999), at http://www. ccrkba.org/EthanAllenBrief.htm. (Accessed March 1, 2003.)

184. *United States v. Emerson,* 46 F.Supp. 2d 598 (5th Cir. 2001), *cert. denied,* 122 S.Ct. 2362 (2002).

185. *United States v. Warin,* 530 F.2d 103, 106 (6th Cir. 1976).

186. *Gillespie v. City of Indianapolis,* 185 F.3d 693, 711 (7th Cir. 1999).

187. *Hickman v. Block,* 81 F.3d 98, 101 (9th Cir. 1996).

188. *Silveira v. Lockyer,* 312 F.3d 1052 (9th Cir. 2002).

189. *Cases v. United States,* 131 F.2d 916, note 19 (1st Cir. 1942).

190. *United States v. Rybar*, 103 F.3d 273, 286 (3d Cir. 1996).

191. *United States v. Hale*, 978 F.2d 1016, 1020 (8th Cir. 1992), *cert. denied*, 507 U.S. 997 (1993).

192. *United States v. Oakes*, 564 F.2d 384 (10th Cir. 1977).

193. *United States v. Wright*, 117 F.3d 1265 (11th Cir. 1997).

194. *United States v. Emerson*, 46 F.Supp. 2d 598 (5th Cir. 2001), *cert. denied*, 122 S.Ct. 2362 (2002).

195. 18 U.S. Code sec. 922(g)(8).

196. Ibid.

197. Ibid.

198. Brief for the United States in Opposition in *Emerson v. United States*, 19–20, U.S. Supreme Court, no. 01–8780, at http://news.findlaw.com/hdocs/docs/gunlawsuits/emersonvs502sgopp.pdf. (Accessed May 7, 2003.)

199. John Ashcroft letter to James Baker, May 17, 2001 at http://vpc.org/studies/ashapa.htm. (Accessed March 6, 2003.)

200. Ibid.

201. Appendix A to Brief for the United States in Opposition in *Emerson v. United States*.

202. Section I(F) of Government's Brief in *United States v. Emerson*, no. 99–10331 (5th Cir. 1999), at http://www.ccrkba.org/EmersonAppealGovt1.html. (Accessed March 6, 2003.)

203. Section I(B), Brief Supporting Appellee of *Amicus Curiae*, National Rifle Association, in *United States v. Emerson*, no. 99–10331 (5th Cir. 1999), at http://www.ccrkba.org/NRAbrief.htm. (Accessed March 1, 2003.)

204. Section II(C), Brief of Appellee in *United States v. Emerson*, no. 99–10331 (5th Cir. 1999), at http://www.saf.org/EmersonMainBrief.html. (Accessed May 6, 2003.).

205. Violence Policy Center Web site at http://vpc.org/studies/ashapa.htm. (Accessed March 6, 2003.)

206. Ibid.

CHAPTER 5

1. U.S. Const. art. I, sec. 8.; "The Congress shall have Power To lay and collect Taxes...."

2. Ibid.

3. In an early case on the subject, the Supreme Court said that the Commerce Clause is not intended to cover the type of commerce "which is completely internal, which is carried on between man and man in a State, or between different parts of the same State, and which does not extend to or affect other States." *Gibbons v. Ogden*, 9 Wheat. 1, 189–90 (1824).

4. 18 U.S. Code, sec. 922(g).

5. *Gillespie v. City of Indianapolis*, 185 F.3d 693, 706 (7th Cir. 1999).

6. *United States v. Lopez*, 514 U.S. 549 (1995).

7. Ibid.

8. White House press release at http://ed.gov/PressReleases/05-1995/gunfree.html (May 10, 1995). (Accessed March 8, 2003.)

9. 18 U.S. Code, sec. 922(q).

10. History of ATF from Oxford University Press, Inc. 1789–1998 U.S., at http://www.atf.treas.gov/about/history.htm. (Accessed May 7, 2003.)

11. Programs: Firearms, at http://www.atf.treas.gov/about/programs/profire.htm. (Accessed May 7, 2003.)

12. Ibid.

13. http://www.atf.treas.gov/about/programs/license.htm. (Accessed June, 2002.)

14. *Federal Firearms Regulations Reference Guide* (Washington, D.C.: Bureau of Alcohol, Tobacco, and Firearms, Firearms Program Division, 2000).

15. Ibid.

16. Joe Waldron, *Armed and Considered Dangerous: Bureau of Alcohol, Tobacco, and Firearms in the 1990's* (July 24, 1995) at http://ccrkba.org/pub/rkba/articles/general/polabuse.txt. (Accessed March 7, 2003.)

17. Budge Williams, "Commentary, Williams: Waco Incident," *Online Athens* (October 23, 1999) at http://www.onlineathens.com/stories/102399/opi_1023990034.shtml. (Accessed May 7, 2003.)

18. Gerry Spence, *From Freedom to Slavery: The Rebirth of Tyranny in America,* Chapter 2, The Trial of Randy Weaver, at http://www.localsov.com/abuses/justice/spence.htm. (Accessed March 7, 2003.) See also Jim Oliver, *The Siege at Ruby Ridge* at http://www.powernet.net/~eichl/rr.html. (Accessed March 7, 2003.)

19. Joe Waldron, *Armed and Considered Dangerous: Bureau of Alcohol, Tobacco, and Firearms in the 1990's* (July 24, 1995) at http://www.ccrkba.org/pub/rkba/articles/general/polabuse.txt. (Accessed March 7, 2003.)

20. Osha Gray Davidson, *Under Fire: The NRA and the Battle for Gun Control* (Iowa City: University of Iowa Press, 1998), 51–53.

21. Federal Register, January 24, 2003 at http://www.ttb.gov/regulations/td487.pdf. (Accessed March 7, 2003.)

CHAPTER 6

1. See Michael A. Bellesiles, *Arming America: The Origins of a National Gun Culture* (New York: Vintage, 2001).

2. For state to state differences in laws regarding gun ownership, concealed weapons permits, and vehicle transportation of firearms, see J. Scott Kappas, *Traveler's Guide to the Firearms Laws of the Fifty States* (Traveler's Guide, 2001, www.gunlawguide.com). (Accessed March 8, 2003.)

3. Alan Korwin with Michael P. Anthony, *Gun Laws of America* (Phoenix, Ariz.: Bloomfield Press, 1999), 247; 26 U.S. Code, sec. 5845(a).

4. 26 U.S. Code, sec. 5845(a)(8) and (b).

5. 26 U.S. Code, sec. 5811 and 5812.

6. 26 U.S. Code, sec. 5802, 5844, and 5861.

7. Gun Control Timeline at http://usgovinfo.about.com/library/weekly/aa092699.htm. (Accessed March 7, 2003.)

8. Osha Gray Davidson, *Under Fire: The NRA and the Battle for Gun Control* (Iowa City: University of Iowa Press, 1998): 30.

9. 18 U.S. Code, sec. 921 *et seq.*

10. The Commerce Clause appears in Article I, Section 8 of the U.S. Constitution. It says, "The Congress shall have Power...To regulate commerce...among the several states...."

11. 18 U.S. Code, sec. 922(a).

12. Ibid., sec. 922(b).

13. Ibid., sec. 922(a)(3).

14. Ibid., sec. 922(a)(5).

15. Ibid., sec. 922(b)(3)(B).

16. Ibid., sec. 922(a)(6).

17. Ibid., sec. 922(b)(1).

18. Ibid., sec. 922(x).

19. Ibid., sec. 922(g).

20. Ibid., sec. 922(d).

21. Ibid., sec. 922(g)(8) and (g)(9).

22. Ibid., sec. 922(n).

23. Ibid., sec. 922 (a)(7).

24. Ibid., sec. 922 (a)(8).

25. Ibid., sec. 921(a)(17)(B).

26. Ibid., sec. 922 (l).

27. Ibid., sec. 929.

28. Ibid., sec. 922 (b)(5).

29. Ibid., sec. 926(A).

30. For a compilation and summary of state laws see Kappas, *Traveler's Guide to the Firearms Laws of the Fifty States.*

31. One author calls this the "lost National Right to Carry" which he asserts is guaranteed by the Second Amendment, but needs legislative lobbying to reinstate. See Korwin with Anthony, *Gun Laws of America*, 188.

32. 18 U.S. Code, sec. 926.

33. Dave Kopel, "The Cheney Glock-n Spicl," *National Review Online* (July 27, 2000) at http://www.nationalreview.com/kopel/kopel-archive.asp. (Accessed March 8, 2003.)

34. Davidson, *Under Fire*, 96.

35. Ibid., 97.

36. See discussion of the activity of the National Rifle Association's Institute for Legislative Action in Chapter 8.

37. 18 U.S. Code, sec. 922(p).

38. Kopel, "The Cheney Glock-n-Spiel."

39. Davidson, *Under Fire*, 112.

40. Former 18 U.S. Code, sec. 922(q)(1)(A).

41. *United States v. Lopez*, 514 U.S. 549 (1995).

42. Ibid.

43. Ibid.

44. White House press release at http://ed.gov/PressReleases/05-1995/gunfree.html. (May 10, 1995). (Accessed March 8, 2003.)

45. *United States v. Lopez,* 514 U.S. 549 (1995).

46. 18 U.S. Code, sec. 922(q)(2)(B).

47. Ibid., sec. 922(q)(3)(A).

48. Davidson, *Under Fire,* 194.

49. Ibid., 17, 200.

50. Ibid., 200.

51. Ibid., 18.

52. Ibid., p. 211.

53. Ibid., 207.

54. Ibid., 210.

55. *Federal Firearms Regulations Reference Guide* (Washington, D.C.: Bureau of Alcohol, Tobacco, and Firearms, Firearms Program Division, 2000): 126.

56. Davidson, *Under Fire,* 209.

57. Ibid., 209–210.

58. Wayne LaPierre, *Guns, Crime and Freedom* (New York: HarperPerrenial, 1995): 56.

59. Erik Larson, *Lethal Passage* (New York: Vintage Books, 1995): 72.

60. 18 U.S. Code, sec. 922(v).

61. Ibid., sec. 921(a)(30).

62. Ibid., sec. 922(v)(3).

63. Ibid., sec. 922(w).

64. Ibid., sec. 921(a)(31).

65. David Lampo, *Gun Control: Myths and Realities,* CATO Today's Commentary, at http://www.cato.org/dailys/05-13-00.html. (Accessed March 8, 2003.)

66. David Kopel, *Guns: Who Should Have Them?* (Amherst, NY: Prometheus Books, 1995): 93.

67. See *Federal Firearms Regulations Reference Guide,* 92–96 and 147–151.

68. *Printz v. United States,* 521 U.S. 898 (1997).

69. *Federal Firearms Regulations Reference Guide,* 93.

70. Ibid.

71. Christopher Newton, "Group Says Many Illegal Buyers Missed by Sloppy Firearms Background Checks," *The Oregonian* (January 17, 2002): A3.

72. 18 U.S. Code, sec. 922(t).

73. 28 Code of Federal Regulations, sec. 25.

74. Ibid., sec. 25.9.

75. *Federal Firearms Regulations Reference Guide,* 149.

76. Ibid.

77. Eric Holder, Jr., "Keeping Guns Away from Terrorists," *Washington Post* (October 25, 2001): A31.

78. Ibid.

79. 18 U.S. Code, sec. 922(g).

80. Ibid.

81. Ibid.

82. Marjolijn Bijlefeld, *People For and Against Gun Control: A Biographical Reference* (Westport, Conn.: Greenwood Press, 1999): 91.

83. Jacob Sullum, "Can't Bear It," Reason Online, at http://www.reason.com/sullum/080598.html. (Accessed March 8, 2003.)

84. 18 U.S. Code, sec. 922(x).

85. Korwin with Anthony, *Gun Laws of America,* 335.

86. 18 U.S. Code, sec. 922(g)(9).

87. Ibid., sec. 922 (g)(8).

CHAPTER 7

1. Robin Wright, "World Population Expected to Hit 6 Billion This Weekend," *The Oregonian* (July 17, 1999): A1.

2. http://www.bradycampaign.org. (Accessed March 8, 2003.)

3. Sarah Brady, Merrill McLoughlin, and Laura Hicks, *A Good Fight* (New York: Public Affairs, 2002).

4. Osha Gray Davidson, *Under Fire: The NRA and the Battle for Gun Control* (Iowa City: University of Iowa Press, 1998): 176.

5. http://www.bradycampaign.org/about/index.asp. (Accessed March 8, 2003.)

6. http://www.vpc.org. (Accessed March 8, 2003.)

7. http://www.helpnetwork.org. (Accessed March 8, 2003.)

8. Ibid.

9. Ibid.

10. http://www.helpnetwork.org/frames/membership_orgs.html. (Accessed March 8, 2003.)

11. http://www.csgv.org. (Accessed March 8, 2003.)

12. http://www.gunfree.org/content/action/action_studact_atwood.html. (Accessed March 8, 2003.)

13. http://csgv.org/content/coalition/frame_coal_intro.html. (Accessed March 8, 2003.)

14. http://csgv.org/content/coalition/coal_aboutus.html. (Accessed March 8, 2003.)

15. http://www.millionmommarch.org/about/index.asp. (Accessed March 8, 2003.)

16. Ibid.

17. Ibid.

18. Oregon Revised Statutes, sec. 166.438.

19. http://www.goal.org. (Accessed March 8, 2003.)

20. http://www.goal.org/Member/home2.shtml. (Accessed March 8, 2003.)

21. Ibid.

CHAPTER 8

1. Militia of Montana at http://www.militiaofmontana.com. (Accessed March 8, 2003.)

2. The Missouri Fifty-first Militia at http://www.mo51st.org. (Accessed March 8, 2003.)

3. Southern Michigan Regional Militia at http://www.michiganmilitia.org. (Accessed March 8, 2003.)

4. Marietta, Pennsylvania, Militia at http://mariettapa.com/marietta_militia. html. (Accessed March 8, 2003.)

5. U.S. Const. art. I, sec. 8, cl. 16.

6. 10 U.S. Code, sec. 311 and 313.

7. Ibid., sec. 311(b)(1).

8. Ibid., sec. 311(b)(2).

9. Anti-Defamation League, *Armed & Dangerous: Militias Take Aim at the Federal Government,* An ADL Fact Finding Report (1994), at http://www.nizkor.org/ hweb/orgs/american/adl/armed-and-dangerous/. (Accessed March 8, 2003.)

10. The Seventh Missouri Militia at http://users.mo-net.com/mlindste/7momilit. html. (Accessed March 8, 2003.)

11. Wayne County Militia at http://www.geocities.com/CapitolHill/1392/ index2.htm. (Accessed March 8, 2003.)

12. The North Carolina Citizen Militia at http://www.ncmilitia.org. (Accessed March 8, 2003.)

13. Missouri Fifty-first Militia at http://www.mo51st.org/thoughts_about_ the_mo_51st_milit.htm. (Accessed March 8, 2003.)

14. "United States 1890s Populism," George Burson Aspen School District, at http://www.jmu.edu/madison/teach/burson/1890.htm. (Accessed March 8, 2003.)

15. Anti-Defamation League, *Armed & Dangerous.*

16. Ibid.

17. Jim Goad, *The Redneck Manifesto* (New York: Simon & Schuster, 1997): 184.

18. Ibid., 190.

19. Anti-Defamation League, *Armed & Dangerous.*

20. Edward R. Fields, ed., *The Truth at Last: News Suppressed by the Daily Press,* at http://www.stormfront.org/truth_at_last/index2.htm. (Accessed March 8, 2003.)

21. Paxton Quigley, *Armed and Female* (New York: St. Martin's, 1989).

22. Ibid., Chapter 3.

23. Erik Larson, *Lethal Passage* (New York: Vintage Books, 1995): 28.

24. Unlawful paramilitary activity: Oregon Revised Statutes sec. 166.660.

25. http://www.saf.org and http://www.ccrkba.org. (Accessed March 8, 2003.)

26. Marjolijn Bijlefeld, *People For and Against Gun Control: A Biographical Reference* (Westport, Conn.: Greenwood Press, 1999): 99.

27. Ibid., 95.

28. Alan Gottlieb, *Politically Correct Guns* (Bellevue, Wash.: Merril Press, 2000): 72.

29. Bijlefeld, *People For and Against Gun Control,* 97.

30. Ibid., 95.

31. Ibid., 93.

32. http://www.2asisters.org/membership/about.html. (Accessed March 8, 2003.)

33. Ibid.

34. Ibid.

35. Ibid.

36. Osha Gray Davidson, *Under Fire: The NRA and the Battle for Gun Control* (Iowa City: University of Iowa Press, 1998): 21.

37. https://www.nrahq.org/history.asp. (Accessed March 8, 2003.)

38. Davidson, *Under Fire,* 22.

39. Ibid.

40. Davidson, *Under Fire,* 27.

41. https://www.nrahq.org/history.asp. (Accessed March 8, 2003.)

42. Ibid.

43. Davidson, *Under Fire,* 30.

44. https://www.nrahq.org/history.asp. (Accessed March 8, 2003.)

45. Ibid.

46. Wayne LaPierre, *Guns, Crime and Freedom* (New York: HarperPerrenial, 1995): 79.

47. https://www.nrahq.org/history.asp. (Accessed March 8, 2003.)

48. Davidson, *Under Fire,* 30.

49. https://www.nrahq.org/history.asp. (Accessed March 8, 2003.)

50. Davidson, *Under Fire,* 35.

51. Ibid.

52. Ibid., 36.

53. Ibid., 245, 246.

54. Ibid., 30.

55. Ibid., 92.

56. Ibid., Chapter 4.

57. Ibid., 194.

58. Ibid., 291.

59. Ibid., 207–210.

60. Ibid., 291–292.

61. Ibid., 292.

62. http://www.nrawinningteam.com/heston.html. (Accessed March 8, 2003.)

63. Ibid.

64. Davidson, *Under Fire,* 157.

65. Ibid., 155.

66. Larson, *Lethal Passage,* 52.

67. NRA Fundraising Letter of Spring 1995 in Bijlefeld, *The Gun Control Debate,* 56.

68. Letter from the NRA president to a Senator in Ibid., 57.

69. Wayne LaPierre, *Guns, Crime and Freedom* (HarperPerrenial, 1995): 17.

70. Ibid., 18.

CHAPTER 9

1. Bill Clede, *Colt's Smart Gun,* http://www.clede.com/Articles/Police/smartgun. htm (1997). (Accessed March 10, 2003.)

2. Ibid.

3. Ibid.

4. Violence Policy Center, *The False Hope of a Smart Gun,* http://vpc.org/fact_ sht/smartgun.htm (1998). (Accessed March 10, 2003.)

5. Clede, *Colt's Smart Gun.*

6. Marjolijn Bijlefeld, *People For and Against Gun Control: A Biographical Reference* (Westport, Conn.: Greenwood Press, 1999): 131.

7. Violence Policy Center, *The False Hope of a Smart Gun.*

8. Ibid.

9. Bijlefeld, *People For and Against Gun Control,* 130.

10. Ibid., 93.

11. Gun Control Timeline at http://usgovinfo.about.com/library/weekly/ aa092699.htm. (Accessed March 10, 2003.)

12. Ibid. See also 18 U.S. Code, sec. 923(d)(1)(G).

13. 18 U.S. Code, sec. 922(g).

14. Ibid., sec. 925(c).

15. Violence Policy Center Web site at http://vpc.org/press/0201relief.htm.

16. *Bean v. Bureau of Alcohol, Tobacco, and Firearms,* 253 F.3d 234 (5th Cir. 2001), *reversed* 123 S.Ct. 584 (2002).

17. The government argued that Bean's Mexican conviction, being foreign, did not trigger the law which would bar him from possessing firearms in the United States, so it is debatable whether he had lost his firearms rights.

18. *Bean v. Bureau of Alcohol, Tobacco, and Firearms.*

19. *United States v. Thomas Lamar Bean,* 123 S.Ct. 584 (2002).

20. Statement of M. Kristen Rand, director of federal policy, Violence Policy Center, on Legislation to Improve and Aid Enforcement of Federal Gun Laws Presented to The Crime Subcommittee of the House Judiciary Committee (April 6, 2000), at http://www.house.gov/judiciary/rand0406.htm. (Accessed March 10, 2003.)

CHAPTER 10

1. Marjolijn Bijlefeld, *People For and Against Gun Control: A Biographical Reference* (Westport, Conn.: Greenwood Press, 1999): 243.

2. "Federal Firearms Regulations Reference Guide," (Washington, D.C.: Bureau of Alcohol, Tobacco, and Firearms; Firearms Program Division, 2000): 1.

3. Section I(B), brief of Texas Rifle Association as *Amicus Curiae* in Support of Appellee, in *United States v. Emerson,* no. 99–10331 (5th Cir. 1999), at http:// www.ccrkba.org/TXRifleBrief.htm. (Accessed March 8, 2003.)

4. Project Safe Neighborhoods at http://www.psn.gov/about.asp. (Accessed March 10, 2003.)

Bibliography

CASES

Adams v. Williams, 407 U.S. 143 (1972).

Atlanta Motel v. United States, 397 U.S. 241 (1964).

Aymette v. State, 21 Tenn. 154 (1840).

Bean v. Bureau of Alcohol, Tobacco, and Firearms, 253 F.3d 234 (5th Cir. 2001), *reversed* 123 S. Ct. 584 (2002).

Cases v. United States, 131 F2d 916 (1st Cir. 1942).

English v. State, 35 Tex. 473 (1872).

Ex Parte Thomas, 21 Okla. 770 (1908).

Gibbons v. Ogden, 9 Wheat. 1 (1824).

Gillespie v. City of Indianapolis, 185 F.3d 693 (7th Cir. 1999).

Hickman v. Block, 81 F3d 98 (9th Cir. 1996).

Hill v. Georgia, 53 Ga. 472 (1874).

Konigsberg v. State Bar, 366 U.S. 36 (1961).

Lewis v. United States, 445 U.S. 55 (1980).

Marbury v. Madison, 1 Cranch. 137 (1803)(Marshall, C. J.).

Miller v. Texas, 153 U.S. 535 (1894).

Perpich v. Dept. of Defense, 496 U.S. 334 (1990).

Presser v. Illinois, 116 U.S. 252 (1886).

Printz, Sheriff/Coroner, Ravalli County, Montana v. United States, 521 U.S. 898 (1997).

Quilici v. Village of Morton Grove, 532 F.Supp. 1169 (N.D. Ill. 1981), *aff'd,* 695 F2d 261 (7th Cir. 1982).

Silveira v. Lockyer, 312 F. 3d 1052 (9th Cir. 2002).

State v. Hirsch, Or.Ct.App. A109091 (Oct. 31, 2001).

State v. Workman, 35 W.Va. 367 (1891).
United States v. Cruikshank, 92 U.S. 542 (1875).
United States v. Emerson, 46 F. Supp. 2d 598 (5th Cir. 2001), *cert denied,* 122 S. Ct. 2363 (2002).
United States v. Hale, 978 F2d 1016 (8th Cir.), *cert. denied,* 507 U.S. 997 (1993).
United States v. Lopez, 514 U.S. 549 (1995).
United States v. Miller, 307 U.S. 174 (1939).
United States v. Oakes, 564 F2d 384 (10th Cir. 1977).
United States v. Rybar, 103 F3d 273 (3d Cir. 1996).
United States v. Thomas Lamar Bean, 123 S. Ct. 584 (2002).
United States v. Warin, 530 F2d 103, 106 (6th Cir. 1976).
United States v. Wright, 117 F3d 1265 (11th Cir. 1997).
Vietnamese Fisherman's Association v. Ku Klux Klan, 543 F.Supp. 198, 210 (S.D. Tex. 1982).

CONSTITUTIONAL PROVISIONS

The Oregon Constitution, Article I, Section 27.
The Pennsylvania Declaration of Rights, Article XIII (1776).
U.S. Constitution, Article I, Section 8.
U.S. Constitution, Amendment I.
U.S. Constitution, Amendment II.
The Vermont Constitution, Article I, Section 15 (1777).

STATUTES AND REGULATIONS

Hening's Statutes, vol. 12, c. 1, p. 9 *et seq.* (Virginia, 1785).
10 U.S. Code, sec. 311 and 313.
10 U.S. Code, sec. 311(b)(1). Defense Link, U.S. Department of Defense at http://www.defenselink.mil/news/May1996/n05161996_9605161.html. (Accessed March 4, 2003.)
10 U.S. Code, sec. 311(b)(2).
18 U.S. Code, sec. 921 *et seq.* (The Gun Control Act of 1968.)
18 U.S. Code, sec. 921(a)(17)(B).
18 U.S. Code, sec. 921(a)(30).
18 U.S. Code, sec. 921(a)(31).
18 U.S. Code, sec. 922(a).
18 U.S. Code, sec. 922(a)(3).
18 U.S. Code, sec. 922(a)(5).
18 U.S. Code, sec. 922(a)(6).
18 U.S. Code, sec. 922(a)(7) and (a)(8).
18 U.S. Code, sec. 922(b).
18 U.S. Code, sec. 922(b)(1).
18 U.S. Code, sec. 922(b)(3)(B).

18 U.S. Code, sec. 922(b)(5).

18 U.S. Code, sec. 922(d).

18 U.S. Code, sec. 922(g).

18 U.S. Code, sec. 922(g)(8).

18 U.S. Code, sec. 922(g)(9).

18 U.S. Code, sec. 922(l).

18 U.S. Code, sec. 922(n).

18 U.S. Code, sec. 922(p).

18 U.S. Code, sec. 922(q).

18 U.S. Code, sec. 922(q)(1)(A).

18 U.S. Code, sec. 922(q)(2)(B).

18 U.S. Code, sec. 922(q)(3)(A).

18 U.S. Code, sec. 922(t).

18 U.S. Code, sec. 922(v).

18 U.S. Code, sec. 922(v)(3).

18 U.S. Code, sec. 922(w).

18 U.S. Code, sec. 922(x).

18 U.S. Code, sec. 922(x)(2).

18 U.S. Code, sec. 922(x)(3).

18 U.S. Code, sec. 923(d)(1)(G).

18 U.S. Code, sec. 925(c).

18 U.S. Code, sec. 926.

18 U.S. Code, sec. 926(A).

18 U.S. Code, sec. 929.

18 U.S. Code, sec. 1132–1132(q).

26 U.S. Code, sec. 5801 *et seq.* (The National Firearms Act.)

26 U.S. Code, sec. 5802, 5844, and 5861.

26 U.S. Code, sec. 5811 and 5812.

26 U.S. Code, sec. 5845(a).

26 U.S. Code, sec. 5845(a)(8) and (b).

26 U.S. Code, sec. 5845(a).

28 Code of Federal Regulations, sec. 25.

139 Cong. Rec. sec. 7884-01 (1994).

Act passed April 4, 1786, N.Y. Laws 1786, c. 25.

Act of May 2, 1792, 1 Stat. 264.

Act of May 8, 1792, 1 Stat. 271.

Act of May 8, 1792, ch. 33, 1 Stat. 271.

Act of April 2, 1794, 1 Stat. 352.

Act of May 22, 1794, 1 Stat. 369.

Former 18 U.S. Code, sec. 922 (q)(1)(A).

The General Court of Massachusetts, January Session, 1784 (Laws and Resolves 1784, c. 55, pp. 140–142).

28 Code of Federal Regulations, sec. 25.

Omnibus Crime Control and Safe Streets Act of 1968.

Oregon Revised Statutes, sec. 161.219.
Oregon Revised Statutes, sec. 161.225.
Oregon Revised Statutes, sec. 161.229.
Oregon Revised Statutes, sec. 166.434.
Oregon Revised Statutes, sec. 166.438.
Oregon Revised Statutes, sec. 166.660.
Texas Government Code Annotated, sec. 431.010.
Texas Government Code Annotated, sec. 431.051.

BOOKS, PERIODICALS, ARTICLES, REPORTS, AND OTHER

Adams, C., ed. *Works of John Adams* (1851).
Adams, Samuel. *The Writings of Samuel Adams*. Vol. 1. Edited by Harry Alonzo
    Cushing. New York: G.P. Putnam's Sons, 1904–1908.
Amar, Akhil Reed. "Second Thoughts." *The New Republic* (July 12, 1999): 24.
Bailey, James E. "Risk Factors for Violent Death of Women in the Home." *Archives
    of Internal Medicine* 157 (1997): 777–782.
Bellesiles, Michael A. *Arming America: The Origins of a National Gun Culture*. New
    York: Knopf, 2000.
Bellesiles, Michael A. *Arming America: The Origins of a National Gun Culture*. New
    York: Vintage, 2001.
Bellesiles, Michael A. "Exploring America's Gun Culture." *The William and Mary
    Quarterly,* 3d ser., LIX, no. 1 (January 2002): 241.
Bellesiles, Michael A. "Gun Laws in Early America: The Regulation of Firearms
    Ownership, 1607–1794." *Law & History Review* 16, (1998): 567.
Bellesiles, Michael. "Suicide Pact: New Readings of the Second Amendment." *Con-
    stitutional Commentary* 16 (1999): 247.
Bernstein, Maxine. *The Oregonian* (March 9, 2001): 1.
Bijlefeld, Marjolijn. *The Gun Control Debate: A Documentary History.* Westport,
    Conn.: Greenwood Press, 1997.
Bijlefeld, Marjolijn. *People For and Against Gun Control.* Westport, Conn.: Green-
    wood Press, 1999.
Bishop, Joel Prentice. *Commentaries on the Law of Statutory Crimes* 497 (1873).
Blackstone, William. *Commentaries.*
Bogus, Carl T. "The Hidden History of the Second Amendment." *University of Cal-
    ifornia Davis Law Review* 31 (1998): 309.
Brady, Sarah, Merrill McLaughlin, and Laura Hicks. *A Good Fight.* New York: Public
    Affairs, 2002.
Brief for the United States in Opposition in *Emerson v. United States,* 19–20, U.S.
    Supreme Court, no. 01–8780.
CNN News, December 12, 2001.
Congressional Record, vol. 139, sec. 7884–01 (1994).
Coxe, Tench. *Federal Gazette* (June 18, 1789).
Cushing, Harry Alonzo, ed. *The Writings of Samual Adams,* vol. 1 (1904–1908): 317,
    318.

Davidson, Osha Gray. *Under Fire: The NRA and the Battle for Gun Control.* Iowa City: University of Iowa Press, 1998.

Driessen, Marguerite. "Private Organizations and the Militia Status." *Brigham Young University Law Review* 1 (1998): 7–8.

Elliot, Jonathan, ed. *Debates in the Several State Conventions* 3 (2d ed. 1836).

Elliot, Jonathan, ed. *The Debates in the Several State Conventions on the Adoption of the Federal Constitution as Recommended by the General Convention at Philadelphia in 1787* (2d ed., 1891, photo reprint, William S. Hein & Co., 1996.)

Elliot, Jonathan, ed. Luther Martin's Letter to the Maryland Legislature. *The Debates in the Several State Conventions on the Adoption of the Federal Constitution* 1, reprint ed. 1941. 1836.

Emery, Lucilius A. "The Constitutional Right to Keep and Bear Arms." *Harvard Law Review* 28 (1915): 473.

"Federal Firearms Regulations Reference Guide." Washington, D.C.: Bureau of Alcohol, Tobacco, and Firearms, Firearms Program Division, 2000.

Flynn, George and Alan Gottlieb. *Guns for Women.* Bellevue, Wash.: Merril Press, 1988.

Franklin, Benjamin. *Benjamin Franklin Papers.* Vol. III.

Freemon, Celeste. *Father Greg and the Homeboys.* New York: Hyperion, 1995.

Goad, Jim. *The Redneck Manifesto.* New York: Simon & Schuster, 1997.

Goodson, Larry P. *Afghanistan's Endless War.* Seattle: University of Washington Press, 2001.

Gottlieb, Alan. *Politically Correct Guns.* Bellevue, Wash.: Merril Press, 2000.

Gross, Robert A. "Forum: Historians and Guns." *The William and Mary Quarterly,* 3d ser., LIX, no. 1 (January, 2002): 203.

Grossman, Lieutenant Colonel Dave. *On Killing.* Boston: Back Bay Books, 1996.

Grossman, Lieutenant Colonel Dave, and Gloria DeGaetano. *Stop Teaching Our Kids to Kill.* New York: Crown Publishers, 1999.

Gruber, Ira D. "Of Arms and Men: *Arming America* and Military History." *The William and Mary Quarterly,* 3d ser., LIX, no. 1 (January 2002): 217.

Halbrook, Stephen. "Personal Security, Personal Liberty, and 'the Constitutional Right to Bear Arms': Visions of the Framers of the Fourteenth Amendment." *Seton Hall Constitutional Law Journal* 5 (Spring 1995): 341.

Halbrook, Stephen "Encroachments of the Crown on the Liberty of the Subject: Pre-Revolutionary Origins of the Second Amendment." *University of Dayton Law Review* 15 (Fall 1989): 91.

Hamilton, Alexander. *The Federalist, No. 29.*

Holder Eric, Jr. "Keeping Guns Away from Terrorists." *Washington Post,* October 25, 2001: A31.

House of Representatives Conference Report. 103–711 (1994).

Howard, Senator Jacob. *Congressional Globe,* 39th Cong., 1st Sess. 2765 (May 23, 1866).

Humphrey, Hubert. "Know Your Law Makers." *Guns* (February 1960): 4.

Independent Gazetteer. (August 20, 1789): 2.

Jefferson, Thomas. *Papers of Thomas Jefferson,* vol. 1.

Kates, Don B. "The Second Amendment and the Ideology of Self-Protection." *Constitutional Commentary* 9 (1992): 87.

Kellermann, Arthur L., Frederick P. Rivara, Norman B. Rushforth, Joyce G. Banton, Donald T. Reay, Jerry T. Francisco, Ana B. Locci, Jancice Prodzinzki, Bela B. Hackman, and Grant Somes. "Gun Ownership as a Risk Factor for Homicide in the Home." *New England Journal of Medicine* 329, no. 15 (1993): 1084–1091.

Kellerman, Arthur L., F. P. Rivara, G. Somes, D. T. Reay, J. Francisco, J. G. Banton, J. Prodzinsky, C. Flinger, and B. B. Hackman. "Suicide in the Home in Relation to Gun Ownership." *New England Journal of Medicine* 327, no. 7 (August 13, 1992): 467–472.

Kellerman, Arthur and Donald Reay. "Protection or Peril? An Analysis of Firearm Related Deaths in the Home." *New England Journal of Medicine.* 314, no. 24 (June 1986): 1557–1560.

Kleck, Gary. "Crime Control through the Private Use of Armed Force." *Social Forces* 35 (1988): 1–22; Table 4, p. 8.

Kleck, G. and M. Gertz "Armed Resistance to Crime: The Prevalence and Nature of Self-Defense with a Gun." *Journal of Criminal Law and Criminology* 86 (1995): 150, 151–152, 174–175.

Kopel, David. *Guns: Who Should Have Them?* Amherst, NY: Prometheus Books, 1995.

Korwin, Alan with Michael P. Anthony. *Gun Laws of America.* Phoenix, Ariz.: Bloomfield Press, 1999.

Landler, Mark. "Kabul Takes Steps toward Disarming Afghan Population." *New York Times,* January 14, 2002.

LaPierre, Wayne. *Guns, Crime and Freedom.* New York: Harper Perrenial, 1995.

Larson, Erik. *Lethal Passage.* New York: Vintage Books, 1995.

Levy, Leonard W. *Origins of the Bill of Rights.* New Haven, Conn.: Yale University Press, 1999.

Lott, John R., Jr. *More Guns, Less Crime: Understanding Crime and Gun Control Laws.* Chicago: University of Chicago Press, 1998.

Lott, J. and D. Mustard. "Crime, Deterrence, and the Right-to-Carry Concealed Weapons." *Journal of Legal Studies* 26 (1997): 1.

Madison, James. *Federalist Paper No. 46.* Heritage Press, 1945.

Madison, James. *Federalist Paper No. 46.* Edited by Edward Mead Earle, 1976.

Madison, James. *The Federalist No. 46.* Edited by C. Rossiter, 1961.

Madison, James. *1st Annals of Congress* (June 8, 1789).

Main, Gloria L. "Many Things Forgotten: The Use of Probate Records in *Arming America.*" *The William and Mary Quarterly,* 3d ser., LIX, no. 1 (January 2002): 211.

Malcolm, Joyce Lee. *To Keep and Bear Arms: The Origins of an Anglo-American Right.* Cambridge, Mass.: Harvard University Press, 1994.

Martin, Luther. *The Genuine Information, Delivered to the Legislature of the State of Maryland, Relative to the Proceedings of the General Convention, Held at Philadelphia, in 1787.* Reprinted in Farrand, *Records of the Federal Convention* 3 (1911).

Meyerhofer, William. "Statutory Restrictions on Weapons Possession: Must the Right to Self-Defense Fall Victim?" *Annual Survey of American Law* 1996 (1996): 219, 226.

Morris, Richard B. *The Forging of the Union.* New York: Harper Row, 1987.

MSNBC, *Explorer,* December 21, 2001.

Newton, Christopher. "Group Says Many Illegal Buyers Missed by Sloppy Firearms Background Checks." *The Oregonian* (January 17, 2002): A3.

Polsby, Daniel D. "The False Promise of Gun Control." *Atlantic Monthly* (March 1994).

Quigley, Paxton. *Armed and Female.* New York: St. Martin's, 1989.

Rakove, Jack N. "Words, Deeds and Guns: *Arming America* and the Second Amendment." *The William and Mary Quarterly* (3d ser., vol. LIX, no. 1, January 2002): 205.

Rather, Dan. *Nightly News.* CBS, July 17, 2001.

Reese, Charley. "Gun Control Isn't about Crime—It's an Elitist Way to Control People," *Orlando Sentinel* (March 31, 1994).

Reynolds, G. and D. Kates. "The Second Amendment and States' Rights: A Thought Experiment." *William and Mary Law Review* 36 (1995): 1737.

Robbins, Tom. *Fierce Invalids Home from Hot Climates.* New York: Bantam Books, 2000.

Robinson, Thomas N., Marta L. Wilde, Lisa C. Navracruz, K. Farish Haydel, and Ann Vardy. "Effects of Reducing Children's Television and Video Game Use on Aggressive Behavior: A Randomized Controlled Trial." *Archives of Pediatrics and Adolescent Medicine* 155 (January 2001): 17–23.

Roth, Randolph. "Guns, Gun Culture, and Homicide: The Relationship Between Firearms, the Uses of Firearms, and Interpersonal Violence." *The William and Mary Quarterly* 3d ser., vol. LIX, no. 1 (January 2002): 223.

Saltzman, L. E., J. Mercy, P. O'Carroll, M. Rosenberg, and P. Rhodes. "Weapon Involvement and Injury Outcomes in Family and Intimate Assaults." *Journal of the American Medical Association* 22, no. 267 (1992): 3043–3047.

Slaughter, Thomas. *The Whiskey Rebellion.* Oxford, NY: Oxford University Press, 1986.

Stephenson, Carl and Frederick George Marcham, eds. *Sources of English Constitutional History.* New York: Harper Row, 1937.

Storing, Herbert J., ed. *The Complete Anti-Federalist.* Vol. 7. Chicago: University of Chicago Press, 1981.

Story, Justice Joseph. *A Familiar Exposition of the Constitution of the United States* (1893).

Story, Justice Joseph. *Commentaries on the Constitution* 2 (5th ed. 1891).

Szatmary, David P. *Shay's Rebellion: The Making of an Agrarian Insurrection.* Amherst: University of Massachusetts Press, 1980.

Tribe, Laurence. *American Constitutional Law.* 3d ed., vol. 1, 2000.

Veit, Helen E., Kenneth R. Bowling, and Charlene Bangs Bickford, eds. *Creating the Bill of Rights: The Documentary Record from the First Federal Congress.* The George Washington University, Washington, D.C.: The First Federal Congress Project, 1991.

Ventura, Jesse. *Ain't Got Time to Bleed.* New York: Villard Books, 1999.

Washington Post (May 19, 1999).

Wills, Gary. "To Keep and Bear Arms." *New York Review of Books* (September 21, 1995).

Wright, James D. and Peter Rossi. *Armed and Considered Dangerous: A Survey of Felons and Their Firearms* (1986).

Wright, Robin. "World Population Expected to Hit 6 Billion This Weekend," *The Oregonian* (July 17, 1999): A1.

Zimiring, Franklin, E. Firearms, Violence, and Public Policy, *Scientific American* (November, 1991): 21.

WEB SITES

About the Brady Campaign at http://www.bradycampaign.org/about/index.asp. (Accessed February 24, 2003.)

Amended Brief of Second Amendment Foundation as *Amicus Curiae* in Support of Defendant Appellee, in *United States v. Emerson,* no. 99–10331 (5th Cir. 1999), at http://www.ccrkba.org/EmersonSAF.htm. (Accessed March 1, 2003.)

Americans for Gun Safety Foundation, Parents Guide to Firearm Safety (no date), at http://w3.agsfoundation.com/safety/parents.html#facts. (Accessed February 25, 2003.)

Amicus Curiae brief of Center to Prevent Handgun Violence, in *United States v. Emerson,* no. 99–10331 (5th Cir. 1999), at http://www.ccrkba.org/CenterTo PreventHandgunViolencebrief.htm. (Accessed February 25, 2003.)

Amicus Curiae brief of David Yassky in *United States v. Emerson,* no. 99–10331 (5th Cir. 1999), at http://www.potomac-inc.org/yass.html. (Accessed March 1, 2003.)

Amicus Curiae brief of the State of Alabama, in *United States v. Emerson,* no. 99–10331 (5th Cir. 1999), at http://www.ccrkba.org/ALABAMAbrief.htm. (Accessed February 25, 2003.)

Anti-Defamation League, "Armed & Dangerous: Militias Take Aim at the Federal Government, An ADL Fact Finding Report" (1994), at http://www.nizkor.org/hweb/orgs/american/adi/armed-and-dangerous/. (Accessed March 8, 2003.)

John Ashcroft letter to James Baker, May 17, 2001 at http://vpc.org/studies/ashapa.htm. (Accessed March 6, 2003.)

"Attorney General Nominee Ashcroft Member of National Rifle Association," Violence Policy Center Web site at http://vpc.org/press/0101ash3.htm. (Accessed February 25, 2003.)

Baker, James J. In "The News: Americans for Gun Safety Is a True Anti-Gun Group," at http://www.nraila.org/newscenter.asp?FormMode=Detail&ID=683. (Accessed March 1, 2003.)

Bonderman, Judith. "Firearms and Domestic Violence." *The Impact of Domestic Violence on Your Legal Practice: A Lawyers Handbook.* The American Bar Association Commission on Domestic Violence. http://www.abanet.org/cle/clenow/dv/intersta.html. (Accessed February 24, 2003.)

Brady Campaign at http://www.bradycampaign.org. (Accessed March 8, 2003.)

Brief of *Amici Curiae* Ethan Allen Institute, Heartland Institute, in *United States v. Emerson*, no. 99–10331 (5th Cir. 1999), section II(B), at http://www.ccrkba.org/ EthanAllenBrief.htm. (Accessed March 1, 2003.)

Brief *Amici Curiae* of the Independent Women's Forum and Doctors for Responsible Gun Ownership, in *United States v. Emerson*, no. 99–10331 (5th Cir. 1999), at http://adnetsolfp2.adnetsol.com/ss1__claremont/doc/drgoamicusbrief000107. cfm. (Accessed March 6, 2003.)

Brief of *Amicus Curiae*, Law Enforcement Alliance of America, Inc., in United States v. Emerson, no. 99–10331 (5th Cir. 1999), at http://www.ccrkba.org/LEAAbrief. htm. (Accessed March 6, 2003.)

Brief of *Amicus Curiae* Texas Justice Foundation in Support of Timothy Joe Emerson, in *United States v. Emerson*, no. 99–10331 (5th Cir. 1999), at http:// www.ccrkba.org/TXJusticeBrief.htm. (Accessed March 1, 2003.)

Brief of Appellee, in *United States v. Emerson*, no. 99–10331 (5th Cir. 1999), at http://www.saf.org/EmersonMainBrief.html. (Accessed May 6, 2003).

Brief of Texas State Rifle Association as *Amicus Curiae* in Support of Appellee, in *United States v. Emerson*, no. 99–10331 (5th Cir. 1999), at http://www.ccrkba .org/TXRifleBrief.htm. (Accessed March 8, 2003.)

Brief for the United States in Opposition in *Emerson v. United States*, 19–20, U.S. Supreme Court, no. 01–8780, at http://news.findlaw.com/hdocs/docs/gunlawsuits/emersonvs502sgopp.pdf. (Accessed May 7, 2003).

Brief Supporting Appellee of *Amicus Curiae* Academics for the Second Amendment, in *United States v. Emerson*, no. 99–10331 (5th Cir. 1999), at http://www.ccrkba .org/EMERSONacadsecd.html. (Accessed February 28, 2003.)

Brief Supporting Appellee of *Amicus Curiae*, National Rifle Association, in *United States v. Emerson*, no. 99–10331 (5th Cir. 1999), at http://www.ccrkba.org/ NRAbrief.htm. (Accessed March 1, 2003.)

Bureau of Alcohol, Tobacco, and Firearms at http://www.atf.treas.gov.

Citizen's Committee for the Right to Keep and Bear Arms at http://www.ccrkba.org.

Clede, Bill. "Colt's Smart Gun" at http://www.clede.com/Articles/Police/smart gun.htm(1997). (Accessed March 10, 2003.)

Coalition to Stop Gun Violence at http://www.csgv.org. (Accessed March 8, 2003.)

Cole, Lewis. "Violence and the Media: The Wrong Controversy?" at http://www. columbia.edu/cu/21stC/issue-1.2/Media.htm. (Accessed February 25, 2003.)

Defense Link, U.S. Department of Defense at http://www.defenselink.mil/news/ May1996/n05161996__9605161.html. (Accessed March 4, 2003.)

Federal Register, January 24, 2003, at http://www.ttb.gov/regulations/td487.pdf. (Accessed March 7, 2003.)

Fields, Edward R., ed. "The Truth at Last; News Suppressed by the Daily Press," at http://www.stormfront.org/truth_at_last/index2.htm. (Accessed March 8, 2003.)

Government's Brief in *United States v. Emerson*, no. 99–10331 (5th Cir. 1999), at http://www.ccrkba.org/EmersonAppealGovt1.html. (Accessed February 28, 2003.)

Gun Control Timeline at http://usgovinfo.about.com/library/weekly/aa092699
.htm. (Accessed March 7, 2003.)

Gun Owners Action League at http://www.goal.org.

Halbrook, Stephen P. "Deconstructing the Second Amendment," *NewsMax.com* at
http://www.newsmax.com/archives/articles/2000/11/3/220439.shtml. (Accessed
March 1, 2003.)

HELP Network at http://www.helpnetwork.org. (Accessed March 8, 2003.)

"Hilary Clinton Offers Support for Gun Licensing Bill," *CNN.com* (June 2, 2000).
http://www.cnn.com/2000/ALLPOLITICS/Stories/06/02/lazio.bustour/. (Accessed February 25, 2003.)

History of ATF from Oxford University Press, Inc. 1789–1998 U.S., at http://
www.atf.gov/about/history.htm. (Accessed May 7, 2003.)

John Hopkins Center for Gun Policy and Research at http://support.jhsph.edu/
departments/gunpolicy/.

Kappas, J. Scott. "Traveler's Guide to the Firearms Laws of the Fifty States" *Traveler's
Guide* (2001), www.gunlawguide.com. (Accessed March 8, 2003.)

Kopel, Dave. "The Cheney Glock-n-Spiel," *National Review Online* (July 27, 2000),
at http://www.nationalreview.com/kopel/kopel-Archive.asp. (Accessed March 8,
2003.)

Korwin, Alan. "Gun Law Updates," at http://www.gunlaws.com. (Accessed March 4,
2003.)

Korwin, Alan. "The Noble Uses of Firearms," at http://www.gunlaws.com/
noble.htm (Accessed March 6, 2003.)

Lampo, David. "Gun Control: Myths and Realities," *CATO Today's Commentary,* at
http://www.cato.org/dailys/05-13-00.html. (Accessed February 24, 2003.)

Landler, Mark. "Kabul Takes Steps toward Disarming Afghan Population," *New York
Times* (January 14, 2002), at http://www.nytimes.com/2002/01/14/international/
asia/14AFGH.html. (Accessed February 25, 2003.)

Marietta, Pennsylvania, Militia, at http://mariettapa.com/marietta_militia.html.
(Accessed March 8, 2003.)

Militia of Montana, at http://www.militiaofmontana.com. (Accessed March 8,
2003.)

Million Mom March, at http://www.millionmommarch.org. (Accessed March 8,
2003.)

Missouri 51st Militia, at http://www.mo51st.org/thoughts_about_the_mo_51st_
milit.htm. (Accessed March 8, 2003.)

National Rifle Association, at https://www.nrahq.org.

National Rifle Association Volunteer Web site, at http://www.nrawinningteam.com.

New Group, "Same Old Lies," vol. 8, no. 7, NRA-ILA FAX ALERT (February
16, 2001), at http://www.nraila.org/grassroots/20010216-AntiGunGroups001.
shtml.

New York State Division of Military and Naval Affairs, "The Seventh New York and
the Naming of the National Guard," at http://www.dmna.state.ny.us/historic/
articles/7th.htm. (Accessed March 2, 2003.)

Oliver, Jim. "The Siege at Ruby Ridge," at http://www.pwernet.net/~eichl/rr.html. (Accessed March 7, 2003.)

Oxnard Police. "Toy Guns: A Deadly Game" (December 20, 2001), at http://www.oxnardpd.org/toyguns.htm. (Accessed February 25, 2003.)

Poe, Richard, "What's Wrong with Toy Guns?" *FrontPageMagazine.com* (October 5, 2000), at http://frontpagemag.com/Articles/ReadArticle.asp?ID=3634. (Accessed February 25, 2003.)

Presidential Debate at Wakeforest University, October 11, 2000. http://www.debates.org/pages/trans2000b.html. (Accessed February 25, 2003.)

Programs: Firearms, at http://www.atf.gov/about/programs/profire.htm. (Accessed May 7, 2003.)

Project Safe Neighborhoods, at http://www.psn.gov. (Accessed March 10, 2003.)

Quotable Quotes from Chuck Heston, NRA President. http://nrawinningteam.com/hestquot.html. (Accessed March 8, 2003.)

Rand, Kristen as quoted by Eggen, Dan. "Ashcroft: Gun Ownership an Individual Right," *The Washington Post Online* (May 23, 2001), at http://www.washingtonpost.com/wp-dyn/articles/A66898-2001May23.html. (Accessed February 25, 2003.)

Rand, M. Kristen. Statement, Violence Policy Center, on Legislation to Improve and Aid Enforcement of Federal Gun Laws Presented to the Crime Subcommittee of the House Judiciary Committee (April 6, 2000), at http://www.house.gov/judiciary/rand0406.htm. (Accessed March 10, 2003.)

Reiss Jr., Albert J. and Roth, Jeffrey A. "Firearms and Violence" at http://sun.soci.niu.edu/~critcrim/guns/gun.viol. (Accessed February 24, 2003.)

Reply Brief for Appellant, in *United States v. Emerson*, no. 99–10331 (5th Cir. 1999), at http://www.ccrkba.org/EMERSONgovtrepl.html. (Accessed March 1, 2003.)

"Rogue of the Week," *Willamette Week* (June 13, 2001). http://wweek.com/flatfiles/allstories.lasso?xxin=1754. (Accessed February 25, 2003.)

Romanoff, Lance Jonn. "Somebody Call the National Toy Rifle Association," *Liberzine.com* (February 19, 2001) at http://www.liberzine.com/lanceromanoff/010219toyguns.htm.

Second Amendment Foundation, at http://www.saf.org. (Accessed March 8, 2003.)

Second Amendment Sisters, at http://www.2asisters.org. (Accessed March 8, 2003.)

"Shot Full of Holes," Violence Policy Center Web site at http://vpc.org/studies/ashapa.htm. (Accessed February 25, 2003.)

Southern Michigan Regional Militia, at http://www.michiganmilitia.org. (Accessed March 8, 2003.)

Spence, Gerry. *From Freedom to Slavery: The Rebirth of Tyranny in America,* Chapter 2, "The Trial of Randy Weaver," at http://www.localsov.com/abuses/justice/spence.htm. (Accessed March 7, 2003.)

State firearms laws, at http://www.atf.treas.gov/firearms/statelaws/22edition.htm.

Sullum, Jacob. "Can't Bear It," *Reason Online,* at http://www.reason.com/sullum/080598.html. (Accessed March 8, 2003.)

Teret, Stephen. "Critical Commentary on a Paper by Lott and Mustard," The Johns Hopkins Center for Gun Policy and Research, at http://www.asahi-net.or.jp/~zj5j-gttl/teret.htm. (Accessed March 6, 2003.)

The 7th Missouri Militia, at http://users.mo-net.com/mlindste/7momilit.html. (Accessed March 8, 2003.)

The Missouri 51st Militia, at http://www.mo51st.org. (Accessed March 8, 2003.)

The North Carolina Citizen Militia, at http://www.netpath.net/~jeffr/nccm.htm. (Accessed March 8, 2003.)

The Potomac Institute, Maryland, at http://www.potomac-inc.org/emeramic.html. (Accessed March 1, 2003.)

United States 1890s Populism (George Burson Aspen School District), at http://www.jmu.edu/madison/teach/burson/1890.htm. (Accessed March 8, 2003.)

Violence Policy Center, at http://www.vpc.org.

Violence Policy Center, at http://www.vpc.org/nrainfo/index.html. (Accessed March 10, 2003.)

Violence Policy Center, at http://www.vpc.org/studies/ashapa.htm. (Accessed March 6, 2003.)

Violence Policy Center, "The False Hope of a Smart Gun," at http://vpc.org/fact_sht/smartgun.htm (1998). (Accessed March 10, 2003.)

Violence Policy Center, "When Men Murder Women: An Analysis of 1996 Homicide Data." http://www.vpc.org/studies/dvconc.htm. (Accessed February 24, 2003.)

Waldron, Joe. "Armed and Considered Dangerous: Bureau of Alcohol, Tobacco, and Firearms in the 1990's" (July 24, 1995), at http://www.ccrkba.org/pub/rkba/articles/general/polabuse.txt. (Accessed March 7, 2003.)

Wayne County Militia, at http://www.geocities.com/CapitolHill/1392/index2.htm. (Accessed March 8, 2003.)

White House Press Release, at http://ed.gov/PressReleases/05-1995/gunfree.html. (May 10, 1995). (Accessed March 8, 2003.)

Williams, Budge. "Commentary, Williams: Waco Incident," Online Athens (October 23, 1999) at http://www.onlineathens.com/stories/102399/opi_1023990034.shtml. (Accessed May 7, 2003.)

Willing, Richard. "Case Could Shape Future of Gun Control." USA Today (August 27, 1999), at http://www.ccrkba.org/EmersonUSA1.html. (Accessed March 1, 2003.)

www.GoPatGo.org/ "Issues: Right to Keep and Bear Arms" (June 5, 1999).

Yassky, David. Amicus Curiae brief in United States v. Emerson, No. 99–10331 (5th Cir. 1999), at http://www.potomac-inc.org/yass.html.

Young, David. "Emerson Case Letter," at http://www.ccrkba.org/Young.html. (Accessed March 1, 2003.)

Zawitz, Marianne, W. "Guns Used in Crime," FirearmsID.com (September 2000) at http://www.firearmsid.com/feature%20Articles/0900GUIC/Guns%20Used%20in%20Crime.htm. (Accessed March 6, 2003.)

Index

About the Author

CONSTANCE EMERSON CROOKER is a writer and a retired attorney living in Portland, Oregon. Her law practice has included defense of gun crimes. She was director of the office of the Tillamook Public Defender and has also managed a private practice of law, emphasizing criminal defense. She is the author of *The Art of Legal Interpretation: A Guide for Court Interpreters* (1996) published by Portland State University's Continuing Education Press.